The Feast of Immortality

The Feast of Immortality

A Study in Comparative Indo-European Mythology

Written by Georges Dumézil

Translated by Tom Billinge

Published by Sanctus Arya Press

First edition, published February 2026 by Sanctus Arya Press.

This work is copyrighted © 2026 by Tom Billinge.

All rights reserved. No part of this book may be reproduced or used in any manner without prior written permission of the copyright owner, except for the use of brief quotations in a review. To request permission, contact the publisher.

Paperback: 978-1-968394-97-4

Hardcover: 978-1-968394-96-7

Library of Congress number pending.

Editing by Tom Billinge and Benjamin Sieghart.

Layout by Benjamin Sieghart.

Cover art by Tom Billinge.

Inside illustrations taken from the public domain.

More at:

tombillinge.com

sanctusarya.com

Lycurgus attacking the nymph Ambrosia (mosaic from Herculaneum, 45–79 AD)

Table of Contents

Introduction

I. Indo-European Mythology
II. Method
III. Documents
IV. Ambrosia
V. Plan

Part One — Determination of the Legendary Cycle of Ambrosia

Chapter I — The Cycle of Amṛta
Chapter II — The Cycle of the Beer of the Æsir
Chapter III — The Cycle of Ambrosia

Part Two — The Cycle of Ambrosia in the Various Indo-European Mythologies

Chapter One — The Cycle of Ambrosia Among the Hindus
I Traces of the Cycle in the Vedic Period: Deva, Asura and Sóma
II The Cycle in Epic Literature

Chapter Two — The Cycle of Ambrosia Among the Germans
I Hýmiskviða

II Lokasenna
III Þrymskviða

Chapter Three — The Cycle of Ambrosia Among the Iranians
I Amərətāt and Aaurvatāt in the Avesta
II The Prehistory of Amərətāt
III The Cycle of Ambrosia in Later Iranian Literature: The Story of Creation
IV Another Version of the Cycle According to Eznik
V Conclusions
Scheme of the Indo-Iranian Cycle

Chapter Four — The Cycle of Ambrosia Among the Greeks
I Legends Concerning Ambrosia and Retaining Something of the Indo-European Cycle
II The Cycle of the Píthos and of Fire: Indo-European and Aegean Legends
A The Text of Works and Days: The Theft of the Píthos, Pandora
B The Text of the Theogony: The Feast of the Gods, The Theft of Fire, Prometheus Chained
III Traces of Other Versions of the Cycle
Conclusion on the Greek Legends Derived from the Cycle of Ambrosia

Chapter Five — The Cycle of Ambrosia Among the Latins
I The Roman Cycle of Anna Perenna
II The Lavinian Cycle of Anna-Soror
III The Legend of Saint Petronilla
IV Mars and Nerio-Minerva — The Cista of Præneste
V The Feast of the Salii and the Feast of Ambrosia — The Ancile

Chapter Six —The Cycle of Ambrosia Among the Celts
I The Cycle of Ambrosia Among the Irish: The Beer of Goibniu and the Battle of Mag Tured
II The Cycle of Ambrosia Among the Welsh: The Holy Grail
II The Cycle of Ambrosia Among the Gauls: Sucellus, Nantosuelta, The Wolf and Little Red Riding Hood
Conclusion on the Celtic legends of Ambrosian Origin

Chapter Seven — The Cycle of Ambrosia Among the Slavs
I The cycle of Ambrosia and the Western Slavs: The Goddesses Ziva-Zivena and Marena
II The Cycle of Ambrosia Among the Russians: the Bylinas of Mikhailo Potyk
The Cycle Among the Balts?

Chapter Eight — Cycle of Ambrosia Among the Armenians
I Armenian Mythology
II Legends Borrowed from the Iranian World
III The Armenian Festival

Chapter Nine — Cycle of Ambrosia Among the Kucha

Chapter Ten — Indo-European Conclusions

Part Three — The Festival of Ambrosia

The Festival of Ambrosia
Among the Latins and Armenians
Among the Slavs

Among the Germans
Among the Celts
Among the Hindus
Among the Greeks

Essay on the interpretation of the rites and legends of ambrosia
I The Festival of Ambrosia and the Spring Rites
II The Ambrosia Feast and the Potlatch
III Ambrosia and Beer

General Conclusions

Tables of Concordance

Translator's Introduction

Perhaps no other academic has had such a profound impact on Indo-European studies than the great French philologist, linguist, and religious studies scholar Georges Edmond Raoul Dumézil (1898-1986). His work on comparative mythology and the trifunctional hypothesis of Proto-Indo-European mythology and society has left its indelible mark on all subsequent scholarship.

Dumézil fell out of favour in the 1980s following character assassination by left-wing scholars who wished to throw the baby out with the bathwater. The Frenchman briefly supported the right-wing organisation Action Française in the 1930s, and was snubbed by both Henri Hubert and Marcel Mauss, far-left scholars who actively used their powerful influence to advance their own political ideology in place of academic rigour in a open forum of ideas.

From the outset of his career, Dumézil faced left-wing criticism of his personal life, but not of his work, which remains some of the most meticulous scholarship in the field of Indo-European studies. He began studying at École normale supérieure in 1916, but he took his leave from his studies to serve as an artillery officer in the French Army in the First World War, for which he received the Croix de Guerre. As the son of a high ranking general, he saw it as his duty to fight.

Dumézil returned to École normale supérieure in 1919 to continue his studies. *The Feast of Immortality* (*Le festin d'immortalité*), written in 1924 was Dumézil's PhD thesis. This work foreshadows the incredible career and body of work of Dumézil. It focusses on the Indo-European Feast of Ambrosia and its various mythologies and rites in the different branches of the Indo-European family tree.

The work had never been translated into English, which led it to being consigned to obscurity. With the renewed interest in Indo-European studies, I felt it my duty to make *The Feast of Immortality* available to a new generation. It is my great honour to present Dumézil's first work in English for the first time and to breathe new life into it.

I have, to that end, translated the Greek and Latin quotations that were left untranslated in the original to make the text more accessible to a non-academic audience. I have also left the originals next to the translated segments so that those with the inclination to read the original sources are able to do so.

Tom Billinge
Connecticut, October 2025

Introduction

I. Indo-European Mythology

The reaction against the old Indo-European comparative mythology — that of solar myths and approximate etymologies — continues to this day. It is scarcely admitted that comparison allows us to go beyond the Indo-Iranian or the common Germanic stage. The study of Greek material has revealed the complexity of Aegean as well as Oriental elements, within which the conquerors' own legends were absorbed, and has made us more keenly aware of the gulf separating Hesiod or Pindar from the *RgVeda*.

Furthermore, the rapid progress and substantial results of sociological research seem to have relegated to the background—among insoluble or even meaningless problems—the comparative study of Indo-European traditions. In France and abroad, the most distinguished scholars have often expressed themselves clearly on this point: according to them, the ancient legendary themes and myths of India, Greece, and Italy are no closer to one another than they are to the myths and themes of "primitive" peoples of any age.

They express a state of collective thought that recurs, in essentially the same form, throughout the evolution of every society. Since the same causes everywhere produce the same effects, the points of comparison and elements of explanation for the classical legends extend across the entire world and throughout all of history.

Salomon Reinach writes, concerning the old comparative mythology (*Cultes, Mythes et Religions*, I, p. 191):

"*The scholars of that school compared only three or four mythologies and left outside their speculations the vast domain of popular traditions and the religions of uncivilised peoples.*"

Thus, it is not merely the method of that school that he condemns, but its very principle — the idea that the peoples of Indo-European language could have preserved in common, along with their language and certain other well-attested social facts, religious traditions of shared origin.

This view, though usually expressed in less harsh terms, has been accepted by most specialists. It suffices to read the opening pages of Oldenberg's book on Vedic religion, or to leaf through the great German compendia of classical mythology, to gauge the discredit into which the notion of an Indo-European mythology has fallen.

In his recent work on libation in the Scandinavian world, M. Cahen, while successfully applying semantic analysis to religious phenomena, consistently rejects the comparative approach whenever it presents itself.

Above all, it must be acknowledged that comparative mythology brought about its own downfall. The so-called "Vedic mania," in both its forms — naturalistic exegesis (storm myths, solar myths) and ritual exegesis (libation myths, etc.) — completely misled scholars.

Then, just as Latinists and Hellenists long ignored comparative linguistics, mythologists in their turn neglected, and at times even despised, the emerging anthropological and sociological schools. One could easily find, even under the usually restrained pen of Victor Henry, more than one summary execution of totemism.

An original — and unfortunately quite rare — example was set by M. Meillet, who showed that the Indo-Iranian Mitra was not a natural phenomenon, but rather a social phenomenon deified.

In short, it was the so-called "Indo-European mythologists" themselves who, by formulating the problem badly, destroyed their own discipline. They opposed the new ideas and the old ones as though they were two irreconcilable systems, instead of asking whether, as happens with every essential advance in science, the new ideas might not provide a broader framework, a more general classification, within which the old could find their place.

By doing so, they excluded themselves from truth, and each victory of their adversaries only served to make the falseness of their position more evident.

It is therefore hardly surprising that these adversaries — sociologists and folklorists, now the masters of the field — have retained a certain distrust and even a principled hostility toward the notion of an Indo-European mythology.

During the fruitful debate that took place in 1908 in the *Revue de l'Histoire des Religions* between the advocates of the "historical method" and those of the "sociological method" (the latter being described as the "comparative method"), no place was allotted — by either side — to the comparative method in the strict sense of the word, that is, to the comparison of different traditions grouped by linguistic or cultural families (Indo-European, Semitic, etc.).

Common sense, however, calls for reconciliation. When human groups once shared — at a certain time — a social unity such as that implied by a common language, family organization, and so forth, it is highly improbable that, after their separation, they did not retain a considerable part of the body of rites, legends, and abstract ideas that then constituted their religion.

That this body of material was of the same general order as that found among the semi-civilised peoples studied by sociologists is, a priori, quite plausible and may serve as a useful guide for research. But that such a body of traditions did not exist at all, or is completely inaccessible to us, cannot be admitted without at the same time assuming either a gap of several centuries in the religious evolution of a society, or a parallel and total forgetting of ancient traditions by all human groups descended from that society — hypotheses as implausible as that of a perfect preservation of the ancient beliefs.

We are thus led to revise the sociologists' stance: between, for example, an ancient Greek datum and a modern Australian or African one, it is necessary — when the Greek datum has precise correspondences among the Indo-Iranians, Latins, Germans, Celts, Slavs, etc. — to insert the Indo-European datum, defined by these correspondences. It is then this Indo-European datum that must be explained by the sociologist's methods.

The Greek datum, on the other hand, will be explained by distortion, contamination, and similar processes. It cannot, without leading to serious error, be treated as a primary datum.

In short, the aim is to restore — in the prehistory of legends and myths — alongside their social interpretation, a place for the study of their evolution.

II. Method

One will likely grant this theoretical correction easily. Yet, in view of the meagre results of the old comparative mythology, one may wonder whether such ideas are practically applicable. To renew an enterprise in which so much ingenuity and erudition were once wasted would indeed be presumptuous—unless one possessed a method that had not been sufficiently tried.

M. van Gennep, in his book *La Formation des Légendes*, writes on page 16:

"It is not the comparison of themes considered in isolation that provides the key to all the problems raised by the study of so-called popular

literatures, but only the comparison of certain of their well-defined combinations. This was clearly seen by J. Bédier in his studies on the Fabliaux and more recently on the Légendes Épiques: 'Common sense,' he says in regard to one of them, 'indicates that the combination Charlemagne–Otinel–Roland–Belissent–Montferrat–Atilie could not have been formed twice, independently, in the minds of two storytellers.' It is therefore necessary, in such a case, to admit a single inventor and a single place of invention, from which the legend spread through successive borrowings..."

Let us suppose that, in the legends of the various Indo-European peoples, we find the same isolated theme recurring. This observation alone would prove nothing as to the theme's Indo-European character — first, because the number of known themes in the world, however great, is limited, and there is a strong likelihood that the same theme might appear among many other peoples of different linguistic families; and secondly, even if the theme appeared only among Indo-European peoples, such a narrow coincidence could easily be attributed to chance.

However, if the agreement extends to one or several thematic sequences, the intervention of mere chance becomes less probable — especially when those sequences are complex and original, that is, when they combine numerous themes that are not found grouped together anywhere else.

If, finally, we recognise among all Indo-European peoples, and among them alone, several sequences rich in themes, themselves grouped around a common centre, and arranged in a consistent order so as to form what we have called a cycle, then the hypothesis of chance must be ruled out.

But at the same time, the hypothesis of borrowing must also be excluded: from whom, when, and how could such borrowing have taken place so as to cover the entire Indo-European area — and that alone?

We are therefore compelled to admit, as in the case of language, the existence of independent evolutions derived from a common original source.

Our task, then, is clearly defined: it is a complex and precise cycle that we must seek.

We speak here of themes, sequences, and cycles, not of Indo-European gods. It is now generally recognised that the names and personalities of gods or heroes are constantly subject to change. A particular story may be told in identical form for centuries, yet continually attributed to new heroes according to the concerns of the time.

M. van Gennep recalls (op. cit., pp. 66–67) the case of Cinderella, who, when transported among a tribe of the Philippines, keeps her beautiful carriage and horses, but whose fairy godmother is transformed into a female crab. It is unlikely that transformations so radical would be found within the Indo-European domain; yet neither the pantheon of Homer, nor still less that of the Edda, can have preserved much of their ancient state.

Apollon and Thor bear strong national characters and represent no "Indo-European person" whatever. They arose, like Viṣṇu, Herakles, and many others after them, from an enthusiasm for a representative type of a race and period, or from the political ascendancy of a clan, or from other similar causes. They are in no sense primitive.

However, through their exalted status, they have attracted to themselves themes, sequences, and cycles that preceded them and were destined to outlive them. The gods pass away, but the themes endure.

We shall not, therefore, attempt to determine any Indo-European divine personality. It may be that, in the course of our study, certain distinct types will emerge; but we shall never attribute to them an existence independent of the cycle in which they appear, nor any action other than that which is specifically theirs within that cycle.

This means that onomastic etymology, so dear to the old school, will have no place in our method.

If one were to find an important cycle connected in India with Vāruna, and in Greece with Οὐρανός (Ouranos), one could, at the end of the study, conclude that the names are identical; it would then be up to linguists to determine how to reconcile the two forms — which, as is known, do not perfectly correspond.

But to begin from such a hypothetical identity, to make it the foundation of the entire structure, after what has just been said, would be a defiance of common sense.

It is no accident that the names of deities, still determinable in fairly large numbers for the Indo-Iranian period, are reduced, for the Indo-European period, to little more than the single Dyeus ("Sky God"). This does not prove that the Indo-Europeans did not give names to their gods, but simply that the life of the immortals is short.

If themes are independent of the gods, they are also — though to a lesser degree — independent of "philosophies," by which we mean the general body of ideas through which each society at a given time conceives the world.

Consider, for instance, the many reinterpretations of the Prometheus legend throughout historical times: from Hesiod's simple moral lesson of submission to the gods, to the philosophers' Prometheus as demiurge, and finally to the crucified Prometheus glimpsed in Lucian.

This observation must be taken in its full breadth: contemporary philosophies or social sciences, however enlightened they may be, are no more final than the systems of thought that preceded them. The reigning ideas of today concerning the origin of legends and rites, the birth of religions, or the childhood of societies, may already be obsolete, and are certainly subject to change.

We must therefore carefully distinguish between facts and their interpretation — between the themes and cycles we identify, and the explanations they invite. Just as comparative grammar, though it does not ignore the philosophy of language, does not subordinate itself to it, so too comparative mythology, at least in its early stages, must not take its direction from the philosophy of religions.

If the old school left behind so few lasting results, it is because its reasoning rested, at every step, on a philosophy that proved inconsistent upon the first serious test. This is a universal law in the development of any science: the physicist may take an interest in hypotheses about matter, but he first establishes facts independent of speculation — it is then up to dynamism or atomism to accommodate them.

In the same way, the autonomy of mythological phenomena — observable in history with respect to the successive philosophies of peoples — must be maintained in science with respect to the successive theories of scholarly schools.

III. Documents

The conditions of our work are, in part, unfavourable. The old school of comparative mythology willingly made Vedic documents — along with a few Iranian texts and the chaotic corpus of Greek legends — the framework of its constructions. Yet, the current state of scholarship tends to diminish the practical value of these three sources.

The Vedic hymns, as is well known, form part of a liturgical ritual—a collection of utterances necessary for the performance of sacrifices, especially the sacrifice of *sóma*. They constitute the spoken or chanted portion of the ceremonies. This essentially practical purpose does not permit the poet any disinterested elaboration. He does not recount, for the listener's pleasure, the exploits of this or that god; rather, he recalls them to the god himself, in order to glorify him or to urge him to continue acting favourably.

More often — and this is what makes the use of these hymns so delicate for the mythologist — he proceeds only by brief and elliptical allusion: the god knows his own deeds, and a single epithet or verse suffices to show him that men are not ignorant of them. Nowhere does a continuous narrative break the sequence of invocations.

As for the rest of Vedic literature — the *Brāhmaṇas*, *Āraṇyakas*, and *Upaniṣads* — their purpose is no less practical. These vast compilations aim to teach all those who take part in the rites the profound meaning, the reason for being, of their gestures, words, and chants. Among so many commentaries, it is rare for a narrative to appear; and when one does, it is never disinterested.

For example, when the author of the *Śatapatha-Brāhmaṇa* recounts the story of the Flood, it is to clarify the ritual value and sacrificial role of the offering called ilā. It is easy to see that such stories, forcibly bent toward arbitrary ritual purposes, cannot be regarded as "primitive."

Furthermore, although the *Brāhmaṇas* represent the latest portion of Vedic literature, their gods are no longer quite those of the *ṚgVeda*. One notes the new and growing prominence of Viṣṇu

— a sign of his coming supremacy — and, conversely, the decline in importance of the Aśvins. The philosophical atmosphere of the legends, too, has changed; it already foreshadows the speculative schools of later ages.

As Victor Henry observed:

"If one imagines — apart from the strictness of syllogistic method — the Summa Theologica of Saint Thomas ending with the Principles of Spinoza, one will have a fair idea of the impression produced by a Brāhmaṇa followed by its Upaniṣad."

In summary:

There is a great mythological poverty in the hymns; a slightly lesser poverty in the rest of Vedic literature—but one aggravated by an evolution which, though it has not yet overthrown the divine hierarchy, is already profound. It is therefore not surprising that we must sometimes turn to the later epic literature, which, though clothed in the garb of an entirely new religion, has the merit of recounting in detail and coherent form the legends and cycles it preserves—some of which, at least, are not of recent invention.

The Avestan literature proves to be even more disappointing. To begin with, the entire compilation can scarcely be dated earlier than the Sassanian period. Moreover, nothing is less unified or coherent than the *Avesta* itself: almost all its parts form, as Meillet put it (*Journal Asiatique*, Jan.–Feb. 1916, p. 125 ff.), *"a heap of disparate fragments, where scraps of texts have been placed side by side almost without order."* One can never be sure that two neighbouring pages or consecutive verses represent the same state of religious thought.

It is true that the *Gāthās*, whose language is more archaic and whose composition is no doubt older than that of the other books, survive among these materials. But precisely because of their antiquity, the *Gāthās* bear more deeply the imprint of the Zoroastrian reform: they exclude the naturalistic and ritual elements of the old Indo-Iranian religion. Haoma is not mentioned in the *Gāthās*, which thus stand at the opposite extreme from the Vedic mentality, entirely focused on *sóma*.

On the other hand, by carrying to their conclusion the tendencies inherent in Iranian religion, the *Gāthās* bring to the forefront, around Ahura Mazdā, the "Lord Wisdom" already present before Zoroaster, the curious abstract beings known as the Ameša Spənta. Questions of good and evil, the fate of souls, and the Last Judgment are the sole preoccupations of this profoundly moral doctrine. Hence, for the mythologist, there is almost no material to be found: a reformer has passed through, purging the sacred texts of their ancient traditions.

It is therefore to the later *Avesta* that we must turn. But what exactly does it represent? It dates from the time when, with the Sassanian monarchy and the nationalist reaction it embodied, Zoroastrianism — until then a sect without official standing — became the state religion of the country. The doctrine of this *Avesta*, which claims to be Zoroastrianism, is no longer that of the *Gāthās*: as it spread, such an abstract faith inevitably lost its purity.

As Meillet observed (loc. cit.), the *Avesta* offers "a compromise between Zoroastrianism proper and the prevailing beliefs — some being old Indo-Iranian survivals, others Zoroastrian ideas emptied of their precise doctrine and popularised." The Ameša Spənta are no longer, or soon cease to be, mere personified abstractions; they also become genii of specific material elements. Haoma regains his cult, and his *Yašt* ranks among the most important. The Indo-Iranian deities excluded from the *Gāthās* reappear, and Mithra begins his prodigious career.

One thus finds some mythological content, but after so many revolutions, restorations, and contaminations, these materials cannot have escaped alteration. How can one rely on such disjointed and fragmentary evidence? The later Pahlavi books are the first to offer continuous narratives, but in the interval the theologians — those great nibblers of mythologies — cannot have remained idle. A priori, it is impossible to say how much, for example, the *Bundahišn* may have preserved in its cosmogony from the old systematisations.

In general, then, in our studies the Iranian evidence will serve little for reconstruction; at most, it may occasionally confirm, in certain instances, the Indo-Iranian character of the Hindu testimony.

As for the Greek evidence, whose richness at first fascinated researchers, it was soon realised that it is difficult to use. Greece is not a country, but a world — infinitely divided, itself the heir of an earlier world that likely possessed no greater unity, and exposed to the influence of many neighbouring civilisations.

From the very first literary and archaeological documents, one encounters only the results of combinations and reconciliations, whose component elements are most often indiscernible. It is thus impossible, directly and a priori, to determine within them what portion may represent genuine Indo-European survivals.

No more than the Iranian evidence does the Greek evidence allow us to reconstruct the past; rather, it is the Greek material that, afterward, will need to be illuminated in the light of comparisons drawn from elsewhere.

We thus arrive at a conclusion that is only seemingly paradoxical: the oldest testimonies within the Indo-European world do not allow us to reconstruct the common original state of things.

The explanation is simple: wherever we possess such ancient documents, it is because civilisation and intellectual development appeared early—but precisely for that reason, the ancient materials have not merely evolved as all oral traditions do, through gradual and unsystematic distortion. Instead, they have participated in the general ferment of thought and culture.

What reaches us, therefore, is no longer the primitive form, but a revised, reinterpreted, and often relegated version of the original traditions. From its very first steps, history encounters Brahmanic mysticism, Zoroastrian moralism, and the "Greek miracle."

There remain, then, the Latin, Germanic, Celtic, and Slavic sources. Except for the Latin ones, all share the disadvantage of being late, almost entirely from the Christian era. The oldest Eddic texts date only from the 9th century; the chief Irish source, the Book of Invasions (*Lebor Gabála Érenn*), is a composition of the 11th century; and the great Russian epic tales (*byliny*) were not collected before the 18th century. Earlier reports concerning these traditions — preserved by travellers or monks — amount to very little.

Nevertheless, it must be emphasised that among these peoples Christianity was not the outcome of an internal religious evolution, as were Brahmanism or Zoroastrianism, but rather the result of a conversion to a foreign doctrine. Consequently, the beliefs and legends associated with their ancient cults met a different fate from those of the ancient East. Except for some minor contaminations, they were not absorbed into the new religion.

Among the Scandinavians, these traditions survived for several centuries without capitulating, then almost completely disappeared; the entirety of our Eddic texts date from this period of survival. Among the Celts and Slavs, they quickly degenerated into popular tales, transforming the old gods into heroes — in one case into the Tuatha Dé Danann, in the other into the paladins of Vladimir the Sun — and thus preserved their autonomy for a long time.

Accordingly, these various testimonies deserve special consideration: though very recent, they represent a tradition unbroken by any reform or religious reorganisation. It is the compensating privilege of those peoples who, longer than others, remained barbarian.

The position of Latin legends is a special one, yet—despite their dates—more comparable to that of Germanic, Celtic, and Slavic traditions than to that of Greek or Indo-Iranian traditions.

Latin thought did not undergo a process of internal transformation; it did not, through philosophical ferment, transmute its own religious elements as happened in Greece or in the Indo-Iranian East. The Roman mind — that of peasants and soldiers — was practical rather than speculative. The only development visible in early times, perhaps partly under Etruscan influence, is the multiplication of rites, ceremonies, priests, and priestly colleges.

In all these transactions between men and gods, the old legends and myths had little direct application. They survived on the margins, as popular tales, disguised as historical stories about the early days of the city; while they continued to speak of the gods, they lost their properly religious character.

The invasion of Greek thought during the last centuries of the Republic — comparable in more than one respect to the Christianisation of the Germanic and Slavic worlds in the Middle Ages — completed the transformation of the old native religious legends into folk tales, which thus survived without artificial distortion, on the periphery of the works of rhetoricians, scholars, and poets.

The effort of Ovid in his *Fasti*, and the results he achieved, are highly instructive in this regard. Wishing to collect the neglected treasure of Roman traditions, he often ends up — especially when dealing with a properly religious legend — retelling, consciously or not, a Greek story. Conversely, when a genuinely native tale appears, it is generally clothed in historical form: such as Anna Perenna provisioning the plebeians on the Sacred Mount; Numa tricking Jupiter and obtaining the miraculous *ancile*; or Juno ending the sterility of the Sabine women abducted by Romulus.

Here lies the indigenous foundation, comparable in its origins to the Slavic *byliny*, where we must look for the remains — more or less humanised, more or less secularised — of Latin "mythology."

In short, the earlier paradox may now be more precisely stated: if we had at our disposal only the *Vedas*, the *Gāthās*, and Homer, our task would be impossible, for lack of sufficient mythological material. If, on the other hand, we possessed only Ovid's *Fasti*, a few Eddic poems, and some *byliny*, our task would be difficult and uncertain, yet in principle attainable.

Certainly, we would still need to filter out, from among the Germanic and Slavic traditions, the many legends of non–Indo-European or non-native origin that had crept in. But we would be justified in hoping that, beneath these foreign deposits, the ancient substratum endured; setting aside questions of chronology, the problem would be one of overabundance rather than absence of material.

Here lies the profound methodological difference between comparative grammar and comparative mythology: the antiquity of documents, which is crucial in the former, is not of the same importance in the latter. Language evolves in a more mechanical and linear fashion than do the psychological or social phenomena it expresses.

In fact, the situation is not so dire. Alongside the Latin and Germanic evidence, the post-Vedic Indian material, controlled and illuminated by the *Vedas*, provides a rich body of data. It is at the intersection of these three lines of evidence — India, Italy, and the Germanic North — that we shall find, as can already be foreseen, our first certainties.

IV. Ambrosia

Among the terms used by the Indo-European languages to designate "man," there are two that arise from the same conception: man is called either "the earthly one" or "the mortal one" — obviously in contrast to beings conceived as non-earthly or non-mortal, that is to say (to abbreviate and without presuming any other qualities), to the gods.

It is noteworthy that these two designations appear to be mutually exclusive. For some peoples, man is "the earthly one" (cf. Latin *humus*; Greek χαμαί); Lithuanian *žemė*; Old Church Slavonic *zemlja*), but in that case he is not called "the mortal one." This is the case among the Latins (*homō, hominēs*), the Germans (Gothic *guma*, Old High German *gomo*), the Lithuanians (*žmuo*, plural *žmonės*), and the Tocharians (Tocharian B *caumo*, plural *cāmna*).

Among others, however, man is "the mortal one" (cf. the root mer- "to die"), and the name "earthly one" does not appear. Thus with the Greeks (βροτός, ἄνθρωπος in Hesiod), the Armenians (*mard*), the Iranians (Avestan *mareta, mashyō*; Old Persian *martiya*), and the Hindus (Sanskrit *martya, marta*).

Does this mean, then, that we must oppose as two irreconcilable conceptions the idea of man as the earthly being — ruling from Rome to Kucha — and the idea of man as the mortal being — ruling from the Aegean to the Himalayas? Obviously not.

As we have said, the principle underlying these two designations is essentially the same, and the Latin gods or Scandinavian Æsir are no less immortal than the Suras of India. But above all, the disappearance of the root meaning "to die" or of a word for man derived from this root can be easily explained by a linguistic taboo, a universally practiced euphemism.

For example, remaining within the Indo-European domain: Celtic, except for one isolated word (Old Irish *marb*, "dead," adjective), has lost the root *mer-*; and the same is probably true of Tocharian B, the language of Kucha, where death is expressed by a new, metaphorical term: *srūkalyne* (from the root *sreu-*, "to flow"?).

The disappearance of the word does not prove that of the idea, but only the fear of giving it reality by invoking it. All the more remarkable, then, that over a large part of the Indo-European world, human beings retained a name of ill omen. There must have been a powerful tradition, well-rooted legends and myths, for the Greek, the Armenian, and the Ārya to have continued to call themselves "the Mortal."

We now encounter another dual grouping — another kind of "isogloss," if not an "isomyth" — in connection with the Drink of the Gods.

For the Indo-European gods, the "non-earthly" or "immortals," possess a special beverage: the Hindu *amṛta* (compare the Iranian Amərətāt, the genius of sustenance and immortality); the Greek ἀμβροσία; the "beer of immortality" of the Irish Tuatha Dé Danann; and, finally, the ale (*öl*) of the Scandinavian Æsir — all of these serve as clear attestations of the same idea.

But what was the precise relationship between this drink of the non-mortals and non-earthly beings and their immortality? Did the drink confer immortality, or was it merely a special privilege belonging to a class of beings already and independently conceived as immortal?

Did the Indo-Europeans regard it as a necessary and sufficient cause of immortality — or rather as a consequence, a kind of external sign of it?

There is uncertainty here. For while the *amṛta* is indeed, like the Irish beer, the "drink of immortality," the Greek ambrosia (ἀμβροσία) and nectar — as we shall see later — seem, already in the Homeric texts, to mean merely the "drink of the immortals." Similarly, the Scandinavian ale nowhere appears as being directly connected with the immortality of the Æsir.

The answer to this question will emerge from other considerations.

Where ambrosia is understood as a drink of immortality — as in India — it is accompanied by a cycle of legends that is more famous, richer, and more coherent than in those cases where the drink is merely "divine" in a vague sense, as among the Scandinavians and Greeks.

This observation must also apply to Indo-European prehistory: the ambrosia must have played a very important role in the religious thought of the time if it served to separate the two worlds, the mortal and the immortal. Conversely, it played a much lesser role if it was merely an attribute of the beings of the other world.

Thus, depending on which of these two situations reflects the original Indo-European state, one might suppose either that the cycle of *amṛta* was the result of specifically Indian innovations, or, on the contrary, that the cycle of the Æsir's beer, for example, merely reproduces in an impoverished form the older pattern of the *amṛta* cycle.

In other words, if we can identify a true "Cycle of Ambrosia," this would imply that Ambrosia — in the Indo-European worldview — possessed the full and genuine value of a drink of immortality.

And, consequently, this would also explain the importance of the notions of "death" and "non-death" (mortal and immortal) in the classification of beings.

In that original system of thought, the distinction between mortals and immortals would not have been merely descriptive, but rather the result of an essential difference — a substance-based separation sustained by the possession or deprivation of the Ambrosia, the drink that ensures eternal life.

V. Plan

Now, this Cycle of Ambrosia does indeed exist. It is clearly found in India, where the cycle of the *amṛta* is well known to all. It is no less evident among the Scandinavians, where two successive Eddic poems, the *Hymiskviða* and the *Lokasenna*, together form a Cycle of the Beer that is almost exactly superimposable on the Indian one.

Moreover, this cycle is present throughout the entire Indo-European world. Even where the idea of a divine drink has disappeared — as among the Latins or the Slavs — or has been altered in some way — such as among the Greeks — the cycle itself has often undergone deviations, but everywhere it has preserved, along with its "nourishing" and "enduring" significance, the characteristic sequence of its themes.

Thus, it remains recognisable everywhere, a persistent mythic structure that marks the boundary between mortals and immortals, and whose central element — the divine drink — symbolises both sustenance and eternal life.

Our plan thus presents itself clearly: since the Indian and Scandinavian sources are the most explicit, we shall begin by using them to form a provisional and as complete as possible reconstruction of the Indo-European cycle.

This first part will be purely constructive, not historical — that is to say, we will compare the earliest Indian and Germanic testimonies directly, without concern for the later evolution of the *amṛta* cycle or of the Æsir's beer cycle.

Our goal, in this stage, is not to trace transformations or influences, but to reconstruct the original framework — the fundamental mythic structure common to both traditions — before examining how later developments modified or obscured it.

The second part, by contrast, will consist of a series of historical studies. We will examine what the Indo-European cycle became over time, and how it evolved among the various peoples of the Indo-European family.

At the same time, this comprehensive review of evidence from every source will serve a double purpose: it will not only trace the transformations of the myth, but also clarify certain points within the original Indo-European cycle that may have remained obscure or uncertain after comparing only the Indian and Germanic data.

Thus, while the first part aims to reconstruct the primordial structure, the second will seek to illuminate its later history — revealing both the divergent developments of each tradition and the persistent unity underlying them.

In a third part, we will examine whether the legendary Cycle of Ambrosia corresponded, among the Indo-Europeans, to a set of rites or a festival — as is clearly the case among several peoples of the same linguistic family.

We will then attempt to illuminate both rites and legends through the analogy of non–Indo-European traditions.

In other words, this final stage will aim to reconstruct not only the mythic narrative but also its ritual expression — to determine whether the drink of immortality was celebrated through a ceremonial re-enactment, and how this ritual may have embodied the symbolic division between mortals and immortals.

By comparing Indo-European evidence with analogous myths and ceremonies from other cultures, we will seek to clarify the religious meaning of the cycle as a whole — where cosmic order, divine privilege, and human destiny are all bound together by the mystery of the Ambrosia.

We will not apologise for publishing, on so vast a subject, a work that in many respects is but a "sketch."

Indeed, we have not sought to make an exhaustive survey of all the ambrosial memories preserved throughout every branch of the Indo-European family, but rather to gather and arrange sufficient evidence to place beyond doubt the original existence of an Indo-European cycle of Ambrosia.

We are fully aware, moreover, of the enormous task that remains — the effort required to pursue, from the Indus to Wales, the full scope of the Ambrosian question.

Our work, therefore, should be seen as a foundation rather than a conclusion: a framework on which future research may build, expanding the comparative study of myth to encompass the entire Indo-European world, and perhaps beyond.

But even this sketch would not have been possible without the kindness and constant guidance of our teachers.

M. Meillet graciously received and helped shape the project while it was still formless and supervised its sometimes reckless growth to the very end. M. Maurice Cahen, M. Vendryes, and M. Bourguet offered their advice and insights on the Scandinavian, Celtic, and Greek chapters. M. Michalski, professor of Sanskrit at the University of Warsaw, guided us in the study of the Indian material, and without the teaching of M. Boyer, the Slavic domain could not have been explored.

To all these masters, we offer here the testimony of our deepest gratitude. We also extend our heartfelt thanks to M. J. Hackin and Cl. E. Maître, administrators of the Musée Guimet, who graciously agreed to include the work of a beginner in their collections. Finally, we shall endeavour to show ourselves worthy of the benefit granted by the University of Paris, which for two years maintained us with the favour of a research fellowship.

Thetis anoints Achilles with ambrosia, by Johann Balthasar Probst (1673–1748)

PART ONE

Determination of the Legendary Cycle of Ambrosia

Chapter One

The Cycle of the *Amṛta*

The *Vedas* know of the *amṛta*. But they know above all the *sóma*; and the plant with its precious juice has successfully outshone the older mythical drink. The *Ṛg Veda* (VI, 44, 23) still knows that the *amṛta* is hidden beyond the lights of the third heaven. But most often the word has only a transparent etymological meaning, which easily adapts to very different objects: it means "immortality," or "the community of the immortals"; or else it is the "immortal essence" conferred by the *sóma*; or again — later on, no doubt (*Atharva-Veda*, VIII, 7, 21, 59) — it is the virtue of longevity that the seed of Parjanya (the rain) has placed in plants and which is made to be absorbed by the sick through the juice of these plants.

All these interpretations were born from the word itself and cannot have preserved much of the ancient legends.

Besides, as we explained in the Introduction, it is not in the *Vedas* that we must look for any Cycle whatsoever: the form as well as the purpose of that literature — of that liturgy — left the poets little leisure for lengthy legendary developments. It is to the epic literature that we must turn.

There we find a new generation of gods: the Śiva, the Viṣṇu, and, not to mention Brahmā, take on the leading roles that, in a Vedic redaction, would certainly have been held by Indra and Agni. But we know that beneath these changes of divine "personnel," the themes and cycles may be preserved; and it will suffice for us to disregard the specifically Brahmanic traits and colouring to extract, from an epic or *Purāṇic* text, a legendary substance that is doubtless much older.

No one today will be surprised by what, a few years ago, would have been considered scandalous: we readily admit that legends could have passed through the Vedic period without leaving any trace in the texts that survive, and then reappeared, thanks to popular or at least oral tradition, in the later literature. This is no more surprising than finding, in the *Edda* of the 9th or 10th century, themes and even a cycle of Indo-European origin.

Besides, do the Vedic books represent the entirety of the religious thought of their age? Obviously not. The Breviary does not contain all the ideas, nor all the legends, of Catholicism.

✷✷✷

The first epic text — also the most substantial, and doubtless the source of many others — is found in the Book of Beginnings (*Ādiparvan*) of the *Mahābhārata* (*ślokas* 1095–1179). It is the *Amṛtamanthana*, the "Churning of the *Amṛta*."

In its present form, this episode is certainly not among the oldest parts of the poem. Lassen, in his edition (*Anthologia Sanscritica*, 2nd ed., 1868, pp. 71–80), points out several indications of this relative youth. First, its metrical form; then, the epithet *Kirīṭin* ("adorned with a diadem"), applied here (in the final *śloka*) to the *divum numen* Nara — whereas it is ordinarily reserved for the hero Arjuna (ibid., p. XI).

But the antiquity of the underlying material is beyond dispute. By the Brahmanic period, this was an extremely famous tradition, one to which poets frequently allude, when they do not devote entire works to it. And as we shall soon see, in every case where there is disagreement among the many versions, it is the *Mahābhārata*'s version that preserves the most ancient form of the legend.

So, for the moment, before examining the first account, we shall simply list the principal authors.

First comes, with some interesting variations but in a much more condensed form, a narrative from the *Rāmāyaṇa* (Book I). Then, since the *Viṣṇu Purāṇas* could hardly have omitted a cycle so glorious for their hero, we find it again, fully developed, as an episode in the *Bhāgavata Purāṇa* (Book VIII) and in several others.

Here now is the substance of the *Amṛtamanthana*, stripped of those sumptuous epithets which make the beauty of Sanskrit poetry — but only in Sanskrit.

⁂

A. Preparation of the *Amṛta*

1. The Gods' Deliberation on the Food of Immortality

The Suras (gods) once assembled upon a peak of Mount Meru, "bound by vows and penances," to deliberate on how they might obtain the drink of immortality.

Then Viṣṇu-Nārāyaṇa said to Brahmā:

"Let the gods, together with all the Asuras, churn the Vase of the Ocean.
For it is there, in the great ocean being churned, that the amṛta will be born.
Therefore, O gods, strew every herb and every pearl within the sea, and set it in motion. Thus shall you obtain the amṛta."

2. Preparations – The Gods Visit the "Lord of the Waters"

The gods go to the Master of the Waters and take possession of the Ocean. They then attempt, but in vain, to uproot the gigantic Mount Mandara, which is to serve as the churning rod. Seeing their failure, Viṣṇu causes his serpent Vāsuki to tear the mountain from the earth and lift it up. Then, with the mountain in their possession, the gods approach the Ocean and say to him:

"In order to obtain the amṛta, we shall churn your waters."

The Lord of the Waters replies:

"Then grant that I, too, may have a share of the amṛta, for the whirling of Mount Mandara will rub me sorely."

And in the sea, the Suras and Asuras speak to the King of Tortoises, saying:

"May Your Majesty consent to become the support of this mountain."

The Tortoise (Kūrma, Kūrmarāja, a male divinity) accepts and presents his back.

Indra sets the mountain in place, and "with Mount Mandara as the churning stick and the serpent Vāsuki as the rope, the gods begin to churn the Ocean — the vast reservoir of waters."

3. Churning of the Ambrosia. — A long description of the scene follows: all the gods clinging to the tail of the serpent, whose head Viṣṇu, the chief of the operation, holds; the serpent breathing out vapours and smoke that fall back in showers; the rain of flowers, the roaring of the ocean "like the rumbling of great clouds;" the mass death of sea creatures; the crash of trees "filled with birds," and the ensuing fire; Mount Mandara amid the flames, "like a violet cloud surrounded by lightning;" lions and elephants burned alive; and Indra, "the best of the Immortals," quenching the fire with water, daughter of the clouds.

Then comes an entire fantastic chemistry: the resin of the trees and the sap of the herbs, in which resides the virtue of immortality, flow into the ocean (as well as a certain "golden effusion" —

nisravam kâncanasya). The water turns to milk, then to "clarified butter" (*ghṛta*). The Hindu imagination is given free rein.

After a moment of discouragement and exhaustion — which Viṣṇu heals with a single word, at Brahma's request — the following wonders rise from the ocean: the moon-god Soma, "fresh, surrounded by a thousand rays;" Lakṣmī, the goddess of Beauty; Surādevī, goddess of intoxicating drinks; a pale-coloured horse; and finally, the divine jewel Kaustubha.

The last goes straight to the breast of Nārāyana, while Lakṣmī, Surā, Soma, and the Horse join the gods "by the path of the sun."

It is only then that the god Dhanvantari — the physician of the gods — appears, emerging from the waters in human form, holding a white vessel containing the *amṛta*.

When the Dānavas (demons) behold this miracle, a great clamour arises among them concerning the *amṛta*:

"*This belongs to us!*"

Several incidents follow. Notably, the god Śiva saves the world from death by drinking the thick poisonous vapours produced by the excessive churning of the ocean.

B. Theft of the *Amṛta*. The False Goddess (False Bride) Among the Demons

"The Dānava, disappointed in their hopes, begin a great war

(literally, 'hatred,' *vaira*) for the *amṛta* and for Lakṣmī."

(Here the text does not say that the demons succeed in seizing the *amṛta*, but the continuation implies it.)

"Then Nārāyaṇa resorts to a fascinating illusion: he assumes a magnificent form of a woman and goes to the Dānava. All the Dānava and all the Daitya (demons), their hearts distraught, their minds possessed, offer the *amṛta* to this woman; and Viṣṇu, the mighty god, having received the *amṛta*, carries it away from the princes of the Dānava, accompanied by Nara (his usual 'double'). Then he gives it to all the hosts of the gods, who drink it amid a tumultuous confusion."

C. The Demon at the Feast of the Gods. His Punishment

While the gods drink the longed-for *amṛta*, the Dānava Rāhu, having assumed a divine form, slips in among them. But as the *amṛta* enters his throat, the Sun and the Moon, "out of devotion to the gods," expose the deception, and Viṣṇu hurls his discus: the severed head flies into the air with terrifying cries; the Daitya's trunk falls quivering to the ground "and makes the earth tremble with its islands, its forests, and its mountains."

From that time comes the fierce, eternal war that Rāhu's head wages against the Sun and the Moon: he still devours them today. As for the blessed Viṣṇu, having cast off his incomparable womanly form, he terrifies the Dānava with his dreadful features. Then, near the salty sea, a great battle is fought — the most terrible that has ever taken place between the Sura and the Asura.

D. Massacre of the Demons

In a long, grand, and dynamic description, arrows and discs fly through the air; maces and axes strike down; heads fall "without pause," and the great corpses of the Asura lie scattered, "like mountain peaks red with metals." The clamour rises, the Sun grows dark...

Then Nārāyaṇa and Nara enter the battle, and swift Viṣṇu begins hurling again and again his famous discus, Sudarśana, "blazing like a fierce fire." It tears the bodies of the sons of Diti and Danu (= the demons), hews their ranks to pieces, and drinks their blood "like a vampire."

The Asura do not yield. They crush their enemies with mountains and hurl themselves by thousands toward the sky. The mountains, like clouds, crash down upon one another with terrible noise, shaking the Earth. Nara, with his great golden-tipped arrows, fills the paths of the sky, piercing the mountain peaks. At last the Sudarśana discus overwhelms the Asura, who plunge beneath the ground and into the ocean of salty waves.

Then the victorious Sura restore the Mandara to its place; the clouds scatter, and the *amṛta* is carefully hidden away. Indra, the slayer of Bala, in agreement with the Immortals, entrusts its keeping to Viṣṇu.

⁎⁎⁎

The composition is very clear. But the text, as often happens in the Hindu epic, is at times so redundant as to weary the reader, and at other times strangely elliptical. Thus, as we have seen, it does not tell us how the demons seize the *amṛta* as soon as it appears. Likewise, we only learn that Nara accompanied Nārāyaṇa to the demons' abode at the moment of their return. There are even inconsistencies: in one *śloka* (v. 1149), which I have not translated, right in the middle of Viṣṇu's expedition — disguised as a woman — into the demons' ranks, the poem says: "Having taken up their weapons and arrows, the Daitya and Dānava rush at once upon the gods." It is clear that this *śloka* is placed too early, since at that moment the demons are "mad with love," unaware of Viṣṇu's ruse, and therefore have no reason to attack the gods: they actually possess the *amṛta* and believe they also possess Lakṣmī. No doubt, moreover, this is merely a "layout error," due to a careless editor — such mistakes abound in India's epics and have occasionally befallen even Greek and Latin poets.

We will not return to the colour, features, or "Brahmanic" characters of this text. But aside from this general modification, it is evident that the Hindu imagination found in it a subject that captivated it, and that more than one detail, more than one elaboration, can safely be attributed to it. I mean not only the interminable descriptions of Mounts Meru and Mandara — which I have not transcribed — but above all the strangely precise details of the churning itself, and of the transformations undergone by the sea water before producing the *amṛta*. This tireless and sometimes incoherent accumulation of marvels clearly betrays the Hindu spirit, with its characteristic contradiction: a taste for the colossal in the whole, and infinite meticulousness in the detail.

But once this luxuriant vegetation is set aside, and likewise the Brahmanic framework (the divine personages, their hierarchy, etc.) that overlays the story, there remains a tightly connected group of legends concerning the preparation of the *amṛta*, the two thefts attempted by the demons, and the gods' vengeance. This ensemble of interdependent legends forms a "thematic cycle," whose structure we have outlined through a network of titles and subtitles.

The order of episodes is fixed and necessary — except for the two thefts, which could easily be interchanged. The thematic elements are not interwoven but juxtaposed, which makes their study easier and will soon make the analogies more evident.

We shall now set this Hindu cycle of the *amṛta* in parallel with its Scandinavian counterpart — the cycle of the beer of the Æsir.

Chapter Two

The Cycle of the Beer of the Æsir

No one has ever used this term, nor any similar one, to refer to the Eddic poems we are about to discuss — the *Hymiskviða* ("Story of Hymir") and the *Lokasenna* ("Quarrel of Loki"). Nor has anyone ever attached importance to their close connection, which is nevertheless clearly emphasised by a specific prose line at the beginning of the second poem.

Indeed, in the stage of development these Eddic texts represent, the central point — the focus of both poems — is the figure of Thor. Each appears as the account of one of Thor's exploits, in which the beer of the Æsir serves merely as an occasion or dramatic pretext. But this annexation of the legends to the character — to the cycle of Thor — cannot be ancient; it is clearly the result of the growing favour that this god enjoyed among the Scandinavians.

What, then, was originally the centre, the unifying element of these two poems? We shall see that it is enough to restore to the beer — the divine drink — its former dignity to rediscover a cycle exactly corresponding, except for a gap easy to fill, to the Hindu cycle of the *amṛta*.

※
※ ※

A. Preparation of the Beer of the Æsir

1. Deliberation of the gods about their food.

One day, the Æsir gather together to eat. But the fare is meagre. They shake the magic wands and consult the blood of the victims: it is discovered that abundance is to be found at Ægir's, the god of the Sea. Thor immediately looks Ægir in the eyes and says: "You must give a splendid feast to the Æsir."

Ægir then asks that they provide him with the Kettle: "After that," he says, "I shall be glad to brew the beer for you all."

2. Preparations.

Thor and Tyr at Hymir's, god of the winter sea. The conquest of the Kettle of the Sea. — The gods cannot manage to provide the Kettle. But Tyr gives Thor a helpful piece of advice: "To the east of the Elivagar (a mythical region sometimes interpreted as the Milky Way), on the edge of the sky, dwells the wise Hymir, my father; he owns a Kettle, a vast vessel, a league deep... It could be taken, with a bit of cunning..."

This Hymir is the god of the dark and hostile sea (= *humiaz* [*tivaz*]?), while Ægir is the god of the sea itself (= *âguiaz* [*tivaz*]?). As for the Kettle, it has long been recognised that it represents the sea itself, possessed by Hymir throughout the winter. Whatever interpretation may ultimately be given to the poem — and several have been proposed, some quite poetic, such as that of Uhland — its subject now clearly reduces to the conquest of Hymir's Kettle by Thor.

Thor, accompanied by Tyr, arrives at Hymir's dwelling after a day's journey. Hymir's wife receives them, brings them the beer of welcome, warns them of her husband's cruelty, and hides them beneath the immense brewing vat.

Hymir returns, and the ice of his beard is heard creaking; his wife gently tells him of the arrival of his son, accompanied by Thor, the benefactor of mankind. The giant's gaze makes the pillar behind which the gods are hiding collapse. The brewing vat crashes loudly to the ground, and the guests appear.

The presence of Thor, the exterminator of his race, bodes ill for the giant Hymir. Nevertheless, Hymir has a good meal served: three boiled oxen. Thor, true to his reputation, devours two of them by himself. Angered by such gluttony, Hymir says to him: "Tomorrow evening, we shall dine on the spoils of our hunt (= our fishing)!"

Then begins, without the text announcing it, a true contest — or rather, a series of contests — between the god and the giant. Thor wins the first trial: he brings back from the forest the black ox whose head is to serve as bait for the fish. Then he triumphs in the fishing: he hauls up on his line the Miðgarðr Serpent. In the third trial, he manages to shatter, by throwing it against Hymir's very forehead (for nothing is as hard as a giant's head), the cup from which the latter customarily drinks. Finally, in the last trial, Thor hoists the great Kettle onto his shoulders, descends the steps of the hall, and departs. "The host of many-headed giants," trying to pursue him, is destroyed by his dreadful hammer, Mjöllnir. After a few incidents, Tyr and Thor reach the home of the Æsir with Hymir's brewing vat: "Now," seems to conclude the poet, in a stanza of very uncertain reading, "the Æsir can feast mightily in Ægir's hall until winter."

3. Brewing of the Beer of the Æsir in the Kettle of the Sea.

About the brewing of the divine beer, the Eddic poems say little; no doubt because they imagined it to be similar to that of earthly beer — a commonplace process, familiar to all their contemporaries. The *Lokasenna* begins when the beer is being served — or rather, "serves itself," for such is the latest refinement of divine comfort. The gods, Æsir and Álfar, are present in great number: Odin and Frigg his wife; Sif, Thor's wife; and many others. Thor, "delayed by his journey to the East," has not yet arrived.

B. The Demon at the Table of the Gods. His Punishment

But Loki — that complex being, half-god, half-giant, sometimes the ally of the Æsir and sometimes their irreconcilable enemy, by turns beneficent and maleficent — Loki has been excluded from the feast for having killed one of Ægir's servants.

Despite the resistance and warnings of the second servant, Eldir, Loki enters the hall. All the gods fall silent. Loki says:

"Burning with thirst after a long journey, Loptr [= Loki] has come to this hall to beg the Æsir to grant him just a cup of mead. Why this silence, gods so puffed up with pride that you can no longer speak? Give me a place, a seat at your table — or drive me away from here." (Trans. from Bergmann, "Poèmes Islandais," Paris, 1838.)

The god Bragi refuses in haughty terms. Loki appeals to Odin, reminding him of their oath of brotherhood — and Odin, for the sake of peace, has mead served to Loki. Loki then greets all the Æsir and all the Ásynjur, except Bragi. Bragi rises and threatens Loki. The quarrel begins.

The gods and goddesses each in turn try to silence Loki: Idunn, Gefjon, Odin himself, Frigg, Freyja, Njörd, Tyr, Freyr, Byggvir, Heimdall, Skaði, Beyla, and finally Thor, who arrives at the end of the feast. Loki's fury grows; he hurls the most violent insults and threats.

At last, the enraged gods rush upon him. Though he takes the form of a fish and throws himself into the waterfall Franangr, the Æsir catch him in a net, drag him into a cave, and bind him with the entrails of one of his sons. Skaði takes a venomous serpent and holds it above Loki's face, dripping poison upon him. But Sigyn, Loki's wife, sits beside him, catching the drops of venom in a bowl. When the bowl is full, she empties it; during that time, the venom falls on Loki's face, and he writhes so violently against his chains that the whole earth trembles. "That," says the poem, "is what people now call earthquakes."

⁂

These Eddic poems call for the same remarks as the "Brahmanic" poem of the *Mahābhārata*: we are dealing with a religion and a divine pantheon that are highly evolved; the gods who now play the leading roles — Thor in particular — have taken the place of older deities.

Moreover, the presence of Tyr alongside Thor in the expedition to Hymir — while we know that Tyr is the direct and legitimate heir of the one great identified Indo-European god — perhaps allows us to suppose that, in an earlier state of the legend, it was Tyr and not Thor who conquered the Cauldron. In the same way, in India, Viṣṇu very probably replaced Indra, who nevertheless still plays a rather considerable role in the text we have studied.

We can already see, broadly speaking, that the "Cycle of the Beer of the Æsir" clearly corresponds to episodes A and C (Preparation of the *Amṛta* — The Demon among the Gods) from the Cycle of the *Amṛta*.

What remain outside of it are episodes B and D (The Expedition of the False Bride among the Demons — The Massacre of the Demons). We shall soon see that Eddic literature has not lost these episodes, but that, by the late period from which we have our first testimonies, it had already detached them from the cycle of the Beer and linked them instead to another object of "permanence."

But let us first specify more clearly the correspondences we have recognised.

Chapter Three

The Cycle of Ambrosia

We will present, gathered as they arise in turn, the themes and groups of themes common to the Hindu Cycle of the *Amṛta* and the Scandinavian Cycle of the divine Beer.

We will then examine what became, in the Edda, of the two episodes of the *Amṛta* Cycle left aside in the previous comparison: the expedition of the false bride and the massacre of the demons.

Finally, we will provide a schema, as rigorous as possible, of the Cycle of Ambrosia thus defined, and we will note the uncertain points, the questions that the comparison of the Indian and Germanic testimonies leaves unresolved.

⁎⁎⁎

A. Preparation of the Ambrosia

1. Deliberation of the gods concerning their nourishment.

(a) The Hindu gods wish to prepare a food that grants

immortality. The Germanic gods deliberate on a less serious matter: it is merely a question of supplementing a rather meagre meal. Likewise, at the beginning of the *Lokasenna*, in order to obtain his share of beer, Loki simply pleads "his fatigue," whereas Rāhu mingles with the gods to gain, along with them, immortality. This difference comes from the fact that the beer of the Æsir is no longer a drink of immortality like the *amṛta*: the entire Germanic tale is, so to speak, toned down by one degree.

(b) With this reservation made, the parallelism between the two accounts is clear: Viṣṇu decrees that the ocean shall be churned in its vessel; Thor commands the god of the Sea to prepare beer for the Æsir.

2. It is the Sea that will provide the divine nourishment, following a certain operation (churning or brewing).

Among the Hindus, it is the sea as a material element: the gods will churn the ocean in its "vessel" (*Kalaśodadhi*); but the gods also deal with the personified Ocean, who consents to the operation. Likewise, among the Germans, it is both the sea in the literal sense and the personified sea: Ægir, god of the sea, will prepare the beer in Hymir's immense marine "Vat."

There is here, in a distinctive detail, an agreement that cannot be accidental; the only difference is that the Hindu "churns," while the German, a beer drinker, "brews." But to apply this operation to the sea considered as a receptacle — to prepare in the "Vat of the Sea" the food of the gods, to imagine the colossal scene implied by such a human task magnified to divine proportions — all this reveals the common origin of the two accounts: the theme of the "brewing of the sea" is too peculiar to have arisen independently in two mythologies.

3. A god goes to seek, from a marine being, the Vat necessary for the operation.

(a) Both the Hindus and the Germans note the impotence of the gods to find the instruments necessary for the operation. It is the god (Viṣṇu, Thor) who saves the situation.

(b) But here it must be noted that the Hindus and the Germans each developed, according to their distinct genius, this idea of "the conquest of the tools." The Hindu — for whom the operation is a churning, and who, moreover, sees around him very high mountains — is especially interested in the uprooting of Mount Mandara, which must serve as the churning stick; the role played in this uprooting by the serpent Vāsuki sufficiently proves the recency of this invention. The Scandinavian, familiar with the sea and imagining only a brewing, concerns himself solely with the conquest of the Vat.

And here we clearly have an Indo-European motif, since — though only in six verses — the *Mahābhārata* still recounts the expedition of the gods to the marine possessor of the Vessel, to the "Master of the Waters," an expedition that forms the main subject of almost the entire *Hymiskviða*. It even doubles it, with that love of accumulation so characteristic of the Hindu spirit: after having asked the "Master of the Waters" to lend them the ocean, the Sura then ask the Turtle-god to lend them his back, at the bottom of the sea, as a support for Mount Mandara.

(c) Was there a struggle between the messenger of the gods and the possessor of the Vat? Did the messenger have to triumph over a certain number of trials in order to obtain the Vat (Germanic account)? Or did the possessor of the Vat yield it immediately — reluctantly, but without resistance — acknowledging his weakness (Hindu account)?

The details of the trials — the hunt for the black ox, the fishing of the Miðgarðr serpent, the breaking of the cup, etc. — to which Hymir subjects Thor are purely Germanic, and no doubt purely Scandinavian. But is the same true of the idea of a contest in which the Vat is the prize, of a struggle between the god and the marine being? Is the Hindu account truncated, or the Scandinavian one elaborated? There is probably some truth in both hypotheses: India disregarded a detail that the peoples of the North delighted in. To glimpse the ancient state of things, we must here await the testimony of other mythologies.

4. Churning (stirring) of the ambrosia.

The operation is described at length in the *Mahābhārata*. But we have already noted, in these elaborations, a multitude of details that can be attributed with certainty to Hindu imagination: to this fantastic and grandiose scene, which clearly captivated it, it has lavished its most singular embellishments.

For the Germans, on the other hand, brewing being a natural and commonplace activity, it ended up as the part of the story that was sacrificed in the development: the beer is brewed offstage, between the last verses of the *Hymiskviða* and the first words of the *Lokasenna*, which simply inform us that the preparations for the feast are complete.

From this silence, however, it would be premature to conclude that the Indo-European cycle was also silent. Not everything in the Hindu account is necessarily of recent invention. But at present, we have no means of distinguishing the original elements from the later additions.

B. The Demon at the Feast of the Gods

1. The demon among the gods.

(a) The gods, Sura or Æsir, gather around the drink at last prepared — *amṛta* or beer.

(b) A demon (Rāhu–Loki) joins them.

However, in India, the mere fact that *amṛta* is a drink of immortality and Rāhu a demon is enough to make his presence among the gods "unpardonable." Conversely, among the Germans, the far less potent virtue of the Æsir's beer — and also the semi-divine character of Loki — forced tradition to attribute to him a crime, a murder, for which expulsion from the feast would serve as punishment: Loki became the murderer of one of Ægir's servants, just as elsewhere he is made the murderer of Baldr.

These crimes clearly belong to a rather late stage of

Scandinavian mythology; and since, in the simpler version preserved in the Indian account, the demon's excommunication and attempt are far more naturally explained — and above all, far more closely tied to the cycle — than in the Germanic one, we find here new reason to suppose that originally ambrosia truly possessed the full value of an immortalising drink, and that it is Germanic mythology, with its weaker "beer" and its partly divine Loki, that innovated. The crime of Loki thus appears as a detail introduced late to prop up a legend whose coherence was threatened by the diminished power of the Æsir's beer and by Loki's ambiguous nature.

For the rest, the outline of the episode is the same in both cases: the demon — "thanks to his disguise," according to the Indian version; "thanks to the pacifying intervention of Odin," according to the Scandinavian one — manages to drink a "mouthful" ("a cup") of the divine beverage. Then — "betrayed and recognized," say the Indians; "because of his insolence," say the Scandinavians — he enters into a quarrel with the gods.

The Hindu legend has nothing equivalent to the *Lokasenna* proper: the punishment follows immediately after the demon's discovery, and his anger is entirely posthumous. The Germans, on the contrary, developed the "scene of insults" into a long episode, full of meaning and allusions, which there is no need to detail here.

It is important to note the essential role played, at the end of the quarrel and at the moment of punishment, by the god already encountered — who was eventually supplanted by Viṣṇu and Thor: it is Viṣṇu, in the *Mahābhārata*, who executes Rāhu. In the *Lokasenna*, it is with the arrival of Thor that the scene reaches such a pitch of violence that the gods seize Loki and torture him; no doubt, in an earlier form of the text, the intervention of Thor (or of his predecessor) was still more decisive and more personal.

2. The demon punished by the gods.

(a) The punishment differs in the two traditions, and in both the Hindu and the Scandinavian versions it includes details that reveal the particular taste and imagination of each people.

(b) However, one fact already seems certain: the punishment served to explain natural phenomena. The fall of Rāhu's decapitated body, just like Loki's convulsions under the venom, are the cause of earthquakes.

The Hindus further explain eclipses through Rāhu's hatred, whose severed head goes to bite the stars that denounced him — the Sun and the Moon. This legend is already known in the Vedas, where it is attributed to a demon with a characteristic name, Svarbhānu; but there, it appears completely unrelated to the *amṛta* or to the *sóma*. Perhaps this is a later Hindu innovation.

In certain Eddic traditions, one also finds analogous eclipse legends (the wolves threatening the chariot of the moon goddess; the wolf Fenrir who will devour the Moon at the end of time), but these too are nowhere connected with either the cycle of the divine beer or the figure of Loki.

Finally — and most importantly — many other peoples, not of

Indo-European origin, possess similar eclipse myths, entirely independent of any such cycle.

∗∗∗

C. The False Bride Among the Demons
D. The Extermination of the Demons

We have seen that the cycle of the Beer of the Æsir, made up of the *Hymiskviða* and the *Lokasenna*, contains all the episodes of the cycle of the *amṛta* except for two: the expedition of the god disguised as a goddess among the demons who stole the *amṛta*, and the scene of the extermination of the demons.

Now, it is precisely these two episodes that fill the very famous poem *Þrymskviða*. This time, it concerns the theft of Thor's hammer; and since all connection has already been broken, even in the earliest accounts, between this legend and the cycle of the divine beer, we should not be surprised to see Loki — who just now appeared as the enemy of the Æsir — take on here his other aspect, that of a benevolent spirit and companion of the gods.

Here is first the substance of the poem:

Thor, upon awakening, realises that his hammer, Mjölnir, has been stolen — a theft of utmost gravity, for if it is not quickly remedied, it will bring about the ruin of the Æsir (stanza 17). Loki, sent out to investigate, learns that it is the giant Thrym who has stolen the hammer, and that he will not surrender his prize except in exchange for the beautiful goddess Freyja.

Thor and Loki therefore go to Freyja to ask her to go to Thrym, to marry him in order to recover the hammer and save the Æsir. Freyja, furious at the request, snorts with such rage that the entire hall shakes. So, the gods hold an assembly and decide to disguise Thor as a woman and send him to Thrym in Freyja's place. Loki will accompany him, disguised as a handmaiden. They dress Thor in the bridal linen, place Freyja's great necklace around his neck, hang a bunch of keys at his belt, lay heavy jewels upon his chest, and tie up his hair in a bridal knot — and the two false goddesses set out.

They arrive at Thrym's hall, where he welcomes them warmly — but is astonished at Freyja's appetite: she devours an entire ox, eight salmon, and drinks three barrels of mead. The maid (Loki in disguise) explains that Freyja has neither eaten nor drunk for eight days, so eager was she to reach the land of the giants.

Moved, Thrym bends forward to kiss Freyja beneath her veil — but the fiery flash of Thor's eyes makes him leap back to the far end of the hall. The maid again saves the moment, saying that Freyja has not slept for eight nights in her haste. Then the giant's old sister enters, demanding the traditional wedding gifts from Freyja. Thrym orders the hammer to be fetched and placed on the bride's knees for the blessing. But no sooner has Thor regained possession of his hammer than he slaughters Thrym, his old sister, and the whole tribe of giants.

"Thus," the poem concludes, "did the son of Odin win back his hammer."

This is exactly the same motif as Viṣṇu's expedition in disguise, only expanded and enriched with vivid details:

The demons have stolen the *amṛta* and now demand, with loud cries, Lakṣmī, the most beautiful of goddesses. Viṣṇu assumes "the form of a woman of wondrous beauty" (the text does not explicitly say it is Lakṣmī's form, but it clearly implies it) and, accompanied by Nara (probably also in disguise), goes to the demons.

Blinded by love — just as Thrym, who does not recognise Thor either by his appetite or by the flash of his eyes — the demons offer him the *amṛta*, which he carries back to the gods. A few verses later, he casts off his disguise, slaughters the demons with his discus, and contributes more than any other god to the final victory.

The *Mahābhārata* here is very restrained: it devotes only eight verses to Viṣṇu's adventure. We will later see how beautifully the *Bhāgavata Purāṇa* expands on this material; but, as in the *Mahābhārata*, we will find not the slightest comic note in the *Purāṇa* — on the contrary, the scene is marked by a somewhat solemn, even sorrowful gravity.

Thus, we can see, vividly and directly, the contrasting genius of two peoples, two mythologies, two artistic spirits: the Indian, captivated by the colossal and little inclined to smile; the Scandinavian, seizing upon picturesque, often ironic detail for its delight. Both move toward fable, but the one through epic grandeur, the other through lyric and song.

In the final battle, there is a significant difference between the two traditions:

At the end of the *Þrymskviða*, the giants are massacred by Thor's hammer alone — the feat of a single god. In the *Mahābhārata*, by contrast, there is a true battle, a general melee involving all the gods, much like in Hesiod's account of the *Titanomachy*. Thus, while the outcome is the same — the extermination of the demons — the correspondence between the two themes is not exact. It seems clear that the innovation lies on the Germanic side.

*
* *

But a preliminary question arises: was this motif of the "false bride," the "god in disguise," already independent of the cycle in the Indo-European period, as it is in the *Edda*, or did it form an integral part of it, as in the Indian version?

Who, then, innovated — the Indians, by strengthening the cycle with a foreign theme, or the Germans, by impoverishing the cycle through the loss of an episode?

Strictly speaking, we should not yet give an answer. But even aside from any argument of antiquity, there are strong reasons to believe that the Indian version faithfully represents the original tradition.

We already know that the Scandinavian beer had a weakened

meaning: the theft of this beer would not have had, for the Æsir, the same gravity as the loss of Thor's hammer, a loss that, as we've seen, would soon bring about their ruin and replacement by the giants.

Thus, this separation of the "false bride" episode can be easily explained as a new consequence of the weakening of ambrosia into beer: the beer yielded its place, in a legendary motif, to a more significant divine object. But this substitution — at least in its final form — must necessarily be recent: it could only have taken place from the moment when Thor, the possessor of the Hammer, became the great favourite of Norwegian legends.

Before Thor, before the Hammer, the theme of the "false bride" must have been connected with some other divine object, which was also a symbol or instrument of power and permanence. Which one? The ambrosia, which — unlike the Hammer — is an ancient concept, had everything necessary to play that role.

*
**

Let us then admit, as a very plausible hypothesis, that this episode — both in the Indo-European period and in the Hindu legend — did indeed belong to the cycle of ambrosia. The examination of all the other mythologies of the same family will soon justify this conclusion. We can now define the ancient cycle as follows:

A. Preparation of the Ambrosia

1. Council of the Gods

(a) The gods, threatened by death or famine, deliberate: "How can we obtain the drink of immortality?"
(b) One god gives the solution: it is the sea, properly churned (or stirred, or brewed…), that will yield it.

2. Conquest of the Vessel

(a) The gods prove powerless to find the necessary instruments.
(b) A god goes to the marine being who possesses the Vessel,
(c) and, after a struggle (or negotiation?), takes it from him.

3. The Ambrosia is brewed (churned…) in the Vessel of the Sea. [Various incidents?]

B. The Demon Among the Gods (First Theft)

1. Feast of the Gods

(a) The gods gather around the ambrosia and drink.
(b) A demon joins them and drinks a mouthful of the ambrosia.
(c) But he is recognised (or denounced?) as a demon. (Or is there a scene of quarrel?)

2. Punishment of the Demon

(a) The gods torture the demon (bind him to a rock? turn him to stone?).

(b) [Theme of the earthquake, linked to the preceding one?]

C. The False Bride (Second Theft)

1. Theft

(a) A demon has carried off the ambrosia to his own dwelling.
(b) He is also in love with a goddess.

2. Recovery

(a) A god disguises himself as a goddess and goes to the demon as a bride.
(b) The demon, mad with love, gives the cup of ambrosia to the false bride, who brings it back to the gods.
(c) Casting off her disguise, the false bride kills the demon.

D. The Extermination of the Demons

(a) General melee — or massacre of the demons by a single god?
(b) The demons are hurled beneath the sea and beneath the earth — or slaughtered?

In the preceding outline, I have avoided "defining" any divine figures, since my purpose was only to establish the themes. However, both the Hindu and the Germanic accounts—as indeed nearly all those we shall examine later—suggest that it is one and the same god who accomplishes the various individual exploits of the cycle (A, 2 b and c — B, 2 a? — C, 2). Beyond that, we know nothing more about this god.

The order adopted for the two abductions is the reverse of that found in the cycle of the *amṛta*. This reversal is not intended merely to better preserve the unity of the Cycle of the Beer of the Æsir in the narrow sense of the term (*Hymiskviða* + *Lokasenna*); it will be seen that, among all the Indo-Europeans, only the Indo-Iranians and the Slavs (and perhaps the Tocharians) place the episode of the "false bride" before that of the "demon among the gods."

The Greeks, Latins, and Celts have the opposite order, as in the outline.

It is, moreover, quite clear that the notion of "order" here has no logical value but only an expository one, and that, fundamentally, either episode may come first without altering the unity or the meaning of the cycle.

※

To conclude, let us record the principal unresolved points that the comparison of these first two traditions has left in doubt — points that only an examination of the other mythologies of the Indo-European family may clarify:

1. Was there, in the Indo-European legend, cooperation between the gods and the demons in the making of the ambrosia? (A, 3.)

2. Was there a struggle (a contest?) between the marine being

who possessed the Vat and the god charged with seizing it? (A, 2, c.)

3. Was the birth of ambrosia accompanied by the birth of certain divine beings (gods, animals, etc.)? (A, 3.)

4. Were earthquakes and eclipses explained within the cycle? (E, 2, b.)

5. Did the cycle end with a general battle between gods and demons? (D, a.)

These questions will be resolved in the second part, which we are now about to begin, where we will trace the evolution of the cycle among the various Indo-European peoples.

PART TWO

The Cycle of the Ambrosia in the Various Indo-European Mythologies

Before examining what the Greeks and Latins, Celts and Slavs made of the Indo-European Cycle of Ambrosia, it will be useful, in order to clarify certain methodological points and to gauge the degree of rigour such an inquiry allows, to see what became of the cycle in the two mythologies that served us to reconstruct it.

We began from the oldest Hindu and Germanic texts concerning the cycle of the *amṛta* and that of the beer of the Æsir. Yet, even once fixed in poetic form, the legendary content continued to evolve.

In India especially, one can, if not follow this slow metamorphosis completely, at least mark important stages of it — stages that probably extend over ten centuries. Christianity too rapidly and too radically transformed the religious thought of the Scandinavians, and their earliest texts are too recent for us to hope to find in them a development as continuous. Still, the legends we have examined had time to age before they died, and some survive in the form of popular tales or *Volksweisen* (folk songs).

This purely historical study will allow us to verify, through a new kind of experiment, the authenticity of the Cycle of Ambrosia. We shall observe, by following the evolution of the myths in India or in Iceland during the historical period, that this evolution simply continues the process we previously had to assume between the Indo-European cycle and its earliest attested forms.

Where we earlier noted a detail in decline, or a theme in danger of atrophy, we shall now find that the detail has vanished, that the theme has ceased to be understood. Where we observed a loosening of the link connecting a given theme to the cycle, we shall now find that the link has been completely severed.

And finally, wherever we saw a new element — still timid and unobtrusive — added to the cycle for some reason (most often out of popular enthusiasm), we shall now see the intruder expand its place and sometimes draw to itself the attention and favour of later poets.

This continuity between the development we inferred and the development we can actually observe will at once explain the latter and confirm the former.

Chapter One

The Cycle of Ambrosia among the Hindus

I. Traces of the Cycle in the Vedic Period: Deva, Asura, and Sóma

To simplify the exposition, we have so far taken as the Hindu element of comparison the earliest text in which the cycle appears in its entirety and clearly connected to *amṛta* — that is, an epic text. But it would be incorrect to say that the cycle does not appear in the Vedic period: it appears fragmentarily, through several of its most characteristic themes, and is linked not to *amṛta* but to the new Indo-Iranian liquor, *sóma*.

What happened here — though to a lesser degree, since *sóma* always remains a divine drink — is similar to what we were led to suppose about the theft of Thor's hammer: the day when, definitively among the Scandinavians and temporarily within Vedic society, the idea of ambrosia faded, the legends connected with it transferred to some other object more important to the gods or more popular among men.

The Greeks and the Romans will likewise show us themes, or groups of themes, or even the entire cycle, transferred from ambrosia to some other divine nourishment or object.

The Vedic traces we are about to note are clearer in the *Brāhmaṇas* than in the *Vedas* proper. We have already explained in the Introduction this general fact and pointed out the exegetical and liturgical distortion that ancient legends—when they managed to slip into the *Brāhmaṇas* — always suffer in such commentaries: they are there only to justify one or another form or prescription of the sacrifice, and the redactors bend them, willingly or not, with all the subtlety one can expect from priests — and from Hindus — to prove whatever they must prove.

At times, one might think one is already reading those strange analyses of Paul Regnaud and his disciples, where Indra, the Aśvins, etc., are "aspects" of fire, and where *ṛta, bhuvana, namas, manas*, etc., are "names" of Soma or of the libation.

The *Brāhmaṇas* naturally link the themes of ambrosia that they have preserved in soma form to the struggle between the Deva and the Asura.

A detailed study of the notion of Asura at different stages of Vedic literature can be found in an article by Torgny Segerstedt, *Revue de l'Histoire des Religions*, 1908, vol. LVII, pp. 157–203 and 293–326. Although the author's general thesis may be debatable, the numerous facts he collects and organises retain their full value.

In addition, Sylvain Lévi's study, *La Doctrine du Sacrifice dans les*

Brâhmanas (Paris, 1898), contains in Chapter II (*Le Sacrifice et les Dieux*) several valuable quotations relevant to this topic.

1. Soma and the Soma sacrifice in the struggles between the Deva and the Asura:

"Two superior orders of beings were brought forth by Prajāpati: the Deva and the Asura. The right of seniority is undecided between the two groups; primogeniture is assigned sometimes to one, sometimes to the other... They have equal rights to the paternal inheritance, which they share equally. Unfortunately, the sacrifice is an indivisible good, and both parties covet it with equal ardor. The Asura surpass in bodily strength, but sacrifice is a matter of knowledge, and thus the Asura will be vanquished." (S. Lévi, op. cit., p. 36. See the references to the various Brāhmaṇas.)

The sacrifice, in somaic language, is the same thing as the feast of the gods in amṛtaic language. It is known — and we shall return to this point in our third part — that the ritual of the soma sacrifice is expressly addressed, during one of its three pressings, "to all the gods." The sacrifice is truly the food of the gods (*Śatapatha Brāhmaṇa* VIII, 1, 2, 10, etc.; cf. S. Lévi, op. cit., p. 30, n. 1), their very principle of life (*Śatapatha Brāhmaṇa* XIV, 3, 2, 1).

One can easily understand how the political clan, or the sacerdotal caste that so greatly developed the role of the somaic sacrifice in the religion of the *Vedas* and the *Brāhmaṇas*, could quite naturally have transposed to the benefit of its own cult the festival and the themes of ambrosia.

The fear of death haunts the gods and directs most of their actions:

"The gods were afraid of death, which is the end, which is the year, which is Prajāpati. 'May he not, together with the days, lead our life to its end!' They performed sacrifices, but they did not obtain immortality. They performed other rites... but they did not obtain immortality."

Then Prajāpati taught the gods the necessary rites.

"Thus the gods acted, and they became immortal." (Śatapatha Brāhmaṇa X, 4, 3, 3–8. See in S. Lévi, op. cit., pp. 41–42, for other similar texts.)

The search for immortality sets the gods in conflict with the Asura.

"The Deva and the Asura, both born of Prajāpati, were rivals; both were without personal life, for they were mortal, and whoever has no personal life is mortal. Among them all, Agni alone was immortal; and it was from him, the immortal one, that both sides lived. Now, whoever among them was killed would come back to life. Consequently, the gods remained in the end the weaker. They went on worshipping, labouring: 'Ah, if only we could triumph over the Asura, our rivals, who are mortal!' Then they perceived that immortality consisted in the ritual establishment of fire. They established it among themselves, within their inmost being; and when they had established it among themselves, within their inmost being, they became immortal, they became invincible, and they triumphed over their rivals, subject to defeat and death." (Śatapatha Brāhmaṇa II, 2, 2, 8–14; cf. S. Lévi, op. cit., pp. 42–43.)

This account turns toward metaphysics, toward religious scholasticism, like so many other accounts in the *Brāhmaṇas*. It has, at least, the merit of showing that the central role of *amṛta* — even diluted, even reduced to an almost purely verbal value — was not forgotten in the Vedic accounts of the divine struggles.

At times, however, the transformation of these themes took a different direction: the divine conflicts became wars of a more human kind, and Soma appeared personified, as the leader and king of the Deva. His role, moreover, remained essential: the Deva were defeated until Soma placed himself at their head. (*Aitareya Brāhmaṇa*, I, 3, 14.)

In short, under both of its forms — substance of the sacrifice or god of the sacrifice — *sóma* is the essential weapon of the Deva. Scenes of battle are multiplied endlessly in the dense pages of the *Brāhmaṇas*. Can we identify those that derive directly from the Cycle of Ambrosia? Can we distinguish, among so many duplicates, the original archetypes? This task is doubtless not impossible.

For example, there is something like an early echo of the cry of revolt of the demons — as the *Mahābhārata* later presents it — in the exclamation with which the Asura try to oppose the *sóma* sacrifice being performed by the Deva:

"*You must not sacrifice! You must not perform the sacrifice!*"

But then the Deva, says the text, turn toward Indra — as later they will toward Viṣṇu — and say to him:

"You are the greatest and most powerful among us; stand up to these enemies."

And Indra drives out the Asura. (*Śatapatha Brāhmaṇa*, IX, 2, 3, 2.)

2. Collaboration Between Gods and Demons – The Expelled and Punished Demon

But it is within a ritual, one of the preparatory ceremonies of the soma sacrifice, that we find a clear trace of the collaboration and subsequent rupture between Deva and Asura, as well as of the episode of the punished demon.

The *sóma* must be brought to the *Brāhmaṇa* priests by a man from the lowest social class, who is immediately expelled and threatened with blows. Hillebrandt (*Vedische Mythologie*, I, p. 80) already saw in this scene the ritual expression of a characteristic verse from the *ṚgVeda* (I, 105, 6):

"Concerning the sóma, we shall fight with the Asura."

We will return to this point in the third part, in connection with the Ambrosia festival.

3. The Bride Among the Demons — Finally, the episode most explicitly preserved is that of the theft of the *sóma* and the expedition of the Bride to the thieving demon.

This episode, too, has taken on a ritual and even social significance, since it underlies a special form of marriage allowed only to the lower classes — the āsuric marriage — which involves the purchase of the bride. It has also undergone exegetical distortion, most clearly visible in the artificial, abstract name of the Bride: Vāc, "Speech."

The *Aitareya-Brāhmaṇa* (I, 27) recounts how the demon Viśvāvasu — a *Gandharva*, a race only slightly less hostile to the gods than the Asura and particularly known for its sensuality — stole and hid the *sóma*.

The Deva and the divine sages, determined to recover it, realise that since the *Gandharva* are ruled by desire, they can ransom *sóma* by giving the thief a "divine woman," Vāc (Speech). (Cf. Oldenberg, *Revue des Études Védiques*, 1894, p. 247.)

What is this personified abstraction? Brāhmaṇic scholasticism, along with Ilā and Bharatī, makes her one of the deities of the sacrifice, assimilating her to the Vedic Sarasvatī. Yet it is especially clear that here she plays exactly the role of the "feminine form" — a god in disguise or a magical effigy created by the gods' *māyā* — who, in the Indo-European legend, goes to seduce the demon and recover the ambrosia.

We also know that the adventure of Vāc ends badly for the Hindu demons: this is likely the meaning of a long-obscure passage from the *Śatapatha-Brāhmaṇa* (III, 2, 1, 23), according to which the gods, *"having taken Speech (Vāc) from the demons,"* thereby defeated them, causing them to flee uttering inarticulate cries.

In this double story, one cannot fail to recognise the various themes of the Indo-European episode of the Fatal Bride, appearing here in a form that closely resembles the Scandinavian *Þrymskviða*. Yet, already at this stage — as later in the *Amṛtamanthana* — no trace of comedy can be found: the Hindu storyteller recounts, with solemn gravity and without a hint of irony, the rather inglorious bargain that delivers the *sóma* and saves the gods.

Finally, it is noteworthy that many of these Brāhmaṇic stories personify Soma, turning him into "King Soma", either as the leader of the Deva or the prisoner of the *Gandharva*. Through this transformation, the narratives lose their mythical quality, becoming instead simple popular tales — pseudo-historical stories of the sort found among all peoples. Thus is justified the observation with which M. Segerstedt begins the article we cited earlier:

"Despite their theological and liturgical speculations, the Brāhmaṇas have preserved a number of mythical elements and thereby contain more popular representations than those found in the sacrificial hymns of the Ṛg Veda."

This will help us understand how the cycle of the *amṛta* could have been preserved for centuries among certain Hindu tribes, on the margins of the official Soma cult, before appearing in its full scope during the golden age of epic literature.

⁂

II. The Cycle in Epic Literature

It is with the *Mahābhārata*, as we have seen, that the cycle of the *amṛta*, until then obscurely preserved by popular tradition alone, enters epic literature. We shall now examine what became of it there — how it evolved between the text of the *Mahābhārata* and those of the *Rāmāyaṇa* and the *Bhāgavata Purāṇa*.

As for their dates, even approximate ones, this causes little difficulty. Within a few centuries' margin, the first — the *Mahābhārata* — can be placed around the beginning of the Christian era, and the third about a thousand years later, despite the undeserved reputation for antiquity enjoyed by the *Purāṇas*.

As for the passage of the Rāmāyaṇa that concerns us, it belongs to the first book of the poem, which is universally considered a rather recent addition; moreover, we possess several variants of it, likely from different periods.

Broadly speaking, and based more on content than on external evidence, the Rāmāyaṇa version may be regarded as intermediate between that of the *Mahābhārata* and that of the *Bhāgavata Purāṇa*; in this respect, as we shall see, the best indicator is the increasingly important role attributed to Viṣṇu in the three poems.

1. The Cycle in the *Mahābhārata*.

In the account of the *Mahābhārata*, only Brahmā is clearly superior in essence to the Deva; he is certainly above Śiva, who appears only in the episode of the Poison and saves the world "by the word of Brahmā" (*Brahmaṇo vacanāt*, *śloka* 51); and he is also above Viṣṇu–Nārāyaṇa, since it is to him, Brahmā, that the weary gods appeal for help in the midst of the churning, and it is he who instructs Viṣṇu to restore to the gods their former strength (*ślokas* 38–41).

Viṣṇu appears throughout as a god — more intelligent, more steadfast, and more vigorous than the others, the foremost among them in many respects and the one closest to Brahmā, but not essentially distinct from Indra, Agni, and the rest. The poet calls him "deva Nārāyaṇa" (*ślokas* 7, 214, etc.), placing him within a well-defined category of superhuman beings.

Likewise, his omnipotence and activity have their limits: however great his role in the churning, he occupies a definite position, a defined task — he stands at the head of the serpent-cable, to hurl it forward again and again (*śloka* 24). In short, his action remains always individual and localised; he is not yet "the soul of the world."

This is so true that beside him, Indra — the great Vedic god — retains an important role both in the labour and in the struggle: it is he who secures the mountain upon the back of the Turtle god; it is he who extinguishes the fire on Mount Mandara. Finally, at the end of the battle, it is he, Indra, "the conqueror of Bala," who entrusts Viṣṇu with the guardianship of the *amṛta* (*ślokas* 21, 34, and 88). Here he regains all his prerogatives as king of the Deva, and this is doubtless a trace of the essential role he played in the cycle before Viṣṇu's rise to supremacy.

This already characterises the text of the *Mahābhārata*. There is more: the story is indeed fantastic, and we have taken pleasure in exposing the exuberance of Hindu imagination. But, when looked at closely, there reigns in several places a great simplicity that we shall no longer find in the later texts.

For example, the ocean to be churned is truly the ordinary ocean, the "reservoir of waters," belonging to the "Lord of the Waters" (*nidhir ambhasām*, śloka 22; *apām patiḥ*, śloka 19); it is only during the churning that the water, by a first transformation, becomes milk (*śloka* 37). There is not yet any mention of an "Ocean of Milk."

Likewise, the underwater Turtle that supports Mount Mandara during the churning is a well-individualised, autonomous deity who existed before and no doubt continues to exist after the operation. We have seen in the gods' expedition to this Turtle a purely Hindu duplicate of the expedition to the "Lord of the Waters" — a duplicate made necessary by the new idea of churning, of the churning-stick that requires a support, whereas the Indo-European "brewing" required only a vat (*ślokas* 18–20).

In any case, the Turtle, in the account of the *Mahābhārata*, is a being of the same nature and of equally slight importance as the "Lord of the Waters," the "god Ocean." We shall see what metamorphoses this Turtle later had the good fortune to undergo.

Finally, the *māyā* that Viṣṇu assumes in order to reclaim the *amṛta* from the demons must be understood in its most literal sense:

it is an "appearance," a "form" of a wondrous woman — just as, in the Indo-European theme, it was the figure and garb of the goddess demanded by the demons. But the word *māyā* itself is there, and it is impossible that, in the work of some later poet, all that this word contains of philosophy — or of superstition with philosophical pretensions — should not eventually become externalised.

That is what I meant by the "simplicity" of this account: the sea is truly the sea; the Turtle god conceals no other being; Viṣṇu's *māyā* is nothing more than a disguise.

One final remark: in the episode of the battle between the gods and the demons, the description of the combatants, their weapons, and their exploits remains entirely marvellous. The mountains of the Dānavas, the arrows of Nara, and the discus of Nārāyaṇa, the immense corpses of the Asuras, the fighting at the borders of the "paths of heaven" — all this contains only the barest trace of anthropomorphism.

Never, in any case (no more than Hesiod in similar scenes), does the poet forget the superhuman form or power of his heroes. Later on — a feature common to the evolution of the cycle among all Indo-European peoples, as we have already noted in connection with the *sóma* battles of the *Brāhmaṇas* — we shall see the fabulous combat degenerate into a banal, earthly battle.

2. The Cycle in the Rāmāyaṇa

The *Rāmāyaṇa* provides only a very brief account. In the first book, in response to Rāma's questions, Viśvāmitra — "the bull among ascetics" — recounts the great events of the world's youth, among them the churning of the "Ocean of Milk." (Book I, ch. XLV, *ślokas* 12–45. Quoted from the translation by Alfred Roussel, Paris, 1903.)

The role of Viṣṇu, who appears under the names Hari ("the Yellow One," i.e., "the Sun") and Keśava ("the Long-Haired One"), is at once more limited and more powerful. He does not intervene in the deliberation of the gods, nor even at the beginning of the operation. He enters the scene only when the gods are threatened with death by the poison *Hālāhala* and call upon Śiva for help (*ślokas* 22–24), and later, when the mountain-pestle sinks into the ocean (*śloka* 29) — a new incident to which we shall return shortly.

But then, not content with aiding the gods, he multiplies himself — or at least doubles himself: he incarnates as the turtle that supports Mount Mandara, and at the same time, *"he, the soul of the worlds, Keśava, seizing the summit of the mountain with his hand, he, the supreme Puruṣa, standing among the gods, churns the Ocean of Milk"* (*ślokas* 30–31). "The soul of the worlds," "the supreme Puruṣa": such phrases, with their philosophical resonance, mark Viṣṇu's elevation to the rank of a super-deity.

Though he is called, as is also Śiva, "the best of the Sura" (*śloka* 24 for Śiva; *śloka* 25 for Viṣṇu), he is clearly set apart from them: when he has aided them, "he disappears" (*śloka* 25), doubtless returning to Brahmā, who is not mentioned in the text. When the

Sura address him, they say: *"You are the path of all beings, especially of the dwellers in heaven. Help us, O you who are mighty!"* (ślokas 28–29).

Indra is not mentioned at all, except in the final verse (śloka 45), where it is said that, after the destruction of the sons of Diti, Purandara, "the City-Breaker," i.e., Indra, takes possession of sovereignty. This may be due to the summary and necessarily incomplete form of the narrative. Yet his absence serves only to heighten Viṣṇu's exaltation — especially when one recalls the relative positions of the two deities in the *Mahābhārata* version.

To give an idea of how terse this account is, here is the beginning:

"Formerly, during the Kṛta Yuga (the first age of the world), the mighty sons of Diti and of Aditi lived as fortunate heroes, valiant and very virtuous. A thought came to these magnanimous heroes, O tiger among men: How shall we become immortal, free from old age and disease? As they reflected on this, the idea occurred to these sages: by churning the Ocean of Milk, we shall obtain the Rasa (that is, the divine liquor). They resolved to undertake this churning. Then they made a cord of Vāsuki, a pestle of Mandara, and they churned, filled with immeasurable vigour." (ślokas 15–18)

The *Mahābhārata* had devoted fifty verses — with very little "filler" — to saying the same thing.

Among the episodes omitted here, the most important are: the uprooting of Mount Mandara, probably a purely Hindu invention;

the expedition to the "Lord of the Waters" to ask him to lend the ocean, a theme we know to be Indo-European; and finally the parallel expedition to the Turtle god to ask him to support the mountain — a theme we have seen to be a purely Hindu doublet of the preceding one.

In reality, only the first two episodes have disappeared in the *Rāmāyaṇa*. The third, still timidly juxtaposed with the original in the *Mahābhārata*, has here been displaced, expanded, and inserted differently into the story: while the gods are churning, the mountain-pestle sinks and falls into the abyss. Viṣṇu, implored by the gods, then takes the form of a turtle, places the mountain on his back, and lies down in the sea (*ślokas* 29–30).

The Turtle loses its individuality — it is no longer a god, neighbour and companion of the "Lord of the Waters," it is one of Viṣṇu's *avatāra*, and one of the most famous.

It is interesting to see this appear before our eyes: first, the duplication of an Indo-European theme; then, the displacement of the resulting doublet within the cycle; and finally, in this doublet, the replacement of an ancient autonomous deity by an avatar of Viṣṇu. The version in the *Rāmāyaṇa*, both logically and chronologically, is therefore clearly later than that of the *Mahābhārata*.

More than one detail — precisely those in which we noted "simplicity" in the *Mahābhārata* — confirms this conclusion:

Under the influence, no doubt, of the idea of "churning," of a "vessel," the ocean has become the "Ocean of Milk." But (śloka 33), an etymological concern causes the primeval waters to reappear at the moment of the birth of the Apsaras (Apsaras, cf. apas: "the waters"). This same etymological concern governs the birth of all the beings that, already in the Mahābhārata, emerge from the churning of the sea: the Apsaras, says the poet, since they cannot belong exclusively to any one Deva or Dānava, are therefore called Sādhāraṇāḥ, that is, "Common" (śloka 35). Vāruṇī, daughter of Varuṇa, as soon as she is born, sets out in search of a husband; the sons of Diti (the demons) do not possess her, but the sons of Aditi (the gods) do — hence the names Asura and Sura, Surā being another name for Vāruṇī (ślokas 36–38).

By a curious whim, Dhanvantari is born among the first, holding a staff and a vessel; but the ambrosia that ought to be in the vessel does not appear until the very end, after the horse Uccaiḥśravas and the jewel Kaustubha (ślokas 32 and 39). One should not, however, try to draw any conclusion from this, for Hindu poetry readily accommodates such inconsistencies. Finally, Lakṣmī, who plays so great a role in the Mahābhārata account, is not even mentioned here.

The absence of Lakṣmī partly explains the evolution of the episode of "Viṣṇu disguised as a goddess." The notion of Māyā did the rest. The Rāmāyaṇa expresses it thus:

"When the extermination was complete (though, in truth, we are only at the beginning of the battle), Viṣṇu, endowed with great power, quickly seized the amṛta, aided by his bewildering Māyā." (śloka 42)

Here, it is no longer a matter of a disguise; the god uses his Māyā in the magical sense of the word — a kind of spiritual weapon, part fascination, part enchantment. The evolution had been foreseen.

The ending is as summary as the beginning: the battle is told in only a few ślokas (ślokas 41, 43, 44), and the episode of Rāhu is omitted. Nothing should be inferred from this concerning the evolution of the cycle, first because of the "summary" character that marks the entire passage, and second because, in the *Bhāgavata Purāṇa*, we shall find those same episodes expanded and beautified.

This text therefore marks an advance over the *Mahābhārata* through the more clearly "supra-divine" role played by Viṣṇu and through the evolution of the episode of Viṣṇu in disguise. It has definitively forgotten the episode of the expedition to the sea god who possessed the Cauldron — a scene already much reduced in the *Mahābhārata* and one that we shall no longer find in later literature.

It retains, in common with the *Mahābhārata* account, a feature we have not yet pointed out: it is purely a mythological narrative, with no moral concern whatsoever. Viṣṇu aids the gods by means of his power, not by means of his precepts. The gods triumph through strength, not as a reward for virtue. By contrast, this moralising tendency — together with the vastly magnified role of Viṣṇu — is the most striking feature of the *Purāṇic* version.

⁂

Before moving on to the *Bhāgavata Purāṇa*, we must note a variant of the Rāmāyaṇa text just studied. This is the version followed by Fauche and Corresio in their French and Italian translations.

In it, verses 15–18 of our text — which include the deliberation of the gods and the churning — are expanded, "diluted," without adding anything of substance or mythic value. Conversely, verses 18–31, recounting the stories of the Tortoise and the Poison, have disappeared. Verses 33–39, describing the various "births" and their etymological explanations (Apsaras, Sura and Asura), reappear unchanged, followed by verse 32, where the god Dhanvantari appears. We recall the anomaly in the previous version, where the births of Dhanvantari and of the *amṛta* framed all the other births — the first at the beginning, the second at the end. Here, the anomaly is less striking, yet it remains true that "the king of physicians" emerges from the ocean after the *amṛta*.

Next, the episode of the Poison — previously omitted. — reappears in a curious form:

"*After (Dhanvantari) emerged from the churned waters the poison that destroys worlds, which, shining like the blazing sun, was swallowed by all the serpents.*"

Finally, with verses 40, 44, and 45, which are preserved, we witness the battle of the gods and the demons, from which only the episode of Viṣṇu and his *Māyā* has disappeared.

Curiously, Viṣṇu and Śiva are both eliminated. This should not lead us to conclude that the text represents an earlier stage of the legend. On the contrary, it contains etymological wordplays that prove a recent date, and it belongs to a section of the *Rāmāyaṇa* known to have been added late to the main body of the poem.

It should simply be seen as a stronger effort at reduction; this is no longer a summary but a schematic outline. The absence of one episode or another does not prove that, at the time of its composition, such episodes had vanished from tradition.

In short, from this variant, only one point deserves to be retained: the new form taken by the theme of the Poison, to which we shall return shortly.

✱

3. The Cycle in the Bhāgavata Purāṇa.

The cycle of the *amṛta* occupies six chapters of the *Bhāgavata Purāṇa* (Book VIII, Chapters VI–XI, cited here from the edition and translation by Burnouf, vol. III, Paris, 1847). Through the expansion and multiplication of episodes, it has taken on a considerable development and reflects a highly evolved religious thought.

In the *Bhāgavata Purāṇa*, Viṣṇu is the true, supreme god, possessing an "independent course" (VIII, 6, 26). The Sura (gods) appear beside him only as beings on the same plane as the Asura (demons), their natural rivals and equals.

Thus, in the episode of the "disguise", Viṣṇu acts as an impartial arbiter accepted by both sides. During the ensuing conflict, he intervenes only to forbid or neutralise the use of illegitimate or magical weapons (VIII, 10, 51–52).

Though he favours the Sura, at the beginning he goes so far as to advise them to lead the Asura into a fool's bargain. Yet even in doing so, his counsel — warning them against envy, lust, and greed — serves to highlight the immense distance separating his divine nature from theirs.

But the conception of this supreme god is much deeper: it pervades the entire poem and gives it its immense value — whether in the eyes of the Hindu believer or the Western philosopher. Viṣṇu is truly the soul of the world; he no longer acts from without, as a mere being more powerful than the rest — he is the inner life of the universe, moving it from within and through all its parts at once.

Thus, during the churning, he does not merely "duplicate himself," as in the still-timid version of the *Rāmāyaṇa*: after taking the form of a tortoise (VIII, 8), we see him *"to stir up their strength and vigour, mingle with the Asura in the form of an Asura, with the hosts of the Deva in the form of a Deva, and enter into the serpent-chief in an invisible form"* (VIII, 11).

A little later, *"he penetrates all things — even the gods themselves, the mountain, and the rope"* (VIII, 13). Finally, when the *amṛta* appears in the urn of Dhanvantari, the poet takes care to tell us that this being *"owes his existence to a portion detached from part of the substance of the Blessed Viṣṇu"* (VIII, 34).

This concept of immanence necessarily entails that of unity. The entire *Bhāgavata Purāṇa* is imbued with the idea that there is only one God, of whom Brahmā, Viṣṇu, and Śiva are but manifestations.

Our text expresses this clearly. In the hymn of supplication that the Deva address to Śiva, "Mahādeva," during the appearance of the poison, they say:

"When, by means of your energy constituted by the guṇa (qualities), you bring about the creation, preservation, and destruction of this universe, then, O luminous and boundless Being, you take the distinct names of Brahmā, Viṣṇu, and Śiva. You are the supreme and mysterious Brahman; you are both the cause and the effect," etc. (VIII, 7, 23–24).

Śiva is therefore only another form of Viṣṇu, and thus the episode of the Poison — like so many others — is ultimately referred back to him.

By an opposite evolution, the ordinary gods — the Deva — have become completely humanised. Indra is depicted as a king entering into an alliance with a neighbouring chief, Bala (VIII, 7, 27–32). One would scarcely recognise in these two diplomats the fabulous warriors of the *R̥gVeda*.

This humanisation is especially evident during the battle, where the only supernatural weapons wielded by gods or demons are magical artifices; everything else reads like a page from a historical romance. The combatants are arranged in two armies, with drums, kettledrums, horses, and chariots. The commanders engage in duels scarcely more wondrous than those of the Pāṇḍava and the Kaurava (VIII, 10–11).

In sum, Viṣṇu stands beside the gods just as, in an ordinary epic, the gods stand beside men — as counsellor, inspirer, and helper. This explains the frequent exchanges of prayers and sermons that fill every interval of the poem, sometimes to excess.

At the beginning (VIII, 6, 1–16), all the gods prostrate themselves before Viṣṇu, and Brahmā addresses to him a hymn of adoration. Bhagavat replies by advising them to make an alliance with the demons, adding:

"Know, O gods, how to approve yourselves of what the Asura desire; affairs succeed better through gentleness than through violence... Let the objects (that shall be born of the ocean) never awaken in you greed, anger, or desire." (VIII, 6, 24–25)

But the "morality" is often so deeply woven into the narrative that episodes which, until now, appeared to us as complete epic tales seem here introduced only as illustrations of moral precepts.

Thus, when Śiva swallows the poison:

"It is because virtuous men usually suffer for the pain of others; they know that this is the first worship that one can render to Puruṣa, the soul of the universe." (VIII, 7, 44)

And when the Surā obtain the ambrosia, denied to their rivals:

"It is because they sought refuge beneath the dust of the god's feet. Whatever a man does for himself and for his children by means of his life, wealth, activity, heart, and words is fruitless, for all that is done in view of distinction; but those same deeds are beneficial when performed in this spirit — that God is in all things. It is like watering the root, which nourishes the whole tree." (VIII, 9, 28–29)

Neither the *Mahābhārata* nor the *Rāmāyaṇa* had anticipated such an edifying interpretation.

The details of the cycle are fairly well preserved. At most, one should note a multiplication of episodes, always resulting from evident duplications.

We have already seen in the Rāmāyaṇa an episode in which the mountain collapses into the sea, and Viṣṇu, incarnated as a tortoise, supports it. The *Purāṇa* retains this episode (VIII, 7, 6–8), but juxtaposes a doublet: while the gods are carrying Mount Mandara toward the sea, the mountain slips from their weary fingers and falls... Viṣṇu appears, loads the burden onto his winged mount Garuḍa, and plunges with the entire retinue to the bottom of the sea (VIII, 6, 34–39)

Likewise, the goddesses born from the churned ocean are more numerous. There is Śrī-Lakṣmī, who chooses Viṣṇu for her husband, and Vāruṇī, "whom the Asura seize with Viṣṇu's consent" (VIII, 8, 30) — whereas the *Rāmāyaṇa* affirmed that neither the Sura nor the Asura could rightfully possess her.

These duplications have no importance other than to show us, at every stage of the cycle's evolution, the same process of rejuvenation at work.

Here, as in the *Mahābhārata*, the ocean is truly the ocean — the reservoir of waters — though it is sometimes called the "Ocean of Milk" (*kṣīrōdadhi*). The episode of Rāhu has retained both its form and its mythic meaning (the explanation of eclipses).

As we have already seen, the battle between the gods and the demons has taken on a new appearance. What remains is to look closely at the episode of Viṣṇu clothed in his *Māyā*, which moreover possesses great literary value.

Here it is, almost in full, in Burnouf's translation:

"*At the moment when the Asura were carrying away the vase of amṛta, the Deva, discouraged, sought refuge with Hari (= Viṣṇu). Seeing their distress, Bhagavat, who fulfils the desires of his servants, said:*

'*Do not be disheartened. I will ensure your success by sowing, through the Illusion (Māyā) at my command, discord among them.*'

Immediately their passionate desire for the amṛta gave rise to discord among them:

'*It is mine first! Mine first!*' *they cried.* '*Not yours! Not yours!*'

'*The Deva have the right to receive their share, since they took an equal part in the work. It is here, as in sacrifice, a constant rule!*'

Such were the words by which the weaker among the Daitya, yielding to jealousy, sought to restrain the stronger who had seized the vase.

At that moment Viṣṇu, that mighty god to whom no resource is unknown, assumed the form of a woman wondrous beyond all description. Her complexion had the deep hue of a beautiful blue lotus; all her limbs were perfect, her ears equal and adorned with rings, her cheeks lovely, and her nose prominent. Her belly was softened beneath the weight of her breasts, newly perfected by youthful bloom; her eyes wandered, dazzled by the buzzing of bees drawn by the fragrance that escaped her mouth. Her flowing hair held a garland of jasmine blossoms; ornaments covered her lovely neck and bosom, bracelets shone on her fair arms; a brilliant girdle enhanced the beauty of her broad hips, wrapped in a pure garment; anklets rang sweetly at her feet as she walked; her glances, escaping amid the graceful motions of her modestly smiling brows, kindled the fire of love in the hearts of the Daitya chiefs.' (VIII, 36–46)

The Asura, who were quarrelling, perceived the Woman and addressed her with a long entreaty:

'Bring us happiness... Distribute the amṛta equally so that there may be no more quarrel.'

Thus invited by the Daitya, Hari, who had disguised himself in the figure of this woman, said to them with a smile and a sidelong glance full of grace:

'How is it, O sons of Kaśyapa, that you linger over me, a woman of pleasure? The wise man never places his trust in those who think only of

love. It is said, O enemies of the Suras, that the friendship of cats and of wanton women—who, obeying only their passions, are ever seeking a new lover—is fleeting.'

Encouraged by the coquettish words of this woman, the Asura lost their self-control and handed her the vase containing the amṛta. Then, taking the vase, Hari said to them with a voice adorned by a gentle smile:

'If you agree to all that I shall do, whether it be good or evil, I consent to distribute this nectar among you.'

The chiefs of the Asura, hearing these words and unaware of their full meaning, accepted...

The Sura and the Asura then separated "in the hall fragrant with incense." Thinking that to give the amṛta to the Asura—those naturally cruel beings—would be no wiser than giving it to serpents, Acyuta (= Viṣṇu) did not distribute it to them.

He arranged the gods and the demons in order... While, vase in hand, he distracted the Asura with deceptive attentions, he made the gods who were farther off drink the nectar that removes old age and death.

Faithful to the pact they had made, the Asura, enamoured of the goddess, kept silent, fearing to incur reproach by quarrelling with a woman. Enchanted by their excessive attachment to this woman, trembling lest they lose her favour, and bound by the signs of respect she gave them, they uttered not a single word of complaint." (IX, 1–23)

This text, though belonging to an entirely different genre, forms a counterpart not unworthy of the Scandinavian *Þrymskviða*. The comic element of this episode, which had already disappeared in the *Mahābhārata* and even earlier in the *Brāhmaṇas*, does not reappear here: irony is not to the taste of Indian epics. Yet the artistic development of the original theme is all the more original for that reason. Among no other people of the Indo-European family do we find this grave, somewhat melancholy tone within a tale that is, by nature, meant to entertain.

As for the evolution of the myth, only one point concerns us here: a new duplication of the episode. At first, Viṣṇu's Māyā is indeed what the Hindus of that time understood by *māyā* — that semi-spiritual, semi-magical power which we have already encountered in the version of the Rāmāyaṇa. But the episode, so to speak, rebounds: after having provoked through this *māyā* a genuine "social crisis" among the demons, Viṣṇu assumes another *māyā*, to be taken in the most literal sense — a female appearance, exactly as he did in the *Mahābhārata*. Thus, the account in the *Purāṇa* synthesises, at this point, the earlier versions.

The Episode of the Poison

Before closing this chapter, we must clarify the various forms of the curious episode of the Poison, which we have so far set aside.

(a) In the *Mahābhārata*, the poison appears almost immediately after the *amṛta*, "as a result of the excessive churning of the ocean."

The worlds lose consciousness. Brahmā appeals to Śiva, who absorbs the poison.

(b) In the first version of the *Rāmāyaṇa* we studied, it is before the appearance of the *amṛta*, after the first thousand years of churning, that the poison emerges — and it no longer comes from the ocean but from the mouths of the serpent Vāsuki. The gods go to implore Śiva; Viṣṇu supports their plea with an argument of precedence: "You are the first of the gods," he says in substance to Śiva, "and therefore it is right that the first product of divine labor should fall to you." And Śiva complies.

(c) In the second version of the *Rāmāyaṇa*, neither Viṣṇu nor Śiva appear. The poison comes out of the ocean, and it is the serpents who swallow it. Moreover, the episode regains the final position it held in the *Mahābhārata*.

(d) In the *Bhāgavata Purāṇa*, on the contrary, the poison Hālāhala is the first product of the churning. The creatures implore Śiva to save them; Śiva, in order "to satisfy Hari (= Viṣṇu)" and "to do good to all beings," drinks the poison. While he drinks, "the scorpions, serpents, poisonous plants, and other harmful creatures seize what falls from his hand."

It seems clear that this is an ancient element of the Hindu cycle. We shall soon find proof that it already existed in the Indo-Iranian period.

∗
∗∗

Such is the evolution of the Cycle of the *Amṛta*. To trace its full development, we must add a narrative from the *Viṣṇu Purāṇa* (translated by Wilson, p. 75 ff.), which closely resembles that of the *Mahābhārata*.

Only, before the churning, the Deva and Asura cast into the Ocean of Milk various kinds of magical plants. Then, among the marvellous objects produced by the churned waters together with the *amṛta*, appear the cow Surabhī and the celestial tree Pārijāta.

Wilson notes, in a footnote, that in other *Purāṇas*, the number of objects produced rises as high as fourteen.

⁂

4. Conclusions

In summary, what changed from century to century — causing or facilitating many secondary modifications — was above all the conception of the gods, and especially that of Viṣṇu.

These detailed changes merely extend those that had already taken place in prehistoric times: the regressive themes, such as the "Conquest of the Tools," disappeared as early as the *Rāmāyaṇa*. The theme of the Tortoise, derived from the former and still appearing in the *Mahābhārata* as the conquest of an "instrument," took on the independent development we have described. Likewise, the theme of Viṣṇu in disguise followed the evolution of the idea of *Māyā*.

Almost all the new episodes, at whatever period of the evolution, arose from the duplication of existing ones.

But above all, what must be noted beneath these minor variations is the constancy of the cycle, which preserves, in the later as in the earlier epic texts, all the essential episodes with their ancient sequence. Most remarkable still is the fidelity with which the notion of the *amṛta* is maintained to the very end: at the time when the *Bhāgavata Purāṇa* was composed, no other Indo-European people retained such precise memories; for centuries, more than one had already impoverished or transformed the divine drink.

Thus, the testimony of the Hindu epic, however late it may be in relation to the Vedas, has provided us with an aid that nothing else could replace.

Chapter Two

The Cycle of the Ambrosia among the Germans

Naturally, only approximate dates can be assigned to the three poems we have studied. The *Þrymskviða* is one of the oldest parts of the Edda and probably goes back to the end of the 9th century (Golther, *Handbuch der Germanischen Mythologie*, p. 266). The *Hymiskviða*, in which many features reveal a later composition, most likely dates from the end of the 10th century (Golther, ibid., p. 272). The *Lokasenna* seems to occupy an intermediate position (Golther, ibid., p. 233; cf. Ranisch, *Eddalieder* in S. *Göschen*, p. 18).

Within the whole of Scandinavian literature, these three texts therefore take us back quite far in time; moreover, the absence of Odin in the *Hymiskviða*, or his effaced role in the *Lokasenna* and *Þrymskviða*, and the important place given to Tyr in the first poem, confirm this impression of antiquity (Herrmann, *Nordische Mythologie*, p. 379).

However, though ancient within the circle of Germanic testimonies, these dates are very late when compared with what we have just found in India. Only the *Bhāgavata-Purāṇa* offered us something comparable — and even then, it stood at the end of a long poetic tradition, through which we were able to find the cycle almost intact, indeed enriched rather than diminished.

No safeguard of this kind protected the cycle among the Scandinavians. And it is remarkable that, in the 9th or 10th centuries, it does not appear to us more dislocated: only the episode of the god disguised as a goddess had become detached (*Þrymskviða*); but the connection between the other episodes, their order of succession, is still clear enough that we were able, without artifice, to group the *Hymiskviða* and the *Lokasenna* into a genuine "Cycle of the Beer."

A century or two later, the cycle had become completely fragmented, as we shall see; and although each episode retained, for several centuries — and sometimes down to modern times — a certain vitality, the beer, which had once been their common centre, was eliminated, just as it had already been in the *Þrymskviða*. It is thus a precious favour of the gods that they have at least preserved for us this last complete manifestation of the cycle.

The ancient kinship between the episodes of Hymir and Loki, even if no longer attested by literary evidence, is clearly revealed by a remarkable archaeological testimony. The reference is to the bas-reliefs decorating the Gosforth Cross in Cumberland, which date from the 9th century.

The cross itself bears three scenes: Víðarr fighting against the wolf Fenrir, the bound wolf, and the punishment of Loki. A nearby stone at the church of Gosforth bears a fourth scene: Thor and

Hymir on their fishing expedition (Herrmann, *Nordische Mythologie*, pp. 28, 381, 412).

The first two episodes are generally regarded as being of Christian origin, and their presence on the cross is thus not surprising. The other two, however, are clearly of pagan origin, and it is striking that the only scenes of Scandinavian mythology represented at Gosforth are precisely the two episodes of the "Cycle of the Beer."

We can already sense here the ritual significance of the legends we are studying.

⁂

I. Hymiskviða

By the time of the *Hymiskviða*, this first episode of the Indo-European cycle had already absorbed many other themes which, as they gradually developed at the expense of the original ones, would eventually cause it to drift away from the Cycle of the Beer.

Here, for reference, is the list of the primitive themes:

The Council of the Gods
The Cauldron of the Sea, necessary for the gods' feast
The Expedition to the possessor of the Cauldron
The Conquest of the Cauldron (battle?)
A, 1, a, b; 2, a, b, c. (1)

All the other themes are of foreign origin, unrelated to the original cycle:

(a) Thor's journey to the land of the giants and the extermination of the giants
(b) The battle with the Black Ox
(c) The battle with the Serpent
(d) The cup broken on the giant's forehead
(e) The lame goat

(a) From the day Thor claimed for himself the exploit of the "Conquest of the Cauldron," it was natural that his expedition to the possessor of the cauldron should take on the features of all his other journeys to the land of the giants: namely, the chariot drawn by goats, the "day-long" voyage, and, at the end of the tale, the massacre of the giants present or nearby. These traits appear in the *Þrymskviða* as in all the poems recounting Thor's eastern expeditions; they form, as it were, part of his costume, like his hammer — or at least of the setting, the atmosphere, along with the gluttony with which no poet ever fails to burden him.

(c) The battle with the serpent, or fishing for the serpent, was a favourite theme among the *skalds* of the period: in the 10th century, it was treated by Vif Uggason and Eystein Valdason. The serpent appears as well on the bas-relief mentioned earlier from the church of Gosforth. It is this fishing scene, finally, that — once the beer has disappeared — will become the central element of the episode.

Bugge has plausibly suggested that here we may see the

influence of Christian legends in which God the Father or Christ catches the Leviathan encircling the world with a hook. In any case, there is nothing Indo-European in this motif.

(b, d, and e) As for the three other new episodes — the Black Ox tamed, the Cup thrown, and the Lame Goat — the independent origin of at least the last one is well attested. It is the story told at length by Snorri Sturluson (*Gylfaginning*, 44): how Thjálfi and Röskva were given as servants to Thor by their father Egil, to appease the god's anger after Thjálfi lamed one of the two goats.

As for the "cup thrown", it is probably a popular motif, readily attachable to any legend involving a duel with a giant.

Let us for the moment leave unexplained the duel between Thor and the Ox, which likely rests on an ancient scene of shape-shifting combat.

That is how the *Hymiskviða* was composed. All those secondary themes that the poet inserted do not yet break the chain of the older ones. However, on closer inspection, the imbalance begins; there is a real contradiction — at least a break in the subject — within the story. Thor and Tyr go to Hymir's home to win the Cauldron; this is clearly stated. Yet from the moment the gods arrive at the giant's dwelling until the very last trial he proposes to Thor, the object of their journey is forgotten. What provokes the contest is not, as one might expect, Thor's request to take the Cauldron, but simply his gluttony.

Moreover, it is hard to understand how this contest of strength begins: Hymir takes Thor fishing only because he judges his appetite excessive and wishes him to earn his meal by some service; suddenly, without explanation, this practical expedition turns into a sport; it is followed by other equally pointless trials, such as the throwing of the cup. Finally, it is difficult to grasp — whatever Hymir's stupidity — that he should make his last challenge to Thor, "Take the Cauldron," and thus fall into a trap that has not even been set for him.

Everything, on the other hand, becomes clear if one admits that in an older and simpler version, Thor asked Hymir to give him the Cauldron, and Hymir replied: *"You shall have the Cauldron if you are more skilful, stronger, etc., than I."* In the end, defeated in every contest, he would say in exhaustion: *"Take it then, if you can…"*

But the poet's intention, it seems, was to gather into a single narrative many episodes of different origins, which forced him to loosen somewhat the unity of his subject: Thor appears at Hymir's house — just as he does before Thrym and so many other giants — without asking for anything, and triumphs by trickery.

That there are familiar folkloric features in this poem (such as the compassionate giantess) is beyond doubt. But after all that has just been said, one can see how implausible it is to reduce the *Hymiskviða* to a mere fairy tale similar to "The Ogre and Little Thumb", as Bugge first attempted and Golther later developed in more detail (Bugge, *Studien über die Entstehung der nordischen Götter- und Heldensagen*, p. 26 of the German edition, Munich, 1889 — Golther, *Handbuch der Germanischen Mythologie*, p. 273):

"Two brothers arrive at the dwelling of a man-eating giant," says Golther, *"while the master is away; a compassionate woman receives them and hides them; the giant returns and sniffs out human flesh, but his wife calms him with gentle words; the brothers then come out of hiding and are allowed to stay with the giant; in the end, one of them — small and weak though he is — manages to trick or overcome the colossus."*

Nothing is more superficially convincing than such catch-all schemata; yet how can this be applied to the *Hymiskviða*, where at no point does Hymir seem inclined to eat Thor or Tyr, and where at no point is there the opposition of the weak and the strong — quite the contrary? At most, such a tale may have provided the poet with the character of the giant's wife, hospitable to guests and unhappy beside such a husband.

But the essential elements of the story — famine among the gods; the sea cauldron; and so on — clearly correspond only to the first episode of the Ambrosia cycle. Such is the *Hymiskviða* — a disparate work, yet still firmly connected to the cycle of the Æsir's beer.

In the *Edda* of Snorri, from the 13th century, we find a new version of the episode; by this time, the beer has completely vanished, and one of the former secondary themes — the "Fishing of the Serpent" — has taken the place of honour. There is no need to dwell on this distortion; here is merely how the story appears (*Gylfaginning*, ch. 48):

Thor sets out in search of the Miðgarðsormr (the Miðgarðr Serpent) and arrives at the home of a giant named Hymir. Hymir is preparing to go out to sea to fish, and Thor, appearing in the guise of a young boy, asks to accompany him. The giant, noticing his frail appearance, refuses him in a condescending tone.

Thor becomes angry and asks only what bait the giant plans to use. Hymir replies that he must find his own bait; so Thor takes his hammer and immediately strikes off the head of one of Hymir's bulls. They set out to sea together. To the giant's great surprise, Thor rows skilfully — so well, in fact, that despite all of Hymir's protests, he rows beyond the spot where the giant usually stops. They reach the deep waters where the serpent lies.

Thor casts his line, baited with the bull's head, and hauls the serpent up to the surface; but he braces himself so hard that the boat splits apart, and he stands firmly on the seabed. Thor fixes his terrible gaze upon the serpent, which spews its venom. The giant, after a moment of terror, takes advantage of the instant when Thor reaches for his hammer to cut the fishing line. The serpent plunges back into the sea. Thor then strikes Hymir on the ear with his hammer and knocks him overboard.

Thus, the episode has become entirely independent of the beer cycle, retaining from the *Hymiskviða* only what relates to the "Fishing of the Serpent."

***

II. Lokasenna

We need not here discuss the very interesting questions raised by the *Lokasenna*. Whatever the intentions of the artist who composed this "divine comedy in one act," — whether he meant to denounce the corruption of morals or the disbelief of the age, or whether, on the contrary, he wished to satirise the ancient mythology, burdened with indecent fables and immoral exploits; whether he was a militant pagan or a freethinker, a preacher or an ironist — one fact is now certain for us:

He made use of a fragment of the Cycle of the Æsir's Beer, in which a demon was openly at war with the gods, in order to provide a setting and a spokesman for a particular idea. The most beautiful passages of Prometheus Bound were born in just the same way.

Scholars have attempted to separate from the *Lokasenna* the final prose passage that recounts Loki's punishment (see H. Paul, *Grundriss...*, 2nd ed., vol. II, p. 596). Indeed, this prose appears again in a section of Snorri's *Edda*, where the murder of Baldr, committed at Loki's instigation, is narrated.

H. Paul observes that the terrible punishment assigned to Loki fits naturally after a murder but seems disproportionate following a mere verbal quarrel over food; he therefore concludes that the final prose of the *Lokasenna* (in the *Codex Regius*) was borrowed from an older version of Snorri's *Edda* "aus der älteren Fassung der Snorri-Edda."

Yet this is a rather peculiar conclusion, drawn from a purely sentimental reasoning that fails to convince. There was a time when the stolen drink in the myth was nothing less than ambrosia itself; like Rāhu in Indian myth, or Tantalus in Greek myth, Loki pays dearly — and eternally — for a theft no less grave than murder.

The legend of Loki's quarrel is not directly attested after the *Lokasenna*, unlike the legend of Hymir and Thor after the *Hymiskviða*. However, this theme of the "demon at the gods' banquet" did produce counterparts or echoes. Thus, in Snorri's *Edda*, we find the duel between Thor and the giant Hrungnir introduced by a scene in which the motif from the *Lokasenna* clearly reappears.

This duel had already been recounted in powerful verses by the skald Thjódolf at the beginning of the 10th century (*Haustlöng*, stanzas 13–20). At that time, it had no connection with the Cycle of the Beer of the Æsir: Thor simply went to fetch the giant from his dwelling and killed him swiftly.

In Snorri's account (*Skáldskaparmál*, ch. 1), the episode is transformed. Odin, in a wager with Hrungnir about the speed of their horses, lures the giant into Ásgarðr. Thor is away "in the East," as often in his adventures. The gods invite Hrungnir to their table; he enters, asks for drink, and they offer him the cups customarily used by Thor. Hrungnir becomes drunk and boastful: he declares that he will carry Valhalla off to his own land, destroy Ásgarðr, and kill all the gods and goddesses — except for Freyja and Sif, whom he plans to take with him. Finally, he proclaims that he will drink all the gods' beer.

When the Æsir have heard enough of his boasting, they invoke

Thor's name, and the god enters, furious. The duel that follows is only delayed by a few unrelated incidents.

It is highly probable that this story represents a fragment of the Cycle of the Gods' Beer, resurfacing two and a half centuries after the *Lokasenna*. Only the demon's name has changed — yet he remains insolent like Loki, and lustful like Thrym.

⁂

III. Þrymskviða

Finally, we have nothing to add to the earlier hypothesis linking the *Þrymskviða* to the Cycle of the Divine Beer. The independent evolution we have just traced for the episodes of Hymir and Loki offers other, though later, examples of themes breaking away from the original cycle.

In the case of the *Þrymskviða*, the great popularity of the episode must have facilitated its early "emancipation." When telling or singing the story of Thor in disguise, the Scandinavians were not likely to recount the entire Cycle of the Æsir's Beer at once. To make the tale self-contained, it was enough to replace the beer with an object belonging to Thor — and thus the hammer naturally imposed itself.

We have already indicated in the first part certain factors that may have favoured this substitution: notably, in the vital importance the gods attached to Thor's hammer, we can recognise an idea akin to the virtue of ambrosia.

We have excellent proof of the episode's popularity in all periods.

It survived paganism within popular poetry. The Icelandic *Þrymlur* preserve the story, and it reappears in a Danish ballad, *Tord af Hafsgaard*. Finally, other traces of the theft of the hammer have also been reported in Norway.

*
* *

Conclusions

Let us now highlight the general features of the Scandinavian evolution of the cycle; in several key respects, they present the reverse of what we observed in India:

1. The weakening of the notion of ambrosia caused the disintegration of the cycle's unity — the connection between its episodes loosened. The cycle evolved not by maintaining its coherence, as in India, but by breaking apart. It incorporated hardly any new themes; rather, it lost its own themes one by one.

2. The origin of the new motifs found in the "Conquest of the Cauldron" is uncertain. It is commonly accepted — and we have so far assumed — that these are indeed foreign, artificially introduced details, unlike the new elements of the Hindu cycle, which arose by duplication of older details within the same tradition. However, we

may soon need to revise this view. Let us already mention the hypothesis that the Iranian and Greek evidence will soon suggest: the duel between the god and the marine being who possesses the cauldron was originally a contest of metamorphoses, including animal transformations.

It is therefore possible that the Hindu Turtle, the Black Bull, and the Serpent of the *Hymiskviða* are nothing more than petrified, individualised remnants of those successive transformations once enacted by the god's marine adversary.

3. Finally, it should be strongly emphasised that, even in their most anciently attested form, the episodes of the Cycle of the Æsir's Beer are known to us only after the first contacts between the Scandinavian world and Christianity. These contacts, once established historically, rapidly wore away the old mythology; and even before the 9th and 10th centuries, before the age of the *skalds*, that erosion must already have begun.

It is therefore probable that if we possessed testimonies two or three centuries earlier, the cycle would appear to us in a remarkably archaic form. Yet, as it stands, it remains one of the best preserved within the Indo-European family; and no other, when placed side by side with the cycle of the *amṛta*, would have allowed us to identify so clearly or so quickly the principal Indo-European elements.

Chapter Three

The Cycle of the Ambrosia among the Iranians

We explained in the Introduction why the Iranian evidence, a priori, cannot serve as a solid foundation for "reconstruction." The oldest Avestan texts, the *Gāthās*, are the least usable, precisely because they best reflect the thought of Zoroaster, which is as "anti-mythological" as possible. The later *Avesta*, which reintroduces into Zoroastrian doctrine many elements of the ancient Indo-Iranian religion, is hardly more useful since its state is essentially fragmentary and disorganised. Finally, the first texts that offer us continuous mythological narratives are relatively modern and show the Iranian data already filtered through religious reflection and reform, of which we have only a vague idea.

However, we should not dismiss these systematisations too hastily: to establish themselves, they must have drawn on more genuinely Mazdean texts than those we still possess. Such is the case, for example, with the *Bundahišn*, compiled perhaps under the Sassanids, around the third century CE, which has transmitted to us a body of traditions concerning the origins, government, and destiny of the world.

From these remarks, it follows that the *Avesta* cannot provide us with a continuous version of the cycle; but this does not prove that such a version did not exist at that relatively early period. In India, as we have seen, the cycle only appeared — still very close to its Indo-European form — long after the Vedic period. We are therefore justified in seeking later testimonies in Iran as well as in India.

However, in the Iranian case, those "later texts" are found in the *Bundahišn*, and here the utmost caution is required. The *Bundahišn* preserves mythological matter filtered through centuries of Zoroastrian redaction; what remains of the ancient Indo-Iranian cosmogony must be distinguished carefully from later Mazdean theology, which had already reinterpreted or moralised most of the old myths.

On the other hand, the *Avesta* does not transmit to us the Indo-Iranian *amṛta* in its pure state. If there once existed a period when some form such as *amerəta-* or *aməša-* represented the "food of immortality," — and we will soon see that there are indeed clear testimonies and survivals of this — that stage already belongs, even in the oldest texts, to prehistory.

What we encounter instead, from the outset, is not the drink or food of immortality, but rather a "genius of immortality," Amərətāt, closely associated with another genius of "integrity" or "wholeness," Haurvatāt. Both of these are incorporated into the group of six abstract divinities that Zoroaster gathered around the supreme god of the Iranians, forming the circle of the Ameša Spənta

("Bounteous Immortals").

In other words, what in the Indo-European period had been a concrete myth of divine nourishment becomes, in Zoroastrian reform, an abstract moral principle — a transformation from substance to virtue, from ambrosia to immortality personified.

We will first examine what the *Avesta* teaches us about these two twin "essences", Haurvatāt and Amərətāt, and we will try to discern, within their historical abstraction, a few lingering traces of the "substances" or tangible realities from which Mazdean reflection originally abstracted them.

Next, we will investigate whether the later texts have preserved a version—necessarily much evolved, yet still recognisable — of the cycle. In doing so, we shall strive always to read the *Avesta* beneath the *Bundahišn*: whenever, alongside an episode from the latter, we can find in the former a fragment serving as its archetype, it is the Avestan text that we will study.

This, unfortunately, is the only material safeguard possible in a field where it is so easy to lose one's way — a method of constant comparison, checking the mythological elaboration of later Mazdean tradition against the older, purer Avestan nucleus.

I. Amərətāt and Haurvatāt in the Avesta

J. Darmesteter devoted a very detailed study to Haurvatāt and Amərətāt. This monograph is all the more valuable because, unlike his other major work *Ormazd et Ahriman*, it is not permeated with naturalistic concerns or with "storm myths."

Darmesteter established, with abundant textual evidence, that over the course of the evolution of Mazdeism, these two Ameša Spənta gradually changed meaning several times.

1. They first denoted exactly what their names imply: Haurvatāt, meaning "integrity," "salvation," or "health" in the broadest sense; and Amərətāt, meaning "immortality." Were they abstractions or spirits? Both at once, as with all the other Ameša Spənta. It is in this role that we see them invoked, for example, in the *Vendidad* (20.13), "to resist disease and death."

2. But very early on, they received a much more material role, like the other Ameša Spənta. Haurvatāt became the genius (spirit) of the waters, and Amərətāt the genius of plants. Neriosengh, in his Sanskrit translation of the *Yasna* (1.5), defines them as *"apām patim"* and *"vanaspatīnām patim"* — that is, "lord of the waters" and "lord of the trees."

In this function, Khordâd and Amurdâd (their later Pahlavi forms) have as adversaries Tarie and Zarie, demons of thirst and hunger, who are themselves the heirs of two "counter-Ameša Spənta" already known in the *Avesta* (*Vendidad* 18): Taura and Zairika.

Here we see through what transition the geniuses of Health and

Immortality could become the geniuses of water and plants: they are those who, in sustaining living beings, provide drink and food, and above all those who, in the afterlife, prepare the nourishment of the righteous.

For even though the Persians, pushing immaterialism to its limit, believe that the righteous in heaven are sated without eating, a late text such as the *Minokhired* still knows that Ahura Mazdā has exquisite foods served to them (*Minokhired*, ed. Westergaard II, 152).

Moreover, Ahura Mazdā himself says in the *Avesta* (*Yasht* 1.25) that "Haurvatāt and Amərətāt are the reward of the pure who pass into the other life" — and a variant, suggested by Anquetil's translation, even replaces "reward" (*mîdem*) with "food" (*myazdem*): one could hardly be more explicit. (Darmesteter, *Haurvatât et Ameretât*, p. 8.)

Thus, Haurvatāt and Amərətāt, spirits of Health and Immortality, became (or rather rediscovered themselves as) first the geniuses of the celestial foods that conferred these privileges, and then, by a natural extension, the geniuses of all nourishment, both liquid and solid — that is, of waters and plants.

There is, moreover, a more precise origin to which we shall return later: Amərətāt is closely linked to the *Gaokerena*, the king of plants, which grows in the Vourukaša Sea and is the source of immortality. But this points to an even older state of Amərətāt, and we must not anticipate.

Darmesteter wisely emphasises (*Haurvatât et Ameretât*, p. 62) that the division of waters and plants between the two Ameša Spənta is purely arbitrary — there must have been a time when they jointly ruled over the whole realm of nourishment. Furthermore, just as they always appear united, like the divine pairs (*dvandvas*) of the Vedic tradition, so too "waters and plants" are treated throughout the sacred books as an indivisible formula — just as, in Greece, nectar and ambrosia were inseparable, and poets never knew quite which was drink and which food.

3. As spirits of plants and waters, they later took on a new, more abstract meaning, of little relevance to us here — that of geniuses of abundance. Darmesteter provides characteristic examples of this later stage: Haurvatāt and Amərətāt came to symbolise prosperity, plenty, and the fullness of life, rather than the concrete forces that nourish it. Their original link to the material sustenance of beings — water and vegetation — gradually turned into a more metaphysical notion of total well-being and eternal preservation.

4. Finally, to conclude the evolution of these two beings:

Khordâd became, for the Persians, one of the "*Ādars*", that is, one of the supernatural fires that appear to humans under particular forms (Anquetil, *Zend-Avesta*, p. 24 n. 1; Darmesteter, *Haurvatât et Ameretât*, p. 60). Amurdâd, under Arab influence, was transformed into "Murdâd," a kind of Ismāʿīl, an angel of death.

⁎⁎⁎

II. The Prehistory of Amərətāt

At the historical beginning of this evolution, Haurvatāt and Amərətāt are therefore two abstract deities, two personified abstractions, comparable to "Good Thought" (Vohu Manah), "Perfect Order" (Aṣa Vahišta), and the other Ameša Spənta.

By this trait, we easily recognise the method dear to Mazdaism, as to most theologies; but ancient mythology must have once contained, in this very place, a concrete notion, analogous to the Hindu *amṛta*.

This notion reveals itself — as we have indicated — in certain life-giving functions of the two spirits, in their role as "nourishers of the afterlife", and especially, for Amərətāt, in her relationship with the plant of immortality, the *Gaokerena*.

These connections are shown in a passage from the *Little Siroza*, the Iranian calendar, where it is said — regarding the seventh month, dedicated to Amərətāt:

"We worship Amərətāt, the Ameša Spənta;
we worship the fat herds, the abundance of harvests;
we worship the mighty Gaokerena created by Mazdā."

Now, we have seen that it is because Amərətāt was originally the spirit of the "king of plants" that she later became the spirit of plants in general. We are thus here at the concrete core of the abstraction — very likely also its ancient, pre-Mazdean nucleus.

The *Gaokerena* is indeed a plant of immortality: according to the *Bundahišn*, it was created "to repel old age" (19, 19), and whoever eats of it "does not die" (42, 14; 59, 5; see other references in Darmesteter, *Haurvatât et Ameretât*, p. 54).

The very idea of this sacred plant is undoubtedly derived from the influence of the *haoma*, whose Vedic counterpart, the *sóma*, also belongs to the vegetal realm. And just as in the Vedas there was constant confusion — at the expense of the first — between *amṛta* and *sóma*, so among the Iranians the "White *Haoma*" (as opposed to the "Golden *Haoma*," the earthly sacrificial plant) is described as the product of the *Gaokerena*.

Here, then, we find a trace of a common Indo-Iranian tradition, a "somic" tradition from which we must consciously abstract ourselves if we wish to rediscover the purely "ambrosial" elements of the myth. (cf. V. Henry, *Sôma et Haoma*, Paris, 1907.)

The first of these elements is very clear and very important: the Gaokerena grows in the Vourukaša Sea, which naturalist interpreters and Darmesteter wanted to see as the "sea of clouds," the "atmospheric ocean," the stage for all the "storm myths." However, everywhere it actually appears as an ordinary sea of real salt water. This is our Indo-European motif of the sea producing the food of immortality. (A, 1, b.) (See Darmesteter, *Ormazd et Ahriman*, p. 178.)

Other themes persist, connected with this Gaokerena — the themes of theft and of struggle between gods and demons. The *Bundahišn* (42.15) says:

"Ahriman created, against the Gaokerena, in the depths of the waters, a frog meant to destroy the White Haoma. To fight this frog, Ormazd created ten kara fish who swim constantly around the haoma, so that there is always one facing it."

These ten fish, as Darmesteter pointed out, are a later multiplication of a single *kara* fish known to the *Avesta* (*Yašt* 14.29; 16.7). This brings us back to some ancient duel, now unrecognisable under such a disguise.

These traces would already be enough to show that the Iranians had not completely forgotten the ambrosial legends. We will now see whether the later texts allow for more precise conclusions.

⁂

III. The Cycle of the Ambrosia in Later Iranian Literature: The Story of Creation

Before addressing the *Bundahišn*, let us first set our course. The Indo-Iranian cycle of the *amṛta* had to conform — under penalty of exclusion — to the new forms of Mazdean theology. If it was preserved, it could only have been so with certain essential modifications, which we may try to anticipate. Here, I believe, are the three principal ones:

1. There will be no "Cycle of Amərətāt" in the strict sense: Amərətāt and her counterpart Haurvatāt cannot stand alone. They

belong to the group of the six Ameša Spənta, and given the solidarity of these divine beings, along with the meticulous regularity of Avesta's theological developments, we must expect the "Cycle of Amərətāt" to have been expanded so as to include — at least nominally — all the Ameša Spənta and their material attributes. Thus, beside waters and plants, we will also find earth, herds, fire, and others.

Thus framed, the "genesis" and the "cycle" of ambrosia become, in truth, the genesis and cycle of the various elements of the world — that is, the story of creation and of the events that accompanied or followed it. It is therefore within this part of Iranian tradition — the cosmological and cosmogonic narratives — that we are most likely to find traces of the ancient legends of the *amṛta*.

2. The two figures — Ahura Mazdā and Angra Mainyu — especially the former, have absorbed almost the entire ancient essence of the gods and demons. In any case, gods and demons are no longer divine powers but rather the first among created beings. Consequently, the "Cycle" can only be understood now as the first episode in the much larger cosmic duel that dominates Mazdean theology.

Finally, the revolution — at least linguistic — that transformed the *daēva* of the Indo-Iranians into the "demons" of the Avesta could not have occurred without producing disruptions whose extent we cannot predict, though we must expect them. Some exploits once attributed, in the ancient cycle, to a god or a demon may here have changed sides.

Now follows the text of the *Bundahišn* in which we believe we can find the ancient cycle. We will indicate immediately, by means of headings, the divisions and analogies that our commentary will later justify.

⁎⁎⁎

Ōhrmazd has just "spiritually created the necessary creatures" (*Bundahišn* 2.10), and Ahriman opposes him with "a multitude of demons and *druj*, creatures of death."

1. Ōhrmazd offered alliance to Ahriman to free the worlds from death, hunger, and so on: *"Ōhrmazd knew how the matter would end. He went down before Ahriman and offered him peace, saying: 'Ahriman, be beneficent toward my creation, offer it homage; in return, may yours also be freed from death and old age, from hunger and from thirst.'"*

Ahriman, believing that Ōhrmazd offered him peace out of weakness, refused. Ōhrmazd, in his omniscience, and Ahriman, in his blindness, then agreed upon the duration of the struggle, which would last 9,000 years, divided into three well-known Mazdean periods of 3,000 years each: *"And Ōhrmazd knows that the first 3,000 years will go according to his will, the second according to the mingled will of himself and Ahriman, and that in the final 3,000 years Ahriman will be driven out of creation."*

(This is evidently, like the Hindu *"yugas"* and the Greek "ages," a later conception, in which no ancient element should be sought.)

Ōhrmazd recited the prayer called *Ahuna Vairya,* and then Ahriman, "troubled," fell back into the darkness for 3,000 years.

2. Ōhrmazd created the Ameša Spənta from the "good cosmic light," from the waters, the plants, and so on (= A, 3).

"During Ahriman's disturbance, Ōhrmazd created the world. From the good cosmic light he created Vohu Manah (Bahman), then Aša Vahišta (Ardibehesht), XšaΘra Vairya (Šahrevar), Spənta Ārmaiti (Spendārmat), Haurvatāt (Xordād), and Amərətāt (Amurdād) — the six Amahraspands (Ameša Spənta). Ahriman, with the cosmic darkness, created Aka Manah (Akoman), Indar (Andar), Saurva (Šavol), Naŋhait (Nāxit), Tārič (Tārīc), and Zairič (Zāric) — the six counter-Amahraspands. Of the worldly creations, the first was the sky, then came the water, then the earth, then the plants, then the animals, then humankind." (Bundahišn 2.10)

3. The expedition of the Dāēhī (= C 1–2).

The first human had been created: Gayōmart (the Gayōmaretan of the *Avesta*). Ahriman, sensing his powerlessness before him, remained for 3,000 years in dejection. In vain the demons came one after another to implore their father: *"Terrified before the righteous man, he could not cause even a single hair to fall from his head."*

"After 3,000 years came the Dāēhī (a sort of demoness), who said to him: 'Arise, father, that we may carry war into the world, that Ōhrmazd and the Ameša Spənta be plunged into anguish and evil!....' But he did not rise from his dejection. The Dāēhī returned and said to him: 'Arise, father! In this war I will pour poison over the body of the righteous man and over

the ploughing bull, so that they will no longer be able to live; I will cause their light to perish, I will afflict the waters, the tree, the fire of Ōhrmazd, all of Ōhrmazd's creation.' She recounted twice the harm she intended to do, and the heart returned to Angra Mainyu, who sprang up from his dejection." (Bundahišn, 8, 7, ch. 3.)

4. Battle between the gods and the demons. The demon in the sky (= B + D).

"Then Ahriman, with all the demons, marched against the lights... From within the sky, he seized a third; then, like a serpent, he leapt from the sky onto the earth... He came to the waters and worked beneath the earth; he pierced the earth and entered it... Then he came to the plants, then to the Bull, then to Gayōmart, then to the fire... He made the world at full midday as dark as the blackest night. He covered the earth with xrafstar (venomous creatures), with serpents, scorpions, ka̱tvā, frogs... He struck the plants, which immediately withered. He brought need, pain, hunger, and disease upon the bodies of the Bull and of Gayōmart; then he came upon the fire and mingled smoke and darkness within it. The planets, together with thousands of demons, came and struck the sky, and entered into battle with the stars, and the whole creation grew dark like a space filled with smoke from a fire. For ninety days and ninety nights, the celestial yazads fought in the world against Ahriman and the demons. Ōhrmazd put them to flight; the yazads cast them into hell: hell is in the middle of the earth, where Ahriman pierced the earth and made his entry." (Bundahišn II, 9 ff.)

Darmesteter, by comparing certain passages from the Avesta with the end of this account, was led to suppose that originally it was upon Mount Arezūra, at the gates of hell, that Ahriman was bound.

To complete this text, one must compare with it (and restore to its proper place, at the beginning of the episode of the battle) another passage from the *Bundahišn*, where the formation of the Vourukaša Sea is described (*Bundahišn*, ch. 7):

Conquest of the Sea (A, 2–4)

"The day the Enemy made his invasion, Tištrya set about fulfilling his functions. The waters were carried away by the action of the wind. Tištrya had as his auxiliaries Bahman, the Yazata Hōm (= Haoma), the Yazata Borz, and the Fravašis of the righteous. He appeared in three forms—man, horse, and boar—each for ten days and ten nights, hovering in full light and acting. Every drop of water was the size of a cup; the whole earth was flooded to the height of a man. The harmful creatures with which Ahriman had covered it were killed or drowned in the holes of the earth; the poison born from their corruption salted the waters. The wind drove the waters back to their extremities, and thus was formed the sea Vourukaša."

A confused account follows concerning the formation of the "smaller seas," in which several features of the previous tale are repeated, but two new and highly important details appear: Tištrya, incarnated as a white horse, must vanquish in the sea the demon Apaoša, incarnated as a black horse. To accomplish this, he implores Ōhrmazd, who grants him the strength and courage necessary for his task.

Darmesteter (*Ormazd et Ahriman*, pp. 141–142, § 120) does not hesitate to see in these two accounts two doublets derived from a single original narrative, with some details repeated and others redistributed more or less skilfully.

Fortunately, the *Avesta* has preserved the older version of this episode (*Yašt* 8): it is the story of the struggle between Tištrya and the demon Apaoša. Tištrya appears in three forms — as a youth of fifteen years, as a boar with golden hooves, and as a horse with yellow ears and a golden saddlecloth. He battles Apaoša, is at first defeated, and laments; then he implores Ahura, who offers the sacrifice and restores his strength. Apaoša is vanquished.

"Victory!" cries Tištrya. "The torrent of waters shall descend unhindered upon the lands!" And the waters go forth, guided by the winds, along the paths traced for them by Haoma..."

*
* *

Taken from various chapters of the *Bundahišn*, though not in an arbitrary fashion — since Darmesteter, who was not searching for our cycle, had already gathered them — these elements form a coherent whole. One might hesitate, at most, about where exactly to insert the last section (the conquest of the sea), since the introductory phrase, "*On the day when the Enemy made his invasion...,*" is somewhat vague. But taken together, the sequence clearly reveals the Cycle of the Ambrosia.

But this version is, to be sure, one of the most evolved among all those that have appeared — or will appear to us later — across the Indo-European world, even at much later periods. The turbulent history of Iranian religious thought explains this rapid wear and aging of the myth.

Thus, the study we are about to undertake — theme by theme, examining the narrative of the *Bundahišn* and comparing it with the Indo-European cycle — will often leave us in uncertainty. The episode of the "false bride," for example, is almost unrecognisable; that of the struggle with the sea-god and the conquest of the sea is clearer, but has lost its original meaning and purpose. Everywhere we stand before ruins, sometimes before only the faintest traces.

1. Ōhrmazd offers an alliance to Ahriman, and the purpose of this alliance is very specific: to free both creations—the world of demons as well as that of the gods — "from death and old age," "from hunger and thirst." In Mazdean language, this means granting them Haurvatāt and Amərətāt; in pre-Mazdean terms, it is the equivalent of bestowing upon them the *amṛta*, the drink or substance of immortality.

This proposal of alliance corresponds exactly to that which the Suras make to the Asuras in the Indian cycle. But here, the alliance is never consummated: Ahriman, a poor psychologist, mistakes Ōhrmazd's initiative for weakness and refuses, whereas in the Indian myth the Asuras only go to war against the Suras after the *amṛta* has been produced.

It is quite likely that the original Indo-Iranian cycle included such an alliance; but Mazdeism, which is founded entirely on the struggle between the two Principles, could not admit that Ahriman might ever have been Ōhrmazd's collaborator, even at the beginning of time. From the ancient tradition, therefore, only the "offer" has been preserved.

Nevertheless, there may remain a negative trace of the old motif: during Ōhrmazd's creation, Ahriman is said in the *Bundahišn* to be paralysed by the twenty-one words of the *Ahuna Vairya*, but he is not inactive — he, too, completes his own work; and only when both creations are finished does the war begin. Might not this sort of truce, in which each being works separately on his own half of creation without attacking the other, preserve the memory of the ancient, temporary, creative collaboration that once surrounded the making of the Ambrosia?

We will not dwell on the development of obviously recent origin, in which the three periods of three thousand years are defined. The *Rāmāyaṇa* likewise specifies the thousands of years that pass between the various episodes of the churning. Such details are entirely human refinements, despite their fantastic proportions — born of a later desire for order and classification among things that were originally beyond human measure.

2. We should now expect, before the actual creation, the equivalent of the Indo-European theme of the "Conquest of the Sea." Indeed, that is precisely where the episode of the "Conquest of the Vourukaša Sea" originally belonged. However, the later addition of the other four Amahraspands (Ameša Spənta) to

Hordād and Amurdād transformed the making of the *amṛta* into the creation of an entire world, necessarily obscuring the role of the sea.

First of all, since nothing material yet existed — where would the sea be? Moreover, by churning the waters one might well obtain a beverage, but could one bring forth from them earth, fire, and so on? This explains the uncertainty that the author of the *Bundahišn* leaves us regarding the position of this episode, otherwise very well preserved, and to which we shall return later.

Even so, a trace of the ancient state may survive: Ōhrmazd creates the six Amahraspands from "the good cosmic light." How can we fail to recall here the *xᵛarənah*, the *kavaēm xᵛarənah* — "the royal glory," or "sovereign light" — which the *Avesta* places, like the *Gaokerena* and the *haoma*, in the Sea Vourukaša, and for the possession of which Ātar and Aži wage a resounding battle within that sea (cf. Darmesteter, *Ormazd et Ahriman*, p. 103)?

"The Light swells and flows within the Vourukaša Sea," says the *Avesta* (*Yašt* 19.52), which gave the naturist school good reason to speak of an "atmospheric ocean" and a "storm myth."

This sovereign light, contained within the Vourukaša Sea, has in fact a distinct taste of *amṛta*. At the end of the time of trial, it will "attach itself to Saoshyant, the demon-slayer, and to his companions, when he will revive the world, deliver it from old age and death... make it eternally living... when the dead will rise, when the immortality of life will come... when the worlds that follow the law of Aša will be freed from death, when the Druj will vanish so that she can no longer destroy the just…" (*Yašt* 19.89; Darmesteter, *Ormazd et Ahriman*, p. 227).

For Mazdean eschatology projects once more into the future the myths of the past: the conquest of immortality and the battle against the demons will begin again — but this time, forever.

However that may be, the Amahraspands — the Ameša Spənta of the *Avesta* — are now created. Their name, without attempting any new etymology, is at least strikingly appropriate at this point in the cycle: Ameša is the exact equivalent of Indo-Iranian *amṛta*, preserved in Sanskrit. The birth of these beings (one of whom is Amərətāt itself) at precisely the moment in the cycle when the *amṛta* was born may be more than a coincidence.

We are on ground too unstable to draw firm conclusions. Yet, is it not possible that these six Amahraspands correspond to the divine beings whom the Indian legend makes emerge from the ocean at the same time as the *amṛta* — and who, by chance perhaps, are six in number in the *Mahābhārata*? Beyond this purely numerical and formal resemblance, however, comparison cannot go; it is not enough to fix with certainty any precise point of the Indo-Iranian cycle.

3. The episode of the Djahi must have arisen from a curious transformation. It appears exactly where — by analogy with the Indian cycle — we would expect the expedition of the "fatal bride" to the demon (or demons) who have carried off the treasure. The intervention of a female figure, the Djahi — whose nature we will specify later — clearly indicates at first glance that the two episodes

correspond to one another.

But here the roles are reversed: it is no longer from among the gods that the seductress departs, and it is no longer from the demons that she seeks to reclaim the *amṛta*. On the contrary, it is from among the demons that the Djahi sets out, and it is against a part of Ormazd's creation that she goes, to deprive it of health, immortality, and the like.

We know how to explain this phenomenon: it is doubtless connected with the linguistic evolution by which the Indo-Iranian *daēva* became the Avestan demons. The myth remained attached to the name while that name passed from one camp to the other.

The text, to tell the truth, does not recount the actions of the Djahi; it only reports the proposal she makes to her father Ahriman. But, as Darmesteter was led to conjecture (*Ormazd et Ahriman*, p. 180, § 149), and judging from the "doublets" of Tahmurath — whose wife is seduced by Ahriman — and of Kerešāspa, prey to the *pairikā* Knāthaiti (see the texts studied by Darmesteter, *Ormazd et Ahriman*, pp. 170, 176, 182), it is to her that we must attribute the exploit of the loss of Gayōmard, the affliction of the waters and of the trees, etc. — Mazdean substitutes for the ancient *amṛta* and materialisations of Amərətāt.

The Djahi — no more than the goddess Vāc, delivered to the *Gandharva* Viśvāvasu according to the tradition of the *Brāhmaṇas* — is not a masculine being in disguise. She sets out on her campaign to save the world of the demons, and in particular Ahriman, whose intelligent instrument she is; but she remains what she is: a female spirit, a demon of lechery, a fallen and degraded sister of Lakṣmī and Freyja.

This very character of lust must have made the substitution easier: the Djahi does not have the scruples, for example, that make Freyja "sigh and tremble" so violently when Thor asks her to go marry Thrym to recover his hammer. A very natural contamination must have occurred between the ancient episode of the "false demoness" going to seize immortality, and the popular traditions concerning the licentious Djahi.

Finally, let us note that the position of this episode is the same in both the Indian and Iranian cycles. This correspondence, though a detail, is quite significant since it is only among the Slavs (and perhaps among the Kucheans) that we again find the episode of the "fatal bride" placed at the head of the episodes of abduction and combat. The Greeks, Latins, Celts (and doubtless the Germans) instead move it to a later position, after that of the "demon among the gods."

4. The episode of the "demon among the gods" has merged into the general battle between gods and demons. The *Bundahišn* states that Ahriman was able to penetrate the sky, "of which he took a third, and from which he leapt down to earth, in the form of a serpent." That is, admittedly, rather scant material. As for his punishment, it is clearly fused with that of the other demons: only at the end of the battle is Ahriman bound upon the mountain that seals the entrance to hell.

We will not dwell on the usual substitutes for the *amṛta* —

plants and waters in particular — which suffer Ahriman's persecution. It will be more interesting instead to note certain remarkable traces of the Indo-European cycle, or even curious correspondences with the Indian cycle.

1. Eclipses and earthquakes — these two natural phenomena — find both their place and their explanation here:

"Ahriman made the world at high noon as dark as in the blackest night."

"He came upon the fire and mixed smoke and darkness into it. The planets, with thousands of demons, came to strike the sky and entered into combat with the stars, and the whole creation was darkened."

"He worked beneath the earth; he pierced the earth..."

"Hell is in the middle of the earth, where Ahriman pierced it and through which he made his irruption."

To this "seismic theme" we must link the appearance of the mountains, which the *Bundahišn* explicitly attributes to the struggle between gods and demons (ch. 8):

"When Ahriman made his invasion and pierced the earth, the mountains appeared."

The Scandinavians associated only earthquakes with this cycle; the Indians and Iranians — and perhaps also, as we shall soon see, the Greeks — joined to it the eclipses as well.

2. The battle, as in the *Mahābhārata*, takes on a fantastic, superhuman character: combat is waged with planets, just as the Asura in India attempt to conquer heaven by hurling mountains. But, just as in the *Bhāgavata-Purāṇa* we saw the battle later reduced to human proportions, so too, through a natural evolution, we find in another, less "cosmological" passage of the *Bundahišn* (15, 1 ff., ch. 6) a more earthly scene:

"The warriors of Ōhrmazd, mounted on battle-horses, lance in hand, stood behind the rampart of the sky..."

3. A variant of the *Rāmāyaṇa* and the passage from the *Bhāgavata-Purāṇa* (VIII, ch. 7, śloka 46) trace to the cycle of the *amṛta* the origin of venomous beings in the world:

"While Śiva was drinking the Hālāhala poison, the scorpions, serpents, poisonous plants, and other harmful creatures took hold of what fell from his hand."

One cannot separate this *śloka* from the passage in the *Bundahišn* where

"Ahriman covered the earth with xarfaštar — biting, venomous creatures — snakes, scorpions, karvā, frogs..."

This is a case of parallel evolution, rather than a surviving ancient memory suddenly reappearing in later literature. Yet it remains a valuable testimony for the episode of the poison, which we shall study soon: the two mythologies would hardly have each invented, independently, such a precise detail unless the idea of poison from which it derives had belonged to their shared Indo-Iranian tradition.

4. The punishment of the demons, here as in the *Amṛtamanthana*, consists in their being cast beneath the earth, into the infernal regions. If Darmesteter's deduction is correct (*Ormazd et Ahriman*, p. 127, § 109), the punishment of Ahriman is described more precisely and is of particular interest to us:

Ahriman chained to Mount Arzūr is exactly equivalent to Loki bound to his rock — which would seem to indicate that, in the Indo-European tradition, the episode of the "demon among the gods" originally ended with such a Promethean torment, and not with a decapitation like that of Rāhu.

The "ecliptic" legend must therefore have shifted within the Indian cycle, moving from the general battle (where we find it both in Greece and in Iran) to one of the episodes of abduction.

Like Loki defying the gods, like Prometheus on his rock, Ahriman chained was a figure ripe for literary elaboration. The *Avesta* even contains the Lamentations of Ahriman (*Yašt* 3, 14 ff.); but these, clogged with endless, wearying repetitions, devoid of movement or warmth, and as dull as a model confession, remain far below the *Lokasenna* and Aeschylus's tragedy. Mazdaism did not know how to make use of what it possessed.

5. We come, finally, to that curious episode of the conquest of the Vourukaša Sea, which the *Bundahišn* explicitly connects to the

preceding "Cycle," and which indeed belongs to it — for it is none other than the ambrosial theme of the "Sea Conquered."

We explained earlier why the later tradition no longer knows exactly when to situate this episode: it cannot retain its original place, since "the sea" could not exist before Creation itself. Thus, it became a secondary detail, no more important than the appearance of the mountains, within the broader struggle between the Yazatas (Izeds) and the Daēvas.

At the same time, the "Conquest of the Sea" (though the *Gaokerena* still grows there) lost its original meaning: it is no longer a matter of churning it to prepare a drink or food, but merely of obtaining its waters, which ensure the fertility of the world.

Consequently, the once precise idea of the "Vessel of the Sea" had little chance of surviving, and indeed, it seems to have left no trace in the texts that remain to us. These essential alterations make it all the more remarkable that such a theme still appears, in the *Bundahišn*, joined to the rest of the cycle.

It has, moreover, preserved some very ancient details, and this testimony will provide us with valuable insights into the Indo-European state of the episode:

1. Whatever the reason that Ōhrmazd and the gods need the sea, Tishtrya enters the waters, engages in battle with the demon Apaoša, ultimately triumphs, and seizes the waters.

Such is the substance of the Avestan narrative, from which the

Bundahišn drew the twofold version we recalled earlier. In it, one clearly recognises both the expedition of the Sura, who beg the Ocean to lend them its waters, and above all the expedition of Thor to the god of the wintry sea, Hymir, to conquer the Vessel of the Sea.

2. I say "especially" because the Iranian testimony resolves a question left open at the end of our first part: there is a battle. But it is a battle of a very particular kind — a repeated struggle, in which the combatants take on various animal forms.

Tištrya appears (in both the *Bundahišn* and the *Avesta*) first as a youth of fifteen years "with shining white eyes," then as a boar with golden hooves, and finally as a horse with yellow ears and a golden halter. Apaoša, his adversary, opposes him in the form of a black horse, with cropped ears and tail.

Elsewhere (*Bundahišn* 44, 4 ff., ch. 19 init.), the text speaks of the Three-Legged Ass who dwells in the middle of the Vourukaša Sea and differs from Tištrya only in that his role as guardian and purifier of the waters is permanent, instead of belonging solely to the beginning of time.

Elsewhere again, we encounter an animal called the Bull-Fish, mentioned in exactly the same terms as the Three-Legged Ass (cf. Darmesteter, *Ormazd et Ahriman*, pp. 151–152). All this proves how essential to the episode was the idea that the combatants changed their forms, and, in a word, metamorphosed.

We shall find a striking confirmation of this in the "ἅλιος

γέϱων," Proteús of Greek legend, but even now we can perceive that the battle waged by the god against the marine demon is a battle of transformations. And we thus begin to understand the Hindu and Scandinavian developments of the legend.

One recalls that in the *Mahābhārata* the episode appears split in two: first, the gods ask the Lord of the Waters, the Ocean, to consent to the churning; then they ask the submarine Turtle to support the mountain used as the churning-stick. We also know what fate Vaiṣṇavism reserved for this second doublet.

Here is how this division must have occurred: as we saw in Chapter I of this second part, the episode tended to atrophy in India. By the time of the *Mahābhārata*, the scene of combat had already disappeared; yet the poet still knew that the marine demon had taken on several forms, and that the expedition (formerly the battle) had unfolded in several successive "phases." He merely chose to fix what had once been fluid — distributing among two independent beings, the Lord of the Waters and then the Turtle, the successive figures, the incarnations of what had originally been a single entity. This is the very model of *dédoublement*, or mythic splitting.

The Scandinavians preserved the notion of a battle, and of a battle fought in several bouts. But the human figures of Thor and Hymir were too firmly established for either to disguise himself in animal form. As a result, the repeated combat became a contest of successive trials.

However, is it not quite likely that when we see Thor fighting a bull, then a serpent, without directly confronting Hymir himself, these feats actually reflect an older narrative in which Thor's adversary successively assumed the forms of the bull, the serpent, and so on?

Such a hypothesis helps explain the process that turned the *Hymiskviða* into a true mosaic of themes: a single theme was fragmented; a single battle became a series of combats; and naturally, other trials (such as the throwing of the cup) were added to the older ones whose original unity was no longer felt.

All the observations made earlier — regarding, for instance, the Christian elements in Thor's battle with the Serpent — still hold true.

3. The theme of the "initial powerlessness" of the gods reappears here, both in the *Avesta* and in the *Bundahišn* — and this correspondence, too, can hardly be accidental.

Recall the embarrassment of the Æsir in the Norse myth: consulting their magic wands, yet unable to find a cauldron for Ægir, and finally, at the end of the *Hymiskviða*, Týr twice attempting in vain to lift the cauldron before Thor shoulders it with ease. Recall also, among the Hindus, the gods' inability to uproot Mount Mandara, and especially the curious episode of the Churning, where Viṣṇu restores to the weary gods their original strength.

Similarly here, Tištrya is at first unable to contend successfully against the demon. He must leave the Vourukaša Sea, breaking off the combat; then he implores Ahura Mazdā: *"If men invoked me by* name, as they do the other yazatas, I would be strong; I would prevail."

Ahura offers the sacrifice, and says to him: *"I grant you the strength of ten horses..."*

Exactly as Viṣṇu said to the gods: *"I grant strength to all those who have undertaken this task."*

And Tištrya, returning to the fight, triumphs.

Already, in the Brāhmaṇic accounts of the battles between the Deva and the Asura, we have seen that the Deva were first defeated, and regained the advantage only when Soma placed himself at their head.

It would, of course, be difficult to specify in what exact form this episode appeared in the Indo-European or even Indo-Iranian versions; yet the correspondence of details can hardly be a matter of chance.

4. Finally, the theme of poison appears here in a form so close to what we saw in India that it must represent at least an Indo-Iranian element:

"The dead creatures remaining in the earth (beneath the Vourukaša Sea) produced corruption and poison," says the *Bundahišn* (ch. 7). *"To purify it, Tištrya entered the sea..."*

The substitute for Tištrya-the-Horse, the Three-legged Donkey, has the same mission:

"If the three-legged donkey had not been created in the waters," says again the *Bundahišn* (44.4.19; ch. 19 init.), "*all the water of the sea would have been lost through the poison that Ahriman would have put there to destroy the creatures of Ōhrmazd...*"

To be sure, it is by urinating that the Donkey purifies the sea, not, as Śiva does, by absorbing all the poison into his throat. Yet the common elements are considerable: both Hindus and Iranians knew that, at a certain moment in the cycle, the nourishing sea was infected by a poison, and that a god had to intervene to save the world.

⁂

Here then is the cycle, as it seems to be presented by the late *Bundahišn*. Once again, neither the Slavs nor the Celts, despite the later date of their earliest texts, offer us a version as developed as this one. The true — and indeed the only — value of this text lies in demonstrating the Indo-Iranian character of several of its episodes. On various points noted along the way, it confirms and reinforces the testimony of the *Amṛtamanthana* or the Purāṇic narratives. But it tells us little about the history, doubtless a very turbulent one, of the cycle within Iran itself.

⁂

IV. Another Version of the Cycle, According to Eznik

There must have existed, within the Iranian world, other heterodox versions of the cycle — more or less altered than the one that gave rise to the Bundahišn account. A trace of one such variant has been preserved in a few lines from the Armenian bishop Eznik, who, in the fifth century, wrote a *Refutation of Heresies*.

There we find (p. 94 of Le Vaillant's translation), at the very beginning of the conflict between Ōhrmazd and Ahriman, the curious memory of a banquet — forgotten by both the *Bundahišn* and perhaps even the *Avesta*. One should also note the reversal of roles between the two principles: here it is Ahriman who invites Ōhrmazd, and Ōhrmazd who initiates the struggle:

"*Ahrmên invited Ormizd to a meal; Ormizd, having gone there, refused to eat until their sons had first fought; and when the son of Ahrmên had overthrown the son of Ormizd, the two fathers searched for a judge but found none; then they made the sun, that it might become their judge.*"

In all likelihood, these three themes — the banquet, the combat of the sons, and the creation of the sun as judge — correspond to the first part of the Cycle of Ambrosia.

1. Preparation of the feast (A, 1, a).
+ Invitation of the gods to the demons (Indo-Iranian theme).

2. Duel necessary for the preparation of the feast.
= Ancient duel for the conquest of the Vessel, duel of Tištrya–Apaoša, etc. (A, 2, a and c).

3. Collaboration of the gods and demons for the "Creation"

(Sun), formerly for the fabrication of the ambrosia (A, 3 + Indo-Iranian theme of "Collaboration" + Iranian theme of "Creation").

✱✱

V. Conclusions

It will be interesting, in conclusion to this chapter, to set out the Indo-Iranian form of the cycle, as we have glimpsed it many times. We outline here the schema without further commentary, since all the necessary explanations have already been given above. The themes of assured Indo-European origin are reproduced without modification from the previous schema; to indicate the specifically Indo-Iranian themes, the notation (I. I.) will be used. The testimony of other mythologies will later confer upon some of these the Indo-European quality that is not yet recognised here.

Schema of the Indo-Iranian Cycle

A. Preparation of the Amṛta

1. Council of the gods:
    (a) "How can we obtain the *amṛta*?" (I. E.)
    (b) A god gives the answer: "It is the sea, properly churned (?), that will provide it." (I. E.)
    (c) The gods ask the demons for their alliance. (I. I.)

2. Conquest of the Sea:
    (a) The gods' powerlessness to find the necessary

instruments. (I. E.)

(b) A god goes to the marine being who possesses the Vessel of the Waters. (I. E.)

(c) He fights against him under various forms, with alternating success and failure. (I. I. and probably I. E.)

(d) Thanks to a "renewal of strength" granted by another god (I. I.) (India: A, 3, a bis. Persia: A, 2, d), he triumphs and takes possession of the sea. (I. E.)

3. Preparation of the *amṛta*:

(a) Gods and demons churn (?) the sea together. (I. I.)

(b) Birth, along with the *amṛta*, of various divine beings. (I. I.)

(c) A poison emerging from the sea threatens the world with ruin. A god neutralises it. (I. I.)

? (d) Theme of venomous creatures. (I. I.? perhaps to be placed under D?)

B. The False Bride (become: First Theft)

(As in the Indo-European cycle — though note the variant (I. I. ?) — Vāc, Djahi — in which the fatal bride is indeed a woman.)

C. The Demon among the Gods (Second Theft)

(As in the Indo-European cycle.)

D. Extermination of the Demons

1. General battle of gods and demons. (I. I.)

2. Theme of the eclipses: attack of demons against the stars. (I. I.)

3. The demons cast beneath the earth. (I. I.)

Chapter Four

The Cycle of the Ambrosia among the Greeks

One might be surprised at the late place given here to the Greek testimony: through its ἀμβροσία, compared with the Indian *amṛta*, it was this that first made it possible, a priori, to unite the two notions of the divine drink and immortality — whatever the relation may be that this union implies. Then, it is from this source that the common notion of ambrosia has arisen. Finally, Greek mythology, through its richness and antiquity, seems to have an unquestionable right to bear witness among the first.

We therefore wish to offer first a few remarks — some general, others specific to the ambrosial legends — which, by clarifying what we indicated in the Introduction, will justify this departure from the usual order.

⁂

1. Coexistence of multiple variants and doublets.

We have already encountered, along our way, legends and

themes that exist in doublets and variants. But nowhere is this phenomenon as common as in Greece — perhaps first because the documents, from every possible origin, are more numerous there than elsewhere, and also for deeper reasons. The Greek spirit, so enamoured everywhere of clarity and harmony, seems to have taken pleasure in the growing anarchy of its fables; at the very least, it easily resigned itself to it, content later to impose upon it, in the writings of certain mythographers, an uncertain and artificial order. Without claiming to determine in a few lines the causes of this mythological richness and confusion, one may state the main ones as follows:

(a) The predecessors of the Indo-Europeans on Greek soil — autochthons, eastern or Aegean settlers — must have bequeathed to their successors a great number of rites, legends, and local cults.

(b) Foreign peoples — Egyptians, Lydians, Phrygians, Thracians, etc. — must, through various channels (commerce, military expeditions, relations of all kinds), have continued from outside this work of penetration, which can be increasingly observed, perhaps even more powerfully, in the historical period. Contaminations of myths, assimilations of gods, direct borrowings — all these agents of evolution came into play.

(c) The fragmentation of the conquerors into a thousand independent and rival cities favoured the birth of variants and doublets, among which, very early, poets and politicians alike were glad to choose according to their interests or inspiration.

(d) The moral and philosophical preoccupations of the poets, the influence of religious doctrines, early stamped their mark upon legends, many of which had doubtless begun as perfectly "amoral." The ideas of fate, of personal and hereditary nemesis, even of justice, soon animated forms that had not been made for them.

(e) Finally, the rationalist tendency of the Greek mind at all its levels — from the irony of certain pages of Homer to the avowed scepticism of the sophists — greatly facilitated the coexistence of so many diverse elements. Questions of faith or orthodoxy, except in rare cases, did not hinder the free play of individual imagination.

We must therefore expect to encounter very delicate working conditions: originating from different regions and attached to various heroes, appearing at unequal stages of evolution, altered by the writers or scholars who preserved them, at times integrated into philosophical or religious systems, and sometimes surviving only through a single episode. Numerous versions of the cycle must have coexisted, collided, merged, or harmonised — more or less successfully — into independent doublets that became officially accepted. Under such circumstances, it would be both futile and dangerous to aim at completeness. We will enter into detailed study only for the version that seems to us the least altered: the Cycle of the Πίθος and of Prometheus.

2. The notion of ambrosia very early became something rather vague for the Greeks.

The monograph that Wilhelm Heinrich Roscher devoted to *Nectar und Ambrosia* (Leipzig, 1883) gathers all the elements of the question, but organises them in a tendentious way: eager to demonstrate that ambrosia, and its counterpart nectar, were substances analogous to honey, the author downplays or omits inconvenient evidence.

Nonetheless, it remains clear that, very early on — perhaps under Semitic influences — poets and mythographers took great liberties with ambrosia, associating it without hesitation with various pleasant human foods, especially with honey. But this is the result of a natural evolution, not the original point of departure.

What is more characteristic is that the life-giving or immortalising power of ambrosia, though it never disappeared, quickly became obscured. Are ambrosia and nectar sources of immortality? Bergk (*Fleckeisens Jahrbuch*, 1860, p. 377 ff.) argued in the negative, and Roscher (op. cit., p. 52 ff.) only partly refuted him.

No doubt Demeter uses ambrosia to make Demophon immortal (*Hymn to Demeter* 236); no doubt Pindar (*Olympian* I, 91) knows that, having tasted ambrosia and nectar, Tantalos became ἄφθιτος ("incorruptible"); no doubt, later on, we see Lucian (*Dialogues of the Gods* 4) establishing a sort of equation between ἀμβροσία and ἀθανασία ("deathlessness"). But it is remarkable that, in other instances, immortality is acquired not through ambrosia but through fire: thus, Herakles enters Olympus through the pyre; Demeter herself, though she anoints Demophon each day with ambrosia, places him each night in the fire (Apollodoros, *Bibliotheka* I, 31); Thetis does the same with Achilles (Apollodoros, *Bibliotheka* III, 171). It seems that a god may be deprived of his special nourishment without ceasing to be immortal: thus, the god who has violated his oath upon the Styx no longer tastes it for a hundred years; yet he does not die — only, during that time, *"he lies breathless and voiceless on his couch, and a grievous coma covers him."* (Hesiod, *Theogony*, 795–796)

Finally, nowhere does Homer specify any life-giving virtue in ambrosia: to mask the foul odour of the seals, Proteus' daughter makes Menelaus breathe it in without any danger of rendering him immortal; but since she does not make him drink it, that evidence is unusable.

The famous scene (*Odyssey* V, 196–199) where Calypso is served ambrosia and nectar while she herself offers Odysseus human food (οἷα βροτοὶ ἄνδρες δουσιν) only emphasises the existence of two kinds of nourishment — one for mortals and one for the immortal — but does not indicate that immortality derives from ambrosia.

This is not an idle play on words: the uncertainty that seems to have existed early on regarding the effects of ambrosia — this very clear tendency to forget, or at least to diminish, its virtue — must have encouraged confusion and contradiction within the ambrosial legends. Ambrosia ceased to be the fixed, evident, and necessary centre of its cycle, just as the beer of the Æsir, fallen from the same dignity of an immortalising potion, quickly ceased to be the centre of its own. And, by an opposite movement, new legends of ambrosia were born on all sides, without any connection to the old ones.

Thus we see in the Iliad (V, 777) that the Simoïs makes grow the ambrosia which Hera's horses must graze; that Proklos (*in Commentarium*, p. 161) can attribute to Orpheus a tradition according to which it was Demeter who invented ambrosia and separated the double nourishment of the gods; and that the scholiast of Kallimakhos (*Hymn* I, 49) finally makes ambrosia, along with nectar, spring from the horns of the goat Amalthea.

The same uncertainty governs how material qualities are divided between ambrosia and nectar. Which is liquid, which solid? Which is a drink, and which a food? The texts contradict one another. Homer almost always joins the two words in a combination as fixed as σῖτος καὶ ποτός, σῖτος καὶ μέθυ, σῖτος καὶ οἶνος; most poets make nectar the drink, but Sappho (fr. 51 Bergk), Alcman (fr. 100), Euripides (*Hippolytus* 741 sq.), and a few others assign this quality to ambrosia.

The question, however, has no real importance: it has long been agreed that nectar and ambrosia are twin terms, between which the distinction was established late and no doubt arbitrarily. No matter the fanciful etymologies proposed for the word νέκταρ — semantically it is the equivalent of ἀμβροσία. We thus find here the same division between solids and liquids that we have already encountered among the Iranians with the pair Haurvatāt and Amərətāt. The evolution is certainly independent in both cases, but natural enough to have produced identical results.

The preceding remarks determine our method: we will first focus, among the legends that still present themselves as ambrosial — those relating in particular to the origin and the thefts of the ambrosia — on identifying those that derive from one or several episodes of the Indo-European cycle. The others, whatever their origin, have been extensively studied in Roscher's monograph; they do not concern us here.

But once its power was diminished, ambrosia became liable to alteration — even to substitution. Just as in Vedic literature soma took the place of *amṛta*, and in certain Scandinavian legends the "Hammer of Eternity" took the place of the Aesir's beer, we must expect to find some other potion of immortality — some other alimentary talisman — occupying the place of ambrosia in certain versions of the cycle.

Where should we look for these versions? The story of Prometheus will provide us with one that is still very little altered: we will recognise, in the deceptive feast of Mekone, in the thefts of food and the punishment of Prometheus, in the theft of the πίθος (píthos — "storage jar") of immortality and the avenging expedition of the False Woman, Pandora, the expected sequence of ambrosial episodes — mingled with elements of quite different origin and deprived only of the themes of preparation.

We will then examine the far more developed accounts of the Titanomakhies and Gigantomakhies. There again, one can recognise versions — more or less impoverished — of the same cycle. Finally, without any pretence or desire for completeness, we will attempt to gather the scattered traces of other versions of the cycle, or to identify the borrowings that other cycles — of entirely different origin but similar in sense and form (such as that of the divine Apples) — may have made from that of the Ambrosia.

⁂

In this investigation, we must always keep in mind a fact not yet mentioned — but soon to be revealed by other testimonies (Italic, Celtic, Slavic, Armenian) — and already suggested by the well-known festivals of *sóma* and of beer among the Vedic Indians and the Scandinavians: the legendary cycle of Ambrosia arrived on Greek soil accompanied by a ritual cycle — a springtime, communal festival during which, through a magico-religious re-enactment of the myths, men sought to secure for themselves a life long, healthy, and happy.

It is therefore probable that, in Greece as elsewhere, each version of the cycle we encounter was originally the translation of a local festival derived from the Feast of Ambrosia. In certain cases (such as the traces in Athens of a Thesean cycle correlated with the Thargelia), these festivals are attested. More often, we know nothing of them: such is the case for the Promethean version, and above all for the local versions that mythographers drew upon in composing their comprehensive accounts of the Titanomakhy and the Gigantomakhies. Neither Pherekydes nor Apollodoros recorded the rites that must once have corresponded, in certain regions of Greece, to the story of the *píthos* of immortality coveted by the Giants, and to that of the "Artificial Goddess," Athena, who deprived the Giants of their immortality.

I. Legends Concerning the Ambrosia and Preserving Elements of the Indo-European Cycle

1. The Sea and the Ambrosia

Of the origin of the ambrosia — of what became in India the Churning of the Ocean within its vessel, and among the Germans the brewing of the water in the Cauldron of the Sea — there survive in Greece only the faintest traces.

First, a verbal vestige: Ambrosia, the nourishing goddess (nurse of Zeus or of Dionysus), is said to be the daughter of the Ocean (Hyginus, *Fabulae* 182). Another curious tradition makes Ambrosia the daughter of the Oceanid Pleione and of a figure we shall soon meet again: Atlas (Hyginus, *Poeticon Astronomicon* II, s.v. "Taurus").

A fragment by the poetess Moirô, preserved in Athenaeus (491b), says the same thing in other terms: while the infant Zeus was in Crete, "*doves (πέλειαι) fed him in a cave, bringing him ambrosia from the currents of Ocean..*"

ἀμβροσίην φορέουσαι ἀπ' Ὠκεανοῖο ῥοάων,

a tradition which provides a mythological and etymological explanation of the constellation of the Pleiades.

And that is all. We shall explain this scarcity of legends about the making of ambrosia throughout the Greek world, at the conclusion of this study, when we glimpse which ancient human ritual beverage corresponded, among the Indo-Europeans, to the legendary and divine ambrosia: no doubt it was, among the Indo-Europeans, a fermented drink made from cereals — something like beer.

Among the Greeks, this beverage having been eliminated from rites and daily use by the Mediterranean wine, the legendary drink corresponding to it became purely fabulous, and the episodes of its fabrication were soon forgotten.

By a similar evolution, the Vedic Hindus — among whom a new beverage, the soma, had in the same way taken the place of the ancient Indo-European ritual drink — have transmitted to us, in fragments, a somic version of the cycle of ambrosia: a version which contains all the expected themes (the feast of the gods, the expulsion and punishment of the demon who came among the gods, the fatal fiancée, the war of gods and demons), except those of fabrication (the conquest of the Cauldron, the churning).

Italy will show us analogous evolutions. In all these cases, either the episodes relating to the marine Cauldron have become purely fabulous (the epic cycle of the *amṛta*), or they have disappeared, leaving only verbal traces (the Okeanid Ambrosia), or they have taken on a new meaning and purpose. We shall soon encounter, in Arkadia and in Rome, examples of this latter kind of transformation.

2. The theft of the Ambrosia: the demon at the table of the gods; his punishment (crushed beneath a mountain or rocks).

One of the most popular variants of the legend presents Tantalus as a guest of the gods (Horace, *Odes* I, 28, 7) who steals nectar and ambrosia in order to share them with his friends — ἀφείλετο νέκταρ καὶ ἀμβροσίαν (Pindar, *Olympian* I, 98 sq.). Here one recognises the episode of the "demon among the gods."

But other authors, by a process of transformation of which we shall find many further examples, have replaced the divine foods with vague, abstract "state secrets," or else have attributed to him a crime analogous to that of Atreus (see the article Tantalos in Roscher's *Lexikon*).

As for the punishment, among the various traditions two recall the Indo-European punishment of the thieving demon — such as we shall later reconstruct it from the comparison of most testimonies — that is, crushed beneath rocks or a mountain, stoned, petrified, or bound to a mountain (all punishments probably having a seismic meaning).

In Hades, says Apollodoros (*Epitome* II, 1), he has a rock hanging over his head; according to Pausanias (II, 22, 3; V, 13, 7), Zeus crushed him beneath Mount Sipylos in Lycia. We shall encounter analogous punishments in the case of Atlas, long recognised as a doublet of Tantalus.

3. Traces of other episodes?

The other episodes of the cycle have not come down to us in a properly ambrosian form. There may, however, be a trace of the episode of the god disguised as a goddess in the text of Hyginus, where Ambrosia is named among the daughters of Ocean, nurse of Zeus or Dionysus (*Fabulae* 182): Dionysus, seeing Ambrosia and her sisters growing old, turns to Medea (evidently introduced into the legend afterward) so that she might transform them into young men.

Here there is a limited but curious coincidence: to allow a divine being named Ambrosia to regain youth (how?), a god changes sex. Could this be the trace of an aberrant version — a legendary translation of one of the ambrosian rites as practiced in some Greek region?

Mannhardt (*Wald- und Feldkulte*, Berlin, 1875–77) has shown how common this rite of the man dressed as a woman, or the woman dressed as a man, was in spring festivals; now, the festival of ambrosia was the spring festival of the Indo-Europeans, and included a similar disguise.

II. The Cycle of the *Píthos* and of Fire: Indo-European and Aegean Legends

Prometheus, throughout antiquity, appears above all as the thief of fire. In this respect, he is related to other heroes of the Aegean world, notably to Hephaistos, the smith of the Lemnian legends (see K. Bapp's article Prometheus in Roscher's *Lexikon*, and C. Robert's revised edition of Preller's *Mythologie*, vol. I, p. 91 sq.).

There is no need to seek far for the origin of this legend of the theft of fire. From very early times, Prometheus was compared — indeed, to the point of an implausible supposed etymological kinship — with the Vedic fire-thief Mātariśvan (*RgVeda* I, 93, 6; III, 9, 5; VI, 8, 4). But nothing in the Vedic traditions can be directly superimposed on the other parts of the Promethean legend.

The motif itself, moreover, is perfectly natural and appears in similar forms among a great number of peoples. Sir James Frazer, in an appendix to his edition of Apollodoros' *Bibliotheka* (vol. II, App. III, *The Origin of Fire*, pp. 326–350), has collected several dozen versions of this legend, gathered from every continent. It could, therefore, have arisen independently on Greek soil.

Thus, it is not as a thief of fire that Prometheus truly concerns us. Reading his story as told by Hesiod, one sees that fire originally held a rather secondary place in it. Other, far more important episodes appear: the tricked feast of gods and men, rigged by Prometheus to the gods' detriment; the punishment of Prometheus; the theft of a *píthos* that contains "the absence of death"; and the vengeful expedition, against the thief, of a female figure fashioned by the gods.

These are so many episodes that together reproduce the entire Indo-European cycle of ambrosia, except for the preparatory scenes. Everything happens as though the Titan Prometheus had gathered upon himself both the Aegean legends of fire and the Greek legends of ambrosia — or of its vessel, the *píthos*.

※

How could such an accumulation of adventures, such a fusion of legends, have taken place? By what path did the thief of fire come to coincide with the thief of ambrosia? It would be useless to appeal here to the traditions mentioned above, where we see fire benefiting from the increasing uncertainty surrounding the notion of ambrosia: the pyre of Herakles, or the fiery baths by which goddesses render their favourites immortal. Certainly, from very early on, the fire that purifies every stain appeared as the best, the only remedy against the great human stain — mortality. But this is already a reflective, almost philosophical assimilation, which would be surprising in the unspeculative state of mind represented by Hesiod.

Thus, in the case of the Promethean legend, the kinship between the notions of fire and ambrosia is more material, more immediate. We can only specify this point after examining in detail all the Hesiodic texts. Let us say at once, however, that for Hesiod, if Zeus denies fire to humankind and Prometheus steals it for them, it is because the former wishes to prevent humans from cooking their meat, from enjoying their share of food obtained by artifice, while the latter wishes, on the contrary, to prevent them from dying of hunger. The story of Prometheus begins with a feast where the best portion is given to men, an act that provokes the gods' vengeance.

Moreover, when Zeus deprives them of fire, does he not also deprive them of grain, of cereals (*bíos*)? The Promethean fire, before it became — thanks to the genius of Aeschylus and the subtlety of later mythographers — the "civilising fire" or the "animating fire" (as elsewhere the "purifying fire"), was simply what it still is in Hesiod: "the fire that cooks." It is therefore in this alimentary sense that the theft of fire could merge with the Indo-European legends concerning the food of the gods.

Another feature — though admittedly quite obscure — of our Indo-European legends may have helped bring about this confusion. We have not yet mentioned it, because the Hindus seem to have retained no trace of it; but the Germanic, Celtic, and Latin legends all agree in assigning, in the operations that precede and in the thefts that follow the preparation of ambrosia, a variable yet always significant role to a divine smith.

Among the Germans, we have seen the god of fire and of smiths, Loki, play the part of the demon at the gods' table (*Lokasenna*). Furthermore, when the episode of the False Bride detached itself from the ambrosial cycle, it attached itself instead to the Hammer of Permanence, and Loki again accompanies Thor, disguised, to Thrym's hall (*Þrymskviða*).

In Irish belief, as we shall see, the Ale of Immortality was brewed by the smith-god Goibniu; and in the late version of that cycle which has reached us, the marvellous weapons forged by that god have, in part, taken the place of the ale of immortality.

Among the Latins, finally, one version of the cycle gives the demon who collaborates with the gods and later steals the object of perpetuity the traits of the smith Mamurius, celebrated by the Salii in their chants as they made their way to the site of their famous feast. And here again, the quality of smith attributed to Mamurius undoubtedly helped make of the *ancile*, by the classical age, what it had become — a shield.

Prometheus, brother of Hephaistos, the Lemnian smith, and of Hephaistos, the cupbearer of the Olympians, Prometheus who takes part in the preparation of the divine feast at Mekone and then defrauds the gods of their share of food, thus joins Goibniu, but especially Loki and Mamurius. There is, without doubt, an Indo-European trait here whose deeper meaning escapes us, but which helps to explain the union, under the name of Prometheus, of the legends of fire and of those of ambrosia.

*
* *

It is well known that the Hesiodic texts have preserved for us two accounts of Prometheus' misadventure — especially of the Pandora episode. One is found in the *Theogony* (vv. 507–616), the other in *Works and Days* (vv. 43–105).

In the study devoted to the latter work, M. Mazon, comparing the two versions, concluded — and with considerable likelihood — that the conception in *Works and Days*, simpler and more naïve, must be the older one. It matters little that, in the order of composition, the account in the *Theogony*, Hesiod's first work, precedes that in *Works and Days*, a work of his maturity; the fact remains that, in Hesiod's time, two conceptions of Pandora coexisted — one more archaic, the other more evolved (Mazon, op. cit., pp. 50 and 138).

The more archaic is that of the *Works and Days*: this is the one we shall first consider. And the Indo-European, ambrosial elements that we will encounter there will confirm the feeling — the already quite plausible hypothesis — of M. Mazon.

A. The Text of Works and Days. The Theft of the *Píthos*. Pandora

M. Mazon, in his analysis of *Works and Days*, highlights two key features of Hesiod's account.

First, Hesiod proceeds by allusion: he assumes his audience already knows the essential outlines of the Prometheus story. Thus he "recalls" advice given by Prometheus to Epimetheus — though he has never mentioned it before; and, abruptly, in the final part, he speaks of the *píthos* without having introduced it. What we have, therefore, is a summary, not a full narrative.

Second — and closely related — the story is not told for its own sake, but functions as a moral illustration supporting the poem's argument. The point of Works and Days is clear: *"Only through work can man sustain his life. This is the will of Zeus, and to the law of Zeus all must submit; the story of Prometheus proves it."* Prometheus, in attempting to free humankind from Zeus' design, brings about their suffering; thus, man cannot escape the divine will and must obey by working (Mazon, op. cit., p. 48).

This moral, philosophical tone colours the entire passage. Like a refrain (vv. 71, 79, 99), the same expressions recur: "by the will of Zeus" (Κρονίδεω διὰ βουλάς, Διὸς βουλῆσι βαρυκτύπου, αἰγιόχου βουλῆσι Διὸς νεφεληγερέταο). And in the jar — the *píthos* of Epimetheus — will be found, among other things later specified, the χαλεπὸς πόνος, the "hard toil" decreed for mankind.

This was certainly not the original sense or colour of the myth;

the transformation and moral redirection were dictated by the fundamental idea of the poem in which the myth was inserted. The account in the *Theogony*, though in other ways more altered, did not undergo this moral "inflection."

Now follows the tale as told in Works and Days: angered by an earlier deception from Prometheus (which the Theogony will allow us to specify later), Zeus hid bread (βίος) from men, and also fire. Prometheus, once again, deceived Zeus and stole the fire in a hollow stalk (ἐν κοίλῳ νάρθηκι) "for mankind." Zeus, once more enraged, foretold a great evil for him and for future men:

"In exchange for the fire, I will give them an evil in which they will delight, embracing their own ruin with joy in their hearts." (τοῖσ' ἐγὼ ἀντὶ πυρὸς δώσω κακὸν ᾧ χαίροντες αὐτοὶ περιπτυχέονται κακόν).

Then Zeus commanded Hephaistos to take earth and water and fashion from them a virgin body, like that of the immortal goddesses. He instructed Athena to teach her the works of women, especially the weaving of cloth, and Aphrodite to bestow on her grace and all charms. But he ordered Hermes to place within this splendid body "a shameless mind, a deceitful heart" (καρδίην τε νόον καὶ ἐπίφρονα θυμὸν ἀπατηλόν).

The gods obey. Hephaestus shapes the feminine form (πυκνὸν ἰδρώσαντι χερσίν — *"with skilful hands he formed her from moist clay"*). Athena girds her with a belt and adorns her with ornaments; the Kharites (Graces), Peitho (Persuasion), and the Horai (Seasons) deck her in beauty, while Athena gives the final touch to her attire.

Finally, Hermes, precise and punctual, breathes into her *"deceit, cunning thoughts, a lying heart"* (δόλον καὶ ἐπίκλοπον ἦτορ ἔθηκε), and grants her speech — the voice through which all these gifts will be made effective.

Since every god on Olympus has contributed something to equip this fatal creature, she receives the name Pandora, "the All-Gifted."

Zeus ordered Hermes to bring her to Epimetheus. But Epimetheus, forgetting the wise advice of his brother Prometheus, who had warned him never to accept any gift from Zeus, received Pandora — and too late understood (hence his name, Epimētheus, "he who thinks afterward") that she was a curse. For until then, humankind had lived apart from evils, *"free from toil and the grievous sicknesses that bring death"* (ἄτερ τε κακῶν καὶ ἄτερ χαλεποῖο πόνοιο, νούσων τ' ἀργαλέων αἵ τ' ἀνδράσι κῆρας ἔδωκαν).

But this woman, lifting the great lid of the jar (πίθου μέγα πῶμ' ἀφελοῦσα), released sufferings and sorrows upon the world. Only Hope (Ἐλπίς — Expectation) remained within the jar, since Pandora replaced the lid in time, according to Zeus's will.

Now, countless miseries wander among mortals: the earth is full of them, and so is the sea. Diseases of the day, and those that come by night of their own accord, roam among men — bearers of evil, silent all, for wise Zeus did not grant them a voice.

The account in the Theogony will fully illuminate the opening verses of this text. Let us note at once, however, that although the story begins with the theft of fire, this theft is immediately forgotten; the punishment bears no direct relation to the offence, nor does it repair it — for humankind keeps the fire. Any other transgression of Zeus's law might have received a similar punishment.

There is therefore a break in the logical, almost moral continuity of the narrative — a disjunction that the text itself, in its final section, allows us to understand: in reality, two legends have been combined. There are two thefts — the theft of fire, preserved here merely by tradition, and the theft of the *píthos*, to which Hesiod, trusting in his readers' prior knowledge, merely alludes.

Here again, M. Mazon has provided all the essential elements of the problem (op. cit., pp. 52–53):

"What was this jar? Did Pandora find it already in Epimetheus's house, or did she bring it herself? The text does not say — obviously because every listener of Hesiod must have known it. We are less well informed. I do not believe, however, that Pandora brought the jar herself: the 'gift of the gods' is Pandora herself; Hesiod does not show the gods, when she leaves Olympus, handing her the fatal jar.

"Therefore it must have already been in Epimetheus's cellar. According to the scholia, he had received it from Prometheus, who in turn had obtained it from the Satyrs.

"This means that by the fifth century the legend had become the subject of a satyric drama, whose plot we may conjecture as follows: Zeus had planned to pour the contents of the jar of evils upon the earth;

Prometheus then had it stolen by the Satyrs and gave it to Epimetheus, warning him never to open it; but Pandora, once introduced into Epimetheus's house, furtively lifted the lid.

"It is unlikely that this was the original form of the legend to which Hesiod alludes, yet it would be even less likely that the Athenian poet, whoever he was, would have contradicted the traditional version on an essential point, such as the origin of the jar. We must therefore think that the jar was already standing — 'planted in the ground' — in Epimetheus's cellar when Pandora entered the house."

Certainly — here the author observes that even if we reconstruct the plot of that satyric drama somewhat differently, one fact is firmly established by the scholia: the *píthos* was already in Epimetheus's possession, and it was Prometheus who, directly or indirectly, had stolen it from Zeus.

From that moment, the parallel with the Indo-European cycle of the ambrosia becomes unmistakable. The scene corresponds point for point to one of its most distinctive episodes: a female form, specially created by the gods for the purpose, is sent to the dwelling of a demon who holds a jar stolen from the gods. By the power of her charm, she neutralises and undoes the benefit of the theft.

In other words, Pandora plays the same role here as the "Fatal Bride" or "False Fiancée" of the ambrosia cycle: she is the divine instrument sent to recover, or at least to render vain, the stolen substance of immortality.

All the more since the jar itself, with its strange contents, still clearly corresponds to the vessel and the ambrosia stolen by the Indo-European demon: once the jar is opened, a thousand plagues are spread throughout the world — μυρία λυγρά — especially diseases, whereas previously men had lived safe from the *"terrible sicknesses that bring death"* (ἄτερ ... νούσων τ' ἀργαλέων αἵτ' ἀνδράσι κῆρας ἔδωκαν, v. 92).

One can debate endlessly whether the jar contained, as the scholia say, evils — or rather goods — evils that had to be kept shut away as dangerous, or goods that had to be kept enclosed as precious. In particular, did it contain health, the absence of mortal illness, or the diseases themselves?

It matters little; however evolved the legend may already be, it still preserves the meaning of its Indo-European prototype: the "female form" comes to take from Epimetheus the immortality that a "jar stolen from the gods" had bestowed upon him. The contents of this jar have, in a sense, become dematerialised, yet their marvellous properties remain the same. It lacks only the name: ἀμβροσία (ambrosia).

Much better: a vase from Oxford (Percy Gardner, *Journal of Hellenic Studies* XXI, 1901, pl. I; Lechat, *Revue des Études Grecques* XIV, 1901, p. 474; Carl Robert, *Hermes* XLIX, 1914, p. 17–38), from which rather risky conclusions have been drawn about the "chthonic" character of Pandora, shows in any case the Woman appearing before the eyes of Epimetheus with the veil and crown of a bride, and, for even greater clarity, surmounted by a winged Eros. This proves that the gods sent Pandora to Epimetheus — the "female form" to the "demon" — not merely as a messenger but as a wife. Hesiod does not say this explicitly, but does he not put in Zeus's mouth, in his threats, those significant words: "Men shall cherish with love their own misfortune?" This idea of "seduction," of "blinding love," accords perfectly with the Indo-European ambrosial tradition of the "fatal bride."

One can note, as a literary curiosity, how closely the episode of Pandora, as it is told in Works and Days, resembles its Germanic counterpart, the Þrymskviða. The gods adorn their creation eagerly, just as the Æsir and the goddesses adorn Thor in disguise; Athena gives her a girdle and jewels, just as Freyja lends hers to Thor; and Hermes leads her to Epimetheus, just as the cunning Loki leads the false goddess to Thrym. Finally, there is the same blindness, the same dazzled infatuation, the same forgetting of all caution in the giant Thrym and in the Titan Epimetheus.

As for Epimetheus, one should not attach much importance to this character: he is merely a reflection, a doublet of his brother Prometheus, born from a play on words whose meaning the story of Pandora reveals. In other versions of the legend, he even disappears: for some (for Hesiod himself, according to Schol. Apoll. III, 1086: *"That Deucalion, the son of Prometheus and Pandora, Hesiod says in the first Catalogue of Women"* ("Ὅτι Προμηθέως καὶ Πανδώρας υἱὸς Δευκαλίων Ἡσίοδος ἐν πρώτῳ καταλόγων φησί). Pandora simply becomes the wife of Prometheus. Among the four brothers mentioned by Hesiod (Theogony v. 508 sq.), the "proud" Menoitios and the "imprudent" Epimetheus are pale figures, serving only to set in sharper relief the stronger personalities of Atlas and Prometheus.

A. The Text of the Theogony. The Feast of the Gods. The Theft of Fire. The Binding of Prometheus

We have said, following M. Mazon, that the episode of Pandora, in the form given it by Works and Days, is more primitive, less developed than the corresponding episode in the *Theogony*. Let us at once settle this question before returning to the beginning of the *Theogony* narrative, which has no counterpart in Works and Days.

This time, the *píthos*, which Works and Days had already mentioned only in passing, disappears completely: it is Pandora herself, by her mere presence, by her very "essence," who executes Zeus's vengeance. She represents "Woman," the great scourge of this earth (*"For from her is the destructive race and tribe of women, a great bane for mortals, dwelling among men, not as helpers in destructive poverty, but in satiety."* τῆς γὰρ 'ολώϊόν ἐστι γένος, καὶ φῦλα γυναικῶν, πῆμα μέγα θνητοῖσι, μετ᾽ ἀνδράσι ναιετάουσιν, οὐλομένης πενίης οὐ σύμφοροι, ἀλλὰ κόροιο, Theogony v. 590–592).

And the gynophobia natural to the Greeks, from this first manifestation, is given free rein in a famous tirade. A very curious, very picturesque evolution of the Indo-European legend, in which the expedition of the False Bride did not unleash such curses upon a sex that was not to blame.

It should be noted that this first evolution of the Pandora myth is the origin of a much greater development of the Prometheus myth: if Pandora embodies "Woman" in general, then the creation of Pandora amounts to the creation of half of humankind. From this arise all those legends whose progression can be traced in historical times, in which we see appearing successively: the creation of Woman by the gods; then by the gods with the collaboration of Prometheus; then the creation of Man by Prometheus, against or with the consent of the gods (here appears a new meaning of the "theft of fire," a theft committed to "animate" the Titan's creature); so that, in the end, Prometheus finds himself…

The mortals thus enjoyed more than one of the privileges of the immortals — and above all, fire, that most precious of all divine possessions.

Yet a day came when gods and mortals separated. They agreed then to determine their respective shares, to fix the tribute of honours or benefits that they would henceforth render to one another. The agreement was concluded in the oldest city of the Peloponnese, in the land where ancient tradition placed the dwelling of a Titan — in Mekone (Sikyon).

Here begins Hesiod's account: the pact is sealed by a banquet prepared by Prometheus, which was to become the model for future sacrifices. Prometheus serves up an ox. But, wishing to favour humankind, he divides it into two parts — one made entirely of meat, which he hides beneath the animal's stomach, a common and unappetising piece; the other composed solely of bones, but wrapped in glistening, tempting fat. Then he lets Zeus choose between them. Zeus sees through the trick but pretends to be deceived and chooses the second portion.

Then he lets his anger burst forth. To avenge himself, he denies fire (οὐχ ἐδίδου) to mortals—without which they cannot roast the flesh. Prometheus, by a second ruse (αὖτις), steals the fire from Zeus.

The text ends, like that of *Works and Days*, with the mission of Pandora. But we know, moreover (*Theogony*, v. 520–525, cf. v. 613–615), that Prometheus suffers a personal punishment — the very one that centuries of literature and philosophy have celebrated: an eagle gnaws at the ever-regenerating liver of the Titan bound to a rock.

Verses 526–534, which mention the deliverance of Prometheus by Herakles, are universally regarded as an interpolation, added in honour of the Argive hero.

It is in this opening part of the story that the mixture of Indo-European and native, pre-Hellenic elements appear most clearly — though the latter are easier to sense than to define. The strange scene of the butchered and falsified ox would by itself reveal a non-Indo-European origin, even if Hesiod did not take care to tell us that it is closely connected to an old, tenacious rite, wholly foreign to the Indo-Europeans:

"From that time on," he says, "the tribes of men have burned white bones to the gods on smoking altars."

We shall soon encounter other cases just as characteristic.

It is remarkable that Prometheus' first offense is committed during a feast — and that it consists in taking away from the gods, to give to their rivals, a certain kind of food. Here lies the clearly Indo-European element of the legend, the trait that allowed the theme of the "tricked feast" to merge with the "ambrosial" themes. Prometheus thus joins Tantalus, the thief and "distributor," so to speak, of divine nourishment.

And the theft of fire takes on a very special meaning: Zeus refuses fire to men, not as an element of civilization, not as the foundation of arts and crafts — all that belongs to Aeschylus, and Hesiod seems not to think of it. His Zeus refuses fire to men quite clearly so that they cannot enjoy their share; it is an alimentary reprisal.

We can now better understand how the theft of fire could merge, within a single cycle, with the ambrosial themes: in both cases, it concerns food, life, "non-death," if not outright immortality. Prometheus, by stealing fire for mankind, simply prevents them from dying of hunger.

Thus is explained, at the beginning of Works and Days, that detail which may have seemed strange: at the same time that Zeus withholds fire from men, he hides in the earth the instrument of life, bread (κρύψαντες γὰρ ἔχουσι θεοί βίον ἀνθρώποισιν... *Works and Days* v. 42 sq.). In reality, Zeus' double gesture corresponds to a single intention: since Prometheus has favoured mankind at the expense of the gods in a matter of nourishment, they will be punished through their food. First, they will have no fire with which to cook the stolen meat, then they will struggle painfully to make their own bread.

This "nutritional" or "food-related" aspect of the Prometheus legend finally helps to explain the curious Orphic development of the Pandora episode. Concerning a sanctuary of Demeter Kabeiria near Thebes, Pausanias (IX, 25, 6) writes:

"It is said that there was once a city there, inhabited by men called the Kabeiroi, and that to one of these Kabeiroi, Prometheus, and to Aitnaios, the son of Prometheus, Demeter came to entrust a deposit." (προμηθεῖ δὲ ἑνὶ τῶν Καβείρων καὶ Αἰτναίῳ τῷ Προμηθέως ἀφικομένην Δήμητρα ἐς γνῶσιν παρακαταθέσθαι σφίσιν.)

For a long time (see Preller, *Philologus* VII, p. 51; Rapp, "Prometheus" in Roscher's *Lexikon*), this παρακαταθήκη — this mystical "deposit" of Demeter Kabeiria — has been plausibly identified with the enigmatic jar of Pandora. Moreover, there can be little doubt that in this gift from Demeter to Prometheus we find some version of the "revelation of grain," which lies at the heart of Demeter's cult.

This tradition takes on its full meaning when we recall that, according to the Orphic traditions, it was Demeter who invented ambrosia and separated the double nourishment of the gods (Proklos, *in Cratylum* 161).

Perhaps this offers a way to reconcile everything we have learned about Pandora with the fairly widespread view that sees in her a chthonic (earth) divinity. Both the ambrosial legends and the cereal (grain) legends corresponded to spring or summer rites. Interference between them was therefore inevitable.

This is the primary meaning of the theft of fire. It is the glory of the Greek genius to have known how to draw from such a material and specific event the philosophical myth we know: Zeus refusing mankind the civilising fire, and Prometheus, through his devotion, correcting the selfish act of the young god.

The humble origin of Aeschylus' drama only highlights more vividly the powerful originality of Greek thought. Nowhere else in the Indo-European world do we see, emerging from the themes of the Ambrosia cycle, a legend comparable in human significance and philosophical richness to that of Prometheus.

⁂

One point remains unexplained: the philanthropy of Prometheus. Everywhere and always, the Titan acts, deceives Zeus, and incurs Zeus's wrath for the benefit of mankind. Zeus, moreover, makes no distinction between Prometheus, his brother Epimetheus, and human beings: he announces (*Works and Days*, v. 57–58) that he will send a plague "upon men," and it is Epimetheus who then receives that plague in the person of Pandora.

What, on the other hand, is this tradition from Sikyon which claims that gods and men once lived together, united and intermingled? Upon reflection, this is the most striking point of the legend. Perhaps we must see here a trace of Kabeiric influence: a passage already cited from Pausanias (IX, 25, 6) speaks of "men called Kabeiroi" who lived near Thebes and identifies Prometheus as one of them. Others (Photius, s.v. Κάβειροι) identified the Titans with the Kabeiroi, and everything else we know about the Kabeiroi presents them as beings close to humanity — prototypes of heroes.

Finally, in the myth of the Races of Men, is not the second race of men that of the Titans (*Works and Days*, v. 127–142; ed. Mazon, p. 65)? And do not all the manuscripts (at verse 141) describe these beings, after the advent of a third race, as ὑποχθόνιοι μάκαρες θνητοί — "mortal blessed ones dwelling beneath the earth"? (Cf. Farnell, *Greek Hero Cults*, 1921, p. 18.)

The θνητοί ("mortals") of the Promethean legend may thus have originally designated only the brothers of Prometheus — the Titans, the vanquished in the great struggle for immortality, those who did not become ἀθάνατοι (immortal) like the sons of Cronus. But this epithet θνητοί, which they shared from then on with ordinary men, must have facilitated the confusion evidenced in Hesiod's text.

And perhaps it is thus that the figure of Prometheus, the benefactor of mankind, was born — a figure whose extraordinary fortune is known across the ages and far beyond Greece. Later (and no doubt already in Hesiod's time), when all precise memory of ambrosia had disappeared from the stories of the struggle between the Titan gods and the Kronid gods, and when immortality no longer appeared as the effect of ambrosia but as a sort of natural, congenital privilege of every divine being, the Titan gods — Prometheus foremost — must have regained their immortality by this very means.

From then on, to whom could the traditional name θνητοί

apply, if not to humans alone? And thus we arrive at the form of the legend as we know it: Prometheus and Epimetheus, working and deceiving for the θνητοί, become "the benefactors of men."

*

A few traces still remain of the Titans, whose place men have taken. Mékoné, Sikyon — where the mixed meal provoking the quarrel is served — was precisely the dwelling place of a Titan (Pausanias II, 11, 5).

A scholium on the *Theogony* (v. 518) explains that this feast took place μετὰ τὸν πόλεμον ("after the war"), that is, after the Titanomakhy. In reality, it must once have formed part of the Titanomakhy itself — at a time when it was the Titans, and not yet men, who sought to appropriate, by trickery, the food of Zeus and the gods.

In any case, one can recognise here the collaboration — the temporary alliance — between gods and demons in the Indo-European tradition, suddenly broken when the time comes to divide between them the wondrous food they had prepared together.

*

We will not dwell on the punishment of Prometheus. It is known that originally — before Orphic influence intervened — this punishment, like that of the other Titans, was meant to be eternal.

The verses of Hesiod that mention his deliverance by Herakles are clearly interpolations.

As for the form of the punishment, it is also known that the eagle did not appear in the primitive legend. Prometheus was simply bound — like Atlas, like Loki, like Ahriman, and no doubt like the demon-thief of the Indo-European cycle — to a pillar or a mountain at the edge of the world. Throughout the surviving drama of Aeschylus, the Titan endures only this elementary torment, and it is not until the second play of the trilogy that Zeus, in an excess of cruelty, adds the eagle to the chains.

Finally, a later tradition explained earthquakes as the convulsions of Prometheus; but since this detail appears only at a late date (Apollonius Rhodios, *Argonautika* III, 862 ff.), it is most likely not an Indo-European remnant, but an independent innovation inspired by the fate of Enceladus and other vanquished giants.

***

All in all, here is how we are led to understand the formation of the legend of Prometheus: it is, above all, the ambrosia cycle — but emptied of the specific notion of ambrosia.

I say "specific," because the legend still retains the idea of the food of the gods, of theft of divine nourishment, and the *píthos* still contains "immortality." But the ambrosia itself, as a brewed drink, has disappeared. We have already suggested earlier the hypothesis

— which will be fully developed at the end of this study — that explains the early loss of the idea of "the beer of immortality" in both the Aryan and Mediterranean branches of the Indo-European family.

Let us note here only the main consequences of that forgetting.

First, everything related to preparation or making has disappeared — at least in Hesiod. Aiskhylos, who drew from other sources, preserved the memory of a collaboration between Prometheus and Oceanus (*Prometheus Bound*, v. 331). But in Hesiod, not a word is said about the origin of the *píthos* (formerly "the conquest of the Vat") or about the making of its contents (formerly "the brewing"). The content of the *píthos* has become completely abstract.

Then, where the Indo-European demon — seated at the gods' table — merely stole the ambrosia for himself or his brothers, the Greeks introduced a similar but distinct and likely Aegean theme: the tricked banquet.

Finally, another pre-Hellenic element entered the legend by an alimentative route: the theft of fire. This element, still limited in Hesiod, eventually became the very centre of the cycle; the episode of the *píthos* shrank and faded, and the myth arrived at this curious outcome that defines its classical form: a single crime (the theft of fire) and two punishments (the chaining of Prometheus and the mission of Pandora).

III. Traces of Other Versions of the Cycle

Aside from the Promethean tale, many Greek legends seem to rest upon an ambrosial foundation. Yet nowhere do we find a witness as unified, explicit, or ancient as Hesiod's double account.

From this point on, we encounter only fragments of the cycle; therefore, all that follows must be presented merely as a series of hypotheses — of uneven solidity — serving as indications of where one should look.

We have, moreover, tried not to abuse the rights of hypothesis, and to risk nothing without the support of a few characteristic facts.

⁂

The Indo-European myth of ambrosia was originally the occasion and very cause of a great conflict between two kinds of superhuman beings — which, for simplicity, we have called gods and demons. It is therefore natural to ask whether the Greek tales of divine battles still preserve something of that ambrosial cycle.

Unfortunately, the conditions for studying this are poor. Even if these Gigantomachies and Titanomakhies do contain ambrosial elements, they also contain many others. Struggles of gods and monsters are the common material of all mythologies and folklores everywhere: stones, mountains, rivers, sacred places, all tend to have their legend of a victorious god and a vanquished demon — in Greece no less than in Brittany or Polynesia. At times, dim historical memories seem to intervene (as with the Pallantids and

Theseus in Attica).

Moreover, the sources that have come down to us are already highly developed. The Greeks tried to arrange all local legends of such struggles into major and minor wars. Apollodoros (*Bibliotheka*, Book I) gives a detailed account of six heavenly revolutions: Ouranos chaining his Cyclopean sons in the underworld; Kronos and the Titans overthrowing Ouranos; Zeus and the Kronid gods overthrowing Kronos and the Titans; the gods fighting the Giants; then Typhon; then the Aloadai.

But this division of combats into great episodes and the grouping of smaller battles as sub-episodes of the great ones is clearly artificial. Just as the hundred exploits of Herakles were organised by clever hands into the framework of twelve Labours, so too the innumerable battles of the gods among themselves or against their foes were fitted into these six wars.

We thus face a twofold difficulty: in the synthetic accounts preserved by late authors, we encounter episodes drawn from widely different regions — often mere artificial doubles, brought together or separated from their local settings by literary systematisation. Most of those local legends have been lost to us.

Then, among these episodes, many are certainly not of ambrosial origin, and their proximity has inevitably blurred and diluted the few that are. We therefore cannot hope to find here anything more than traces of lost versions of the ambrosial cycle.

In his very brief Titanomakhy, Hesiod may have preserved one of these memories. He does not indicate the cause of the conflict between *"the Titan gods and the gods born of Kronos"* (Τιτῆνές τε θεοὶ καὶ ὅσοι Κρόνου ἐξεγένοντο, *Theogony* v. 631). We know only that it lasted for a long time, with victories on both sides, and that there seemed to be no reason for it ever to end.

Then the ambrosia intervened: Zeus and his allies brought back into the light the three Hekatonkheires, who had long been bound at the edges of the earth. And *"when they had given them nectar and ambrosia, with which the gods are nourished, courage burned more strongly in every heart; and when the Hekatonkheires had satisfied themselves with nectar and desirable ambrosia,"* Zeus made with them the alliance that would ensure the ruin of the Titans (*Theogony* v. 639–643).

The Hekatonkheires and the Titans are purely Greek figures; the account is already, without doubt, highly developed. Yet it is striking that ambrosia — and its twin, nectar — appears at the decisive moment of the struggle.

The ambrosia is not the object of the quarrel, but rather, as with the *sóma* in the Vedic legend, it is the means of victory, and Hesiod emphasises this point. Might this not preserve a memory of the role it once played in the ancient conflict? This ambrosial detail is all the more valuable because, in the entire account of the battle, it is the only precise feature that Hesiod records.

But it is in Apollodoros' Gigantomakhy (*Bibliotheka*, Book I, ch. 35–38) that we find the clearest trace of an ambrosial cycle.

This text is admittedly late in date, yet monuments confirm the antiquity of many of its essential details. Even if Apollodoros — or the sources he compiled — merely gathered a series of independent local legends into a more or less coherent whole, those legends were drawn from trustworthy traditions, and their testimony carries great weight.

At the decisive moment of the struggle, they mention a φάρμακον (*phármakon* — "medicine," "poison," or "drug") of immortality, a true ambrosia in everything but name:

"The Earth, having learned that the Giants could be slain only by a mortal, sought a phármakon that would prevent them from perishing, even at the hand of a mortal. But Zeus, forbidding Dawn, the Sun, and the Moon to shine, himself was the first to cut the φάρμακον and, through Athena, called upon Herakles as his ally." (Apollodorus, *Bibliotheka* I 35: Αἰσθομνένη δὲ μὴ τοῦτο, ἐζήτει φάρμακον, ἵνα μηδ' ὑπὸ θνητοῦ δυνηθῶσιν ἀπολέσθαι. Ζεὺς δὲ ἀπειπὼν φαίνειν Ἡοῖ καὶ Σελήνῃ καὶ Ἡλίῳ τὸ μὲν φάρμακον αὐτὸς ἔτεμε φθάσας, Ἡρακλέα δὲ σύμμαχον δι' Ἀθηνᾶς ἐπεκαλέσατο).

Here the *phármakon* — a magical substance conferring imperishability — clearly plays the same functional role as ambrosia in earlier Indo-European myth: the decisive instrument of divine victory.

The word ἔτεμε ("he cut") makes φάρμακον likely mean a magic herb. But the exact sense — whether "herb" or "potion" — doesn't really matter: what's important is that Zeus and Earth, leading their opposing sides (the Gods and the Giants), are fighting over a miraculous substance that guarantees complete immortality.

This strange episode, unrelated to what comes before or after in the narrative, seems to be a faint but direct descendant of the grand old "ambrosial quarrels." Once, gods and demons went to war for the possession of ambrosia itself; here, the ambrosia has changed in nature — it's no longer the cause of the conflict, but a weapon within it, a decisive expedient that determines victory.

As for the role of the Sun and the Moon as saviours of the gods in this episode, it closely recalls their role in the *Amṛtamanthana* (the "Churning of the Nectar") from Indian mythology. It is at least striking that, in both traditions, the motif of eclipses appears in precisely the same place in the story — during the struggle for the substance of immortality.

This parallel is particularly remarkable since Greek mythology is generally very poor in eclipse-related myths. The appearance of such a motif here strengthens the sense that the Gigantomakhy episode preserves a deep Indo-European echo of the cosmic struggle over divine nourishment or immortality.

No less characteristic in this scene is the role of Athena, whose part is far more clearly defined in most Gigantomachy accounts than in Apollodoros' version.

Even in Apollodoros (*Bibliotheka* I, 35–36), she appears several times as the one who removes from the demons their "conditional immortality." When prophecy reveals that the Giants will remain immortal unless the gods find a mortal ally, Zeus sends Athena to summon Herakles. When the Giant Alkyoneus is said to be immortal so long as he fights on his native soil, it is Athena who advises Herakles to draw him away from it. In other versions — no doubt local ones — Athena acts directly: she slays Enkelados; she kills Pallas, then uses his skin as her *aigís* (Apollodoros I, 37); and according to Euripides (*Ion* 987 ff.), she also kills the monster Gorgo, born of Earth to help her sons, and makes the creature's head her *aigís*.

Ancient monuments confirm this central role of Athena. On the archaic Athena of Dresden, among the eleven scenes of gods fighting Giants, only Zeus and Athena are identifiable. The duel between Athena and a Giant likely appeared on one of the mutilated metopes of the Parthenon; and a black-figure amphora shows her in full armour — helmet, spear, aegis with Gorgonion — striking down Enceladus. Thus the goddess appears as Athena γιγαντολέτειρα, γιγαντολέτις "slayer of Giants" (cf. Zeus γιγαντολέτωρ, γιγαντο- λέτης), Athena Nike, the victorious one, sent by Zeus to take from a Giant the conditional immortality he possessed.

This figure unmistakably corresponds to the Indo-European "female form" — the divine woman sent by the gods to take back from a demon the stolen drink of immortality. The parallel grows even clearer with the strange tale of Athena's birth, which one tradition explicitly connects to this moment of the Gigantomakhy. Sidonius Apollinaris (VI, 15 ff.) says that during the Giants' war, the gods were first defeated, and only gained victory when Zeus's head gave birth to Athena, fully armed. On several Greek vases, the birth of Athena directly accompanies the Gigantomakhy scene.

Scholars note that only two myths of Athena go back to the common Hellenic period: her birth and her role in the Gigantomakhy. And this miraculous birth — later turned into the "cranial childbirth" from Zeus's head—closely mirrors the creation of Pandora: likewise a divine female, crafted and armed in every way on Zeus's command, sent not against the Giants but against their counterparts, the Titans, to take away the benefit of the *píthos* of immortality.

Finally, the erotic element sometimes appears here too — Pallas attempting to violate Athena, or Zeus sending the desire of Hera (πόθον Ἥρας) to disarm the Giant Porphyrion. Altogether, these Gigantomakhy tales preserve a Greek version of the ambrosial cycle, lacking only the preparatory "fabrication" episodes and the earlier Indo-European motif of "the demon among the gods."

The Gods and Giants, locked in cosmic war, fight a decisive battle over a *phármakon* — a substance granting full immortality. With the help of the Sun and Moon, Zeus succeeds in seizing this *phármakon*.

Yet some Giants remain conditionally immortal — protected by specific circumstances of place or combat (each variant preserving a local legend). To counter this, Zeus creates from nothing a woman — a παρθένος — whose interventions, told in several different forms, deprive one or another Giant of his conditional immortality, or destroy others by trickery and disguise.

In the end, the defeated Giants are hurled beneath mountains and islands, whose volcanic tremors betray their restless struggles beneath the earth — as told by Apollodoros (*Bibliotheka* I).

We may have here one of the earliest elements of Athena's character: Athena may at first have been nothing more than a Pandora — a divinely fashioned maiden — who later had the good fortune to be adopted, recreated, and transfigured by the Athenians.

⁂

We will later encounter, under the Thargelia, the ancient Indo-European festival of ambrosia, along with several explanatory legends that the Greeks attached to the origins of their rites. Unfortunately, the evidence that survives is very scant. Nevertheless, these fragments allow us to glimpse two local forms of the cycle — two distinct Greek reinterpretations of the old Indo-European myth of ambrosia and its divine conflicts.

First, there is an "Akhillean" form of the myth, though its precise origin is uncertain. What survives corresponds only to the rite of the *phármakos* — the scapegoat who is stoned:

"A man named Pharmakos had stolen the sacred cups of Apollon; captured by Akhilleos and his companions, he was stoned to death." (ὁ Φαρμακός, ἱερὰς φιάλας τοῦ Ἀπόλλωνος κλέψας ἁλοὺς ὑπὸ τῶν περὶ τὸν Ἀχιλλέα κατελεύσθη, καὶ τὰ τοῖς Θαργηλίοις ἀγόμενα τούτων ἀπομιμήματά ἐστιν (Harpokration, p. 180 Bekker, s.v. Φαρμακός.)

Harpokration cites as his source the first book of Ἐπιφανεῖαι Ἀπόλλωνος by Istros.

In this figure we recognise a brother of Tantalus or Prometheus — another divine thief who steals a sacred object. The φιάλαι (libation bowls) of Apollon, like the *píthos* in other myths, are very likely, in Istros' version, heirs of the vessel of ambrosia — the divine container of immortality that the Indo-European demon-hero steals from the gods.

Next comes the "Thesean" form, clearly Athenian in origin. Thanks to Plutarch, we know the parts of it related to the rite of the communal feast, the boys dressed as girls (Oskhophoria), and the procession of Eiresione.

In this version, the old story of the gods and demons has merged with the national legend of Theseus and the Minotaur:

(a) Plutarkhos (*Theseus* XXIII) says that when Theseus set out on his expedition against the Minotaur, under the pretence of delivering the annual tribute of maidens, he disguised two strong youths in women's clothing. Plutarch doesn't tell what happened next, but it is easy to guess: it is the story of Thrym, struck down by his false bride, Thor disguised as a woman. According to Plutarch, this is the origin of the Oskhophoria, during which young men, dressed in female attire, carry branches through the city. It is probably also the origin of the Thargelian procession of Eiresione, since Plutarkhos (*Theseus* XXII) says that Theseus instituted that procession upon his return from Crete, in commemoration of the event.

(b) Plutarch also recounts that upon returning from Krete, Theseus and his companions mixed together all the remaining plant-based provisions, cooked them in a single pot, and shared the meal together ("...*to mix together the leftover food and, having cooked it in a single common pot, to dine together and share the meal with one another.*" ...συμμίξαι τὰ περιόντα τῶν σιτίων καὶ μίαν χύτραν κοινὴν ἑψήσαντας συνεστιαθῆναι καὶ συγκαταφαγεῖν ἀλλήλοις). According to Plutarkhos, this was the origin of the ritual feast of the Thargelia.

The connection between these two legends — one corresponding to the preparation and sharing of a communal sacrificial meal of the gods, and the other to the mission of a god disguised as a goddess — allows us to glimpse the Thesean, Athenian form of the ambrosia cycle, as it was represented in the festival rites of Athens.

We have already encountered traces of versions where Dionysus and Demeter played major roles. These two names open boundless perspectives for the study:

How far did the ambrosian legends and rites — those surrounding the divine food or drink of immortality — influence the myths and rituals of Dionysus and Demeter, and through them, the development of Orphism?

This question marks a turning point: from here, the inquiry expands beyond the purely mythological reconstruction of the ambrosia cycle into the domain of Greek mystery religion — into the Dionysiac and Demetrian mysteries where the promise of blessed immortality reappears in ritual form.

Scholars have long debated this question (see, for example, the article "Dionysos" in the *Realencyclopädie of Pauly-Wissowa*). The theories of Erwin Rohde — who linked the Greek belief in immortality with the Thracian cult of Dionysus (*Psyche: Ursprung des Unsterblichkeitsglaubens. Der thrakische Dionysosdienst*, pp. 295–326) — were strongly criticised. It was said that no ancient evidence truly supports such a connection.

However, later research showed that Dionysus, or at least one of the divine concepts that contributed to his complex figure, was originally the spirit of a fermented drink made from grain (perhaps barley), long before he became the god of wine (see Jane E. Harrison, *Prolegomena*, pp. 414 ff.; cf. below, pp. 282 ff.). And this, as the author will later show, was very likely the old Indo-European form of ambrosia — a sacred fermented beverage granting vitality or immortality.

The Theodaisia (Θεοδαίσια) — Dionysian festivals celebrated in many parts of Greece and sometimes giving their name to springtime months — perhaps preserve the memory of that ancient ambrosian festival, the "Feast of the Gods", where humans ritually re-enacted the divine banquet that conferred renewal and divine life.

There is, of course, no original connection between the ambrosian communion and the omophagy that characterises the cult of Zagreus. But once Orphic theology had merged Zagreus with Dionysus, could there not have arisen inevitable contaminations between the two cycles?

When we are told that the Titans stole Dionysus, that they boiled his limbs in a cauldron (λέβης) in order to eat them, that Zeus sent a goddess — Athene, precisely — to recover from the Titans the vital part of this dreadful meal, the heart, and that he then inflicted upon them the subterranean punishment that the Indo-European demons endured for trying to take from the gods the food of immortality, does not this fable show a fusion of Zagrean and ambrosian themes?

It is a vast question — perhaps insoluble — yet one that must be asked. We even know, in this case, the probable author of the fusion, since the ancients tell us that it was Onomakritos who gave the legend its classical form (Pausanias, III, 37 ff.).

As for the content of Orphic thought — the idea of immortality, the conditions of attaining immortality, and so forth — its origin is certainly complex. Yet it seems unlikely that the old Indo-European ideas reflected in the ambrosian cycle played no role at all in shaping the Greek doctrines of immortality. The subject clearly deserves detailed study.

※

We cannot end this brief survey without noting the curious similarities of theme between the ambrosian cycle and another Greek cycle of entirely different origin, though of analogous meaning — the Cycle of the Apples of the Hesperides.

It has been plausibly suggested, based on fragmentary evidence, that the story of Herakles conquering the apples of fertility and prosperity originated as a mythic transposition of magical-religious rites.

As M. van Gennep writes (*Formation des Légendes*, pp. 140–141):

"The principal cult site of Herakles was in Thessaly, on Mount Oita. The legend places his death there, after Deianira sent him the poisoned tunic of the centaur Nessus. There was a sacred orchard whose apples were the main ritual object. According to the fragmentary information available, the ritual ceremony included a representation of a journey beyond the ocean and a descent into the underworld (as in the Eleusinian and Orphic mysteries), the defeat of a dragon (or a monstrous guardian) that protected the orchard and the sacred apples, and the plucking of a branch laden with fruit. ... When this ritual eventually disappeared, the acts ceased to be performed but continued to be described in narrative form. Thus, several themes in the cycle of Herakles (the Descent into Hades, the Garden of the Hesperides) were originally what I call 'myths', and later became legends."

In other words, the Hesperidean apples — symbols of divine vitality, fecundity, or immortality — occupy in Greek myth a function parallel to that of the ambrosia in the Indo-European tradition: both are sacred substances or objects over which gods and heroes struggle, both mark the border between mortality and divine life.

The material of this myth is quite different from that of the ambrosian cycle. Instead of gods and demons who first share in fellowship and then become enemies in a cosmic struggle over food, which determines the structure of the universe, we are dealing here with a human adventure, whose outcome affects only one individual. The gods, now apart in Olympos, are spectators rather than actors; they follow Herakles' exploit with indulgence, even aiding him — some vase paintings show Athena standing behind Herakles in the Garden of the Hesperides. But once the task is complete, Athena confiscates the prize, and everything returns to order.

Two vase paintings (in the *Annali dell' Istituto*, XXXI, 1859, tav. d'agg. G.H., and Noël des Vergers, *Étrurie*, tab. 4) reveal that in older versions, Herakles' success granted him — and him alone — immortality and entrance to Olympos (cf. Daremberg and Saglio, *Dictionnaire des Antiquités*, s.v. Hercules).

Scholars have long debated the origin of the apple-theft motif. It is neither Indo-European, nor Greek, nor Semitic by origin, but belongs to universal folklore: the apples of life, the fruits of eternal youth or rejuvenation, appear in myths from the most diverse peoples (see Sittig, *Realencyclopädie*, VIII, 1243 ff.).

If, however, it belongs to a particular mythic family, it is likely to that of Semitic myths. The legend is Arkadian in origin — Atlas, his daughters the Hesperides, and the dragon Ladon are all Arcadian figures — and Victor Bérard showed how Semitic settlers influenced Arcadian religion. Moreover, the Babylonian epic of Gilgamesh, describing his journey across the sea in search of the Plant of Life, offers striking parallels to Herakles' voyage across the outer sea (τὴν ἔξω θάλασσαν, Apollodorus) to fetch the Apples of Bliss.

Both heroes traverse the world's limits — Gilgamesh passes by Mount Mashu, which is identified with the *shupuk shame*, the "foundation of heaven," a pointed mountain that supports *illat shame*, the highest point of the sky (Lagrange, *Études sur les religions sémitiques*, p. 312); in the same way, Herakles encounters Atlas, the bearer of the sky.

Gilgamesh crosses the sea in forty-five days; Herakles undertakes a similar transoceanic quest. Gilgamesh forces Utanapishtim, the keeper of the Plant of Life, to reveal its hiding place despite his reluctance; Herakles uses Atlas to fetch the apples for him. And just as a serpent steals Gilgamesh's plant, depriving him forever of immortality, Athena removes the apples from Herakles after he wins them.

Finally, both stories culminate in a descent to the underworld (Gilgamesh visiting the realm of the dead; Herakles' twelfth labour being his descent into Hades).

Whether or not the Arkadian legend is of Semitic origin hardly matters — it expresses the same eschatological anxieties as the Epic of Gilgamesh, which Jensen once opposed to it (*Theologische*

Literaturzeitung, 1901, p. 34):

"Gilgamesh," wrote Jensen, *"is not a Babylonian Herakles; we are not dealing with an epic of heroism, but with a response to the anxious questioning of life and death and the beyond."*

But the story of Herakles, as we have seen, had the same function: it translated into legend a ritual drama, a set of "mysteries" meant — like the Orphic and other initiatory cults — to answer the anxious question of human destiny and immortality.

But whatever its origin, the Arkadian rites and the Arkadian legends of the Apples saw, with the arrival of the Indo-European conquerors, the coming of the rites and legends of the ambrosia. What happened to the rites — doubtless springtime rites in both cases — we do not know. But as for the legends of the Apples, they now appear loaded with various original themes, which have no equivalents in the Epic of Gilgamesh, and which instead cover extremely precise ambrosian themes: the sea duel and the conquest of the Cauldron; the attempted theft and the punishment of Atlas; the expedition of a goddess (always Athena), going to recover the apples.

(a) The sea duel and the conquest of the Cauldron

The Cauldron had a very simple meaning in the ambrosian cycle: a god would go to win it, through a duel involving transformations, against a sea spirit; then the gods would use it to brew their drink. Now, this episode reappears in the story of Herakles, preserved very faithfully in form, but given a new and rather strange purpose: this Cauldron becomes the vessel that Herakles uses to cross the ocean.

The Nymphs advise Herakles to seek information from the sea god Nereus. Herakles surprises Nereus while he is sleeping, and despite the many transformations Nereus tries to assume, Herakles binds him and does not release him until he has learned from him where the Apples and the Hesperides are hidden (*"Having seized him while he was sleeping and changing into all sorts of forms, he bound him, and did not release him until he learned from him where the apples and the Hesperides were to be found."* Συλλαβὼν δὲ αὐτὸν κοιμώμενον καὶ παντοιὰς ἐναλλάσσοντα μορφὰς ἔδησε, καὶ οὐκ ἔλυσε πρὶν ἢ μαθεῖν παρ' αὐτοῦ ποῦ τυγχάνοιεν τὰ μῆλα καὶ αἱ Ἑσπερίδες, Apollodoros, *Bibliotheka* II, 116). But Panyassis (in Athenaeus, 469 D) still knew that the result of the duel had been more concrete: according to him, Nereus had to give Herakles the great Cup, on the order of Helios, because the hero, angered by the excessive heat, had not hesitated to threaten that god with his arrows. According to Peisander (in Athenaeus, ibid.), it is Okeanos himself who gives the Cup to Herakles. We know what this cup became for the Greeks: it is the vessel that Helios uses to return, by night, from the West to the East. Thus the presence of Helios is explained in an episode whose form remains so clearly ambrosian, and whose setting is entirely maritime.

The episode of the sea duel (though separated from the Cauldron, as one might expect, since the episodes of the making of ambrosia had disappeared from Greek tradition in every version) was, moreover, famous throughout antiquity. Apart from the very ancient depictions, we know the story in the *Odyssey* where

Menelaos subdues Proteus (IV, 351–570). There is nothing ambrosian there, except perhaps a faint verbal echo, a kind of "embryonic" detail: the daughter of Proteus, who helps the hero against her father, makes him breathe ambrosia to mask the nauseating smell of the seal skin in which he hides. Likewise, in the *Hymiskviða*, Hymir's wife offers beer to Thor, who has come to subdue her husband — over that same beer.

Certain versions, moreover, recall quite closely — through their almost completely humanised characters — the scene of Thor in Hymir's house (breaking the cup, stealing the Cauldron, etc.). A vase in the Louvre (Campana collection) noted by Furtwängler (*Annali*, 1878, pl. E and pp. 38 ff.) shows a young Herakles received in the house of Nereus: he has seized the trident, and while the old man, raising his arms, reproaches him violently, Herakles overturns and smashes the furniture. It has plausibly been supposed that this depiction of the duel between the god and the hero referred to some satyric drama; by subject and tone, that drama must have been very close to the *Hymiskviða*.

As for the famous sea duel of Aristaeus in the *Georgics*, it is perhaps not, in essence, a mere literary and artificial imitation of Menelaos' duel in the *Odyssey*, but rather a late witness to another version of the same cycle. In any case, it is striking that Aristaeus is one of the few heroes in Greek mythology destined for immortality, and that the object of his quest is, ultimately, honey — honey being, as is well known, one of the substances that the Greeks very early compared to ambrosia.

(b) The attempted theft and the punishment of Atlas. — Atlas is the Arkadian Titan: Dionysius of Halicarnassus (*Roman Antiquities* I, 6) says that he dwells in Arkadia near Mount Thaumasion (Sylburg's correction for Kaukasion in the manuscripts). It is in Arkadia that his daughters are born, and the kings of the country honour him as an ancestor. Under influences no doubt Oriental, this Titan appears as the bearer of the heavens, is identified with a mountain that supports the sky, and, following the usual Semitic conceptions, emigrates to Libya, at the edge of the world (cf. Apollodoros, *Bibliotheka* II, 117).

But his name already links him to a well-known group of demons. Scholars have long noted (Mayer, *Giganten und Titanen*, p. 87; Wilamowitz, *Euripides Herakles* II, p. 130; etc.) the probable identity between the Arkadian Ἄτλας (Atlas) and the Argive Τάλταλος (Taltalos), from which comes Τάνταλος (Tantalos). Their punishments, despite the cosmographic distortion we have just seen in the case of Atlas, are not without resemblance: a huge rock is suspended above Tantalos' head, or else he is crushed beneath Mount Sipylos. Might not the similarity go even further — extending to the crime as well as to the punishment?

But Hesiod (*Theogony* 508–519) says nothing of Atlas's crime. Of the four brothers whose punishments he records — Prometheus, Epimetheus, Menoitios, and Atlas — we know a specific crime only for the first two. Menoitios is punished for his "arrogance," and nothing remains of Atlas's offence. Aiskhylos (*Prometheus Bound* 347 ff.; lines 425 ff. are clearly interpolated) likewise only notes that Atlas's punishment occurred at the same time as Prometheus'.

Later scholars explain that Atlas took part in the rebellion of the

Titans (Servius on *Aeneid* IV 247; Eustathius on *Odyssey* I 52) or even led it (Hyginus, *Fabulae* 150). The Orphics — whose tradition, as we have seen, perhaps contains ambrosian elements — say that Atlas pays for "the theft of Zagreus' food" and the cannibal feast.

Doesn't all this suggest that, like his brothers Prometheus and Epimetheus, and like his namesake Tantalos, Atlas too must once have committed a theft of divine nourishment and suffered the Indo-European demon's punishment?

But while among the Argives the legend of Tantalos kept its ambrosian form, Atlas — upon arriving in Arkadia — encountered a religion, ritual, and set of legends already well established and, as Victor Bérard has shown, largely Semitic in tone. He had to "take on the colour of the country" — his punishment was deformed just enough to make him merge with the image of a mountain supporting the sky; as for his crime — his theft — it followed the fate of the ambrosian version to which it belonged, that is, it became mixed with the local cycle of another divine food, the Apples.

Thus we see Atlas, in a charming fable-like scene, trying to keep the divine Apples for himself, to Herakles' detriment. Yet since it was impossible that a Titan should be punished so harshly merely for attempting to cheat a hero who, after all, was only a man, the link between crime and punishment was lost: the punishment was even placed earlier, pushed back into the distant past. Neither Aiskhylos nor Hesiod nor Apollodoros knows — or says — what fault the gods reproached Atlas with. The ambrosian theft was forgotten, replaced by the theft of the Apples, but this latter was not grave enough to justify a damnation that remained, thereafter, without explanation.

Here again, only the hypothesis of an ambrosian origin — suggested by the Titan's very name and lineage — can restore order to legends disordered by borrowing and contamination.

(c) Athena Taking Back the Apples from Herakles.

The hero who won the Apples, in the Arkadian cycle as in the Babylonian one, was neither a god nor a demon, but a man. If we are right in thinking that a fusion took place between the Arkadian cycle of the Apples and a version of the Indo-European cycle of the ambrosia — where only gods and demons appeared — this man, Herakles, is very likely to have taken on, in various ambrosian episodes, now the role of a god, now that of a demon.

Moreover, since the Arkadian hero, no more than Gilgamesh, probably did not remain in possession of the magic branch he had plucked, Herakles, who takes his place, quite naturally became the victim of a scene closely resembling the ambrosian episode of the Goddess (female form; god disguised as a goddess; or sometimes an actual goddess) reclaiming the divine food from the thieving demon.

This is clear from a very brief passage in Apollodoros:

"Athena took the apples from him and brought them back to their place, for it was not permitted that they be set down anywhere else." (*Bibliotheka* II, 122: ... παρ' οὗ λαβοῦσα Ἀθηνᾶ πάλιν αὐτὰ ἀπεκόμισεν, ὅσιον γὰρ οὐκ ἦν αὐτὰ τεθῆναί που. Pediasimus XI, summarising Apollodorus, specifies: μετατεθῆναι).

Athena's intervention is all the more characteristic since we have already seen this goddess, in the Gigantomakhies as well as in the Orphic Titanomakhy, inherit the role of the fatal goddess charged with reclaiming the divine nourishment.

It seems to us that the best way to explain the presence, in the cycle of the Apples, of these ambrosian themes (of which the first — the Conquest of the Cauldron — is particularly characteristic) is to assume a fusion of two festivals of similar meaning, two narratives comparable in subject and development, but different in their object.

The pre-Hellenic scenario of the Apples continued to form the essential framework of the new cycle; but the Greeks attached to it episodes from the ambrosian narrative — sometimes skilfully modifying their purpose (the conquest of the Cauldron turned into a boat), sometimes more crudely, at the risk of creating inconsistencies (Atlas, the thieving Titan, whose punishment no longer has an explanation), and sometimes by means of detailed analogies (Athena's expedition to recover the Apples).

It is thanks to this blending, we believe, that we have finally been able to find on Greek soil a version of the ambrosian episode of the sea duel fought for the conquest of the Cauldron — an episode that has disappeared (and is the only one to have disappeared) from all the versions that remain properly ambrosian or closer to the ambrosia, and that reappears elsewhere only in isolation, detached not only from the ambrosia but even from the

Cauldron, and without mythic character (as in the Odyssean duel of Menelaos and Proteus).

As for the blending itself — which must have made the Argive Heracles the hero of a pre-Hellenic legend enriched with Indo-European elements — Victor Bérard himself formulated it in the conclusion of his *Cultes arcadiens* (p. 357):

"The Arkadian Pelasgians, after having accepted from the Phoenicians an entire religion, preserved it for centuries almost intact, at least without essential or profound modifications. This religion changed only under foreign influence. It was the intervention of the Hellenes that caused the cults and gods of historical Arcadia to emerge, and this intervention, which came chiefly through Argos, lasted for many centuries. The Arcadians evolved only slowly from their Semitic religion to the cults of the Hellenes."

⁂

Conclusion on the Greek Legends Derived from the Cycle of Ambrosia

We have tried to show some of the many forms that the Indo-European cycle of Ambrosia took in various Greek lands. What all of them share — even those that still retain the name ambrosia — is the forgetting of anything in that idea that might recall a real, tangible, familiar drink.

Sometimes it is personified (the Oceanid Ambrosia), sometimes transformed into a purely fabulous drink (the ambrosia drawn by doves from the ocean). More often, it has yielded its place to a very vague or abstract potion of immortality: in the version used by Apollodoros for his Gigantomakhy, it is replaced by an indistinct *phármakon* of immortality; in the Promethean version, the immortality contained in the stolen *píthos* no longer even has a material form.

In other versions, we do find a food (drink or porridge), but certainly not the ancient brewed beverage glimpsed in the legends of the *amṛta* and of the beer of the Æsir. Thus, in the Thesean version, Theseus and his companions ritually prepare a porridge of grains, which they consume in a communion feast.

We have, moreover, witnessed this elimination of ambrosia in a specific case: the theft of Tantalus, which the earliest texts still link with ambrosia, becomes, in later documents, a theft of "divine secrets."

We have already indicated, and will show later in detail, how this phenomenon seems to be explained: among the Indo-Europeans, ambrosia corresponded to a fermented drink made from cereals (similar to beer), which the southern branches of the family neglected and then forgot in favour of wine when they settled in the Mediterranean basin.

But this "dematerialisation" of ambrosia explains why, in all the versions we have encountered, the themes relating to the preparation of the drink (the conquest of the Cauldron of the sea, the brewing) are either atrophied (with only faint traces remaining of the connection between ambrosia and the sea) or have disappeared entirely: we may perhaps have found the episode of the sea duel and the conquest of the Cauldron only in a very particular case — in a highly contaminated version, where the Cauldron no longer has its original function (the Apple cycle, where it becomes Herakles' boat-cauldron).

Nowhere else, even where we still see a container (the Promethean πίθος, the χύτρα of Theseus, perhaps the Orphic λέβης), do we know how the divine or daemonic figure obtained this vessel.

Chapter Five

The Cycle of the Ambrosia among the Latins

Since scholars began distinguishing, within classical Latin traditions, what derives — directly or indirectly — from Greece and what is genuinely Italic, they have often emphasised the extreme poverty of the ancient native mythology. It seems that the gods only gained personality and lived adventures once they were arbitrarily aligned with Greek types. Indeed, reading Ovid's *Fasti* inspires suspicion: in the midst of a story that one had every right, until proven otherwise, to regard as Italic, Latin, or Roman, one suddenly encounters an episode that is clearly nothing but an evident reminiscence of the Odyssey.

Where does this reminiscence begin? What part of the narrative is due to the learned, Hellenising author?

Nevertheless, we shall find in Latium, and in fairly well-preserved form, the cycle of ambrosia. By a fortunate chance, Ovid has preserved several variants, which can easily be localized: the Romans and the Lavinians knew the cycle and altered it in different but parallel ways — so parallel, in fact, that Ovid himself acknowledged their kinship.

Let us expect no philosophy here — nor even any literary charm such as the Hindu, Germanic, and especially Greek legends have given us. At best, the Lavinian cycle, thanks to the memory of Aeneas, rises somewhat above this humble condition: what we are about to encounter are old wives' tales, coarse peasant humour, with varying degrees of roughness.

Finally, just as in the Greek versions we have studied, ambrosia will no longer appear here as a divine drink modelled after a known human beverage. At Rome and Lavinium, ambrosia has been personified (Anna Perenna), and consequently, the episodes of its preparation have been forgotten. The Sabine cycle has preserved some of the episodes of preparation (the aquatic duel for the conquest of the ancile), but only by completely altering their purpose.

Indeed, in the legends of Anna Perenna and in the Salian rites, we find in good place the expected communal feast, the ritual meal — only, it is a meal that has nothing magical about it: a banquet distinguished merely by the quantity or quality of the food, not by any special material, liquid or solid.

We have already indicated, in speaking of the Greek legends, the probable explanation of this phenomenon common to all southern, especially Mediterranean, branches of the Indo-European family. We shall return to it in the conclusion of this work. But one must always keep in mind this dematerialisation of ambrosia in the legends in order to understand how, among the Romans and their neighbours, the Indo-European cycle evolved.

I. The Roman Cycle of Anna Perenna

In the third book of the *Fasti*, Ovid devotes more than one hundred and fifty lines to the festival of Anna Perenna, which falls on the Ides of March. He first gives a detailed description of the celebration and then, following his usual method — but with even more care and indulgence than usual — he lists the various explanations for the festival that were current in his time.

A few other details are provided by Macrobius, Martial, and the inscriptions, but these are of little importance compared to what Ovid gives us.

Here are the distinctive features of this festival:

It is celebrated near the Tiber (*Fasti* III, 524), probably around the Milvian Bridge, between the Via Salaria and the Via Flaminia (Preller, *Römische Mythologie*, 3rd ed., I, 344; C.I.L. I, 322), in a "fruit-bearing grove" (*nemus pomiferum*, Martial IV, 64, 16 sq.).

The common people (*plebs*) gather in the meadows, either in full sunlight, or under makeshift tents, or beneath leafy arbours. They drink heavily, and each person wishes to live as many years as the number of cups they empty.

"*There are men,*" Ovid jokes, "*who would drink there all the years of Nestor, and women who would become true Sibyls, if their years depended on their cups.*" Then they sing theatrical songs, with gestures, and soon start dancing without restraint.

When they return home, they are far from walking straight; the crowds look on, and the passers-by say: *"They are truly happy!"* (Ovid, *Fasti*, III, 523–540)

Macrobius and Lydus confirm Ovid's description in a few words, and they seem to indicate that prayers for health and long life formed the essential rite of the festival.

Macrobius adds that the public celebration was accompanied by private ones, during which people offered sacrifices *"so that they might live through the years and endure them well"* (*ut annare perennareque commode liceat*). We will return shortly to this liturgical formula.

Finally, if we can believe Martial, the license Ovid already mentions was not limited to songs or light dances.

It is clear that, before theatrical festivals were introduced in Rome, the verse *"There they sing whatever they learned in the theatres"* (v. 535) would not have applied. Ovid himself will later specify (vv. 676, 695) the likely ritual subject of these songs, which predated any dramatic performances.

We also possess a few lines from a mime by D. Laberius entitled *Anna Perenna* (Ribbeck, *Scaenicae Romanorum Poesis Fragmenta*, 3rd ed., II, p. 339), which is likely one of those later stylisations of the old traditional songs Ovid refers to.

Finally, from a lost *Skiomakhía* of Varro, we have preserved the curious invocation: *"Te anna ac perenna,"* which should be compared to Macrobius' formula *"annare perennareque."*

∗∗∗

Of the various explanations Ovid then reports, some eliminate themselves — they are merely etymological wordplays.

"I am," says Anna in one passage, *"the nymph of the gentle Numicius; since I hide in a perennial river (amnis perennis), they call me Anna Perenna."* (*Fasti* III, 653).

Elsewhere:

"There are those who identify Anna with the Moon, because the Moon, month by month, completes the year" — *"sunt quibus haec Luna est, quia mensibus impleat annum"* (*Fasti* III, 657).

Others are clearly nothing more than late inventions by poets steeped in Greek mythology: thus Anna is likened to Themis, or to the heifer who was the daughter of Inachus — *"some think her Themis, others the Inachian cow"* (*pars Themim, Inachiam pars putat esse bovem,* v. 658).

But there remain three identifications worth retaining. Anna is said to be an Atlantid, the nurse of Jupiter. Anna is "the old woman of Bovillae." Anna is "the sister of Dido." In truth, as we shall see, this third Anna is not Roman at all but Lavinian, and we shall examine the pages Ovid devotes to her when we study the Lavinian cycle.

⁂

1. "*You will find people who say that Anna was an Atlantid nymph, and the first nurse of Jupiter.*"

Invenies qui te nymphen Atlantida dicant,
Teque Jovi primos, Anna, dedisse cibos." (v. 659–660).

A fable of Greek fashion and Greek tone, without any doubt. But neither poets nor mythographers have ever counted the daughters of Atlas among the nurses of Jupiter — though it is well known how uncertain the names of these nurses are, and how elastic their number. None of the approximate explanations that have been proposed accounts for this singularity. In particular, the idea of a pun between Anna and the genuine Atlantid Hagnô might, at best, explain the first half of Ovid's line, but by no means the second.

If we turn to the following fable, we may suspect that this "Atlantid" is nothing more than a Greek form hastily imposed by some poet — perhaps by Ovid himself — upon a Latin divinity whom legend portrayed, as the rites of her festival already testified, as a "nourisher."

⁂

2. Here is that second fable — and, as Ovid says, *"it does not depart from the truth."* It was at the time of the plebeians' secession to the Sacred Mount. Then an old woman from the suburb of Bovillae, poor but not lazy, began to make with her trembling hands rustic cakes, which she brought to the people in the morning, still warm. When peace was restored, she was granted, in recognition of her services, the title of "Perenna," and a statue was erected to her because she had warded off famine (v. 661–674).

But that is not the whole legend. Ovid immediately explains why, on that day, the young girls sing lewd songs (*obscena*); for, he says, they gather together (*coeunt*) and sing very specific indecencies (*certa probra*). The poet closely connects this story with that of the old woman of Bovillae: Anna had only just been promoted to the rank of goddess when the god Mars Gradivus came to her and said,

"I have allowed you and your festival to find a place within the month that is mine; grant me, in return, a great favour. I, the god who bears arms, burn with love for the goddess who bears arms, Minerva—and it is not the first time! Arrange to bring together these two divinities so well suited to one another; the task befits you, good old woman."

Anna promises and, with delays and evasions, toys with the foolish hopes of the god. When he grows more insistent, she says, *"I have done what you asked. By my prayers, Minerva has at last yielded."* The lover rejoices; he prepares the bed — and then they bring him Anna, her face veiled, as is proper for a new bride. He leans in to take a kiss, but suddenly sees who she really is… Shame and anger pull at the heart of the deceived god. The new goddess mocks the lovesick suitor of Minerva, and Venus has never laughed so much.

Such, Ovid concludes, was the origin of the ancient games and the lewd songs: people found it amusing that Anna had thus played a trick on so mighty a god (v. 675–696).

***

Here, then, is the cycle of Anna Perenna. It has inspired both ancient and modern scholars to display great ingenuity. All the various explanations that have been offered are carefully catalogued in Meltzer's article on Anna in Roscher's *Lexikon*.

The common flaw in all these interpretations is that each explains only a single aspect — often a minor detail — of the legend. Thus, for Mommsen (*Unteritalische Dialekte*, p. 248 ff.), Anna is a goddess of abundance; for Klausen (*Aeneas und die Penaten*, II, 77–728), she is the goddess of the white water. But then, what becomes of the story of Mars deceived?

According to Preller, she is a lunar divinity, her name "Anna et Perenna" being comparable to the Greek expression ἕνη καὶ νέα ("the old and the new moon"). Yet even this interpretation explains — if it explains anything at all — only the very last portion of the legend.

Usener's explanation — the most appealing — is, in truth, merely ingenious (H. Usener, *"Italische Mythen,"* Rheinisches Museum, N.F. xxx, pp. 182–229). For him, the real name is indeed

"Anna ac Perenna," as in Varro's formula, and the festival is that of the New Year. Anna represents the year to come; Perenna, the year that has passed. Mars, in a sense, is the god of the year itself, standing between Anna and Perenna.

One must read those fifty pages to appreciate the brilliance of mind expended there. Yet, first of all, they are far from explaining everything — particularly the nurturing or nourishing character of the goddess — and then it seems far too subtle to claim, for instance, in order to explain why Mars, born on the first of the month, waits until the Ides before confronting the past year, Perenna:

"The young god must first grow and gain strength before he can conquer, drive away, or kill the old one."

Moreover, these explanations will correct themselves once we have restored Anna Perenna to her proper place within our cycle.

But before that, we must clarify her appearance as an old woman. In all the other identifications proposed — including the Lavinian one with Anna Soror — Anna is either a nymph or, in any case, a young woman capable of inspiring love. It would not be surprising if this transformation resulted from a play on words: *Anus* ("old woman") is not far removed from Anna, just as *Annus* ("year") or *Amnis* ("river") are. The very construction of the couplet (lines 667–668), where *anus* is placed at the end — just as earlier, in line 657, *annus* — seems intended to suggest such an etymological pun.

Perhaps, too, this metamorphosis is the result of the fusion of two legends: an older one, that of Anna Perenna as a nourishing divinity, and a more recent one, that of the old woman who supplied food to the plebs — the first giving the heroine of the final tale her name, and the second her form. In any case, the goddess Anna Perenna retained so firmly in popular imagination the features of the old woman of Bovillae that she produced, within the story of the "false bride," a curious substitution of characters.

The nourishing character of the goddess is well established: the old woman of Bovillae saves the people from famine, just as, in another version, Anna serves as nurse to Jupiter. Finally, certain rites of the festival (*"they pray for as many years as they drink cups"*), as well as certain formulas (*"ut commode annare perennareque liceat"* — *"that one may prosper in living through the years"*), clearly point us in this direction.

Originally, Anna was more than a nourisher — she was nourishment itself, not of long life but of immortality, ambrosia; and the Cycle of Anna Perenna, as we have just seen it, reproduces two of the principal episodes of the Cycle of Ambrosia.

Let us first consider the name: for Anna Perenna to be understood as a personification of ambrosia, her name must preserve, at least in part, the same meaning as that of the divine drink — just as the Iranian Ameša Spənta Amərətāt and the Greek Oceanid Ambrosia do.

In both of those cases, the transition from "substance" to "person" was made easier by the feminine gender of the words involved, yet their original meaning remained transparent. Now, it is exactly the same with Anna Perenna.

The meaning of *perenna* is beyond doubt: a variant form, now lost, of *perennis*, the word can mean only "of infinite duration," "eternal," or rather — like *amṛta* itself, which is strictly speaking a passive form meaning "not dead," hence "immortal," but which has taken on the active sense "that which causes not to die" — "that which gives infinite duration."

As for Anna, it may simply be one of those childish or popular words that the Latins liked to insert, with or without alliteration, into compound names, and to which one should not try to assign a precise meaning (Acca Larentia, etc.; compare also pairs of alliterative but identifiable names such as Dea Dia, or Mutunus Tutunus).

However, it is not impossible that the word has a more specific sense. It appears on several inscriptions where it designates a nurse: in the *Corpus* (III, 2012, 2160, 2450, 2515), the Thesaurus notes, "*anna nutricem videtur significare, ut Mommsen bene annotat.*" Furthermore, the word *annona*, which properly designates the harvest or food supply, connects more plausibly to a root anna relating to nourishment than to annus ("year"). For the derivation *anna — annona*, Usener (loc. cit.) already compares the hypothetical goddess Bonona, suggested by the name of the city Bononia and clearly derived from the Bona Dea.

Anna Perenna, then, must be something like "the nurse of everlastingness," the personification of a nourishment of immortality — a literal translation of the Sanskrit *amṛta* — and corresponds exactly to the *Ambrosía*, nurse of Zeus and Dionysus.

At the same time, this explains both Macrobius's and Varro's quotations, from which Usener began when he divided Anna Perenna into two separate figures.

People addressed the goddess in order *"to have enough to eat and to last as long as one wishes"* — *"ut commode annare perennareque liceat."*

Varro's quotation, though textually uncertain, can be understood in the same way: either *"te anna ac perenna"* should be read as two imperatives of the preceding verbs (*annare* this time being active), or else it is simply an invocation to the goddess, who is both a nurse (*anna*) and eternal (*perenna*).

Now let us compare the cycle of Anna Perenna with that of Ambrosia. Just as the Æsir ask Ægir for beer because their own supply of food is too meagre, and just as the Suras, assembled on Mount Meru, seek to escape mortality through the *amṛta*, so too, when Anna Perenna appears, the people gathered on the Sacred Mount are threatened by famine.

This says much about the religious spirit of the ancient Latins: the plebeians, withdrawn upon their mountain, could easily and naturally take the place of the gods, allowing a mythical legend to be modernised and secularised into a political tale.

How did this transformation occur? It is noteworthy that Livy makes no mention of Anna's intervention, and that, topographically, the festival of Anna is in no way connected with the Sacred Mount nor with the suburb of Bovillae. This suggests that such an adaptation — quite natural on the part of the plebs after their struggles and victories — deceived no one. Indeed, we might already have suspected as much, seeing the many other explanations that Ovid reports alongside this one.

The idea of eternity or perpetuity, still contained in the name of the goddess, disappears within the story: the old woman merely provides cakes, simple daily sustenance, to the plebeians; and what the plebeians, each year, ask of her in celebrating her festival is long earthly life and good health.

This, again, is a natural evolution for a people who, in their beginnings, do not seem to have been distinguished by any taste for metaphysical flights.

The idea of eternity reappears only when the grateful Romans "name" Anna a goddess and call her Perenna — that is to say, when the *anna perenna*, the ambrosia, reappears in the company of the gods whose place the Roman plebeians have taken.

The story of the god Mars shows a rather curious transformation of the "false bride" episode. That the Latins forgot the theft of the ambrosia was to be expected once they had embodied it in the form of an old woman. But then the whole structure of the tale was overturned: if there is no longer a theft, there can be no "recovery" either, and the false goddess sent to the demon must now play a new role.

The Latins turned the matter into a farce: it becomes simply a practical joke played on a lustful god. Yet they still remembered that this legend was part of the ambrosia cycle, that it followed closely upon the birth of ambrosia (*"nuper erat dea facta,"* says Ovid), and that ambrosia itself played a large part in it. So popular imagination gave it a new function — fitting to her aspect as an old woman — and one that nicely completes the comic tone: Anna Perenna (the old woman) took the place of the god who, in the older myth, had disguised himself as a young goddess to recover the ambrosia (the drink).

The disguise remains, but the disguised figure changes; one character vanishes from the legend, but it is not Anna — it is the male god, the brother of Viṣṇu or Thor, and the like. In this way, the whole story becomes quite clear. One may even note very specific details resembling the *Þrymskviða* (such as the scene of the kiss): this is because both mythologies developed the theme in a humorous vein, and so inevitably met in a few particularly striking features. The Roman tale, in keeping with its new spirit, ends not in a massacre, but in general laughter.

Here, Mars inherits the role of a demon. This is an interesting insight into Roman mythology before it came under Greek influence. In this mixed nature, Mars recalls the "Titan gods" of Hesiod, the Sura and Asura, equal in birth and rights, and the Scandinavian Loki, whose ambiguous character makes him at once god and demon.

Impoverished and stripped of all its grand or tragic elements, the cycle of Ambrosia thus reappears in that of Anna Perenna, and through it, the entire tradition can be explained.

The preparation of ambrosia, the episode of the demon among the gods, and the final battle have all disappeared from these plebeian legends, leaving only the themes of "famine," "saving nourishment," and the entire episode of the "false bride."

This, incidentally, is further proof that the latter episode indeed formed part of the Indo-European cycle.

✷✷✷

II. The Lavinian Cycle of Anna Soror

"The cult of Anna, as a nymph, was ancient at Lavinium beside the river Numicius, as well as at Rome beside the Tiber. She was honoured in March, precisely at the time when the springs begin to flow again and the rivers fill with water." (Saglio)

This Lavinian Anna even enjoyed a strange destiny up to modern times. Th.-Victor de Bonstetten, in his *Voyage dans le Latium* (Geneva, Year XIII, 8vo: pp. 196–197 — cf. Saintyves, *Les saints successeurs des dieux*, p. 307), writes:

"Not far from Lavinium, we saw atop Monte di Leva, in the middle of a green field, a white chapel dedicated to Anna Petronilla. The pagan legend had marked the spot where the unhappy sister of the queen of Carthage, Anna, transformed into a nymph, wished to be worshiped; her name had been immortalised by the gayest and most charming of festivals.

Christianity took root, and the Christians, finding in the wilderness a temple dedicated to Anna Perenna, could only think it must be Anna, the mother of the Virgin. Thus Anna Perenna, sister of Dido, continued to receive the worship of the faithful under the Christian name of Anna Petronilla."

Thus Ambrosia, in an unexpected disguise, crossed twenty centuries of Christianity.

Ovid (*Fasti*, III, 545–656) is familiar with this Lavinian Anna, whose festival is celebrated near the Numicius, just as that of the Roman Anna takes place near the Tiber. He identifies her — likely following an already existing literary tradition — with the Phoenician Anna, sister of Dido. Later, Silius Italicus (*Punica* VIII, vv. 28–202) would take up this tale, "on the margins of Virgil," with a fondness that is easy to understand.

Anna Perenna, Anna Soror: this is a learned assimilation, an Aeneid-inspired legend of the highest order, and highly suspect beneath its recent literary veneer. Its interpretation is delicate, for we are no longer dealing with a spontaneous, popular distortion, but rather with an adaptation crafted by scholarly hands.

Yet it is still possible to recognise, beneath Ovid's curious narrative, the major structural elements of the Ambrosia cycle.

After Dido's death, to escape the Africans and Iarbas, Anna takes refuge in the middle of the sea — *"not far from barren Cossyra, on the island of Melite"* (Malta) — with King Battus. But soon the ruthless Pygmalion demands that the sea-king surrender Anna.

Battus, too weak to resist, can only advise the unfortunate woman to flee once more.

She again sets out to sea, enduring twenty storms... At last, her ship is carried to the shores of Laurentum, where Aeneas, newly married to Lavinia, now reigns. Anna lands there. As it happens, Aeneas is walking nearby with his faithful Achates; he recognises her. She tries to flee, but he reassures her with kind words, takes her into his home, and entrusts her to his young wife, Lavinia.

However, Lavinia, jealous of the honours shown to the foreign woman, grows to hate her — *"she prepares traps and seeks revenge, even at the cost of her own life."* Then, one night, the ghost of Dido appears to her sister and tells her to flee that ill-fated house. Anna climbs out through a low window, escapes into the countryside, where a river, the horned god Numicius, takes her into his waters. They search for her in vain — until she reveals herself: *"My name is Anna Perenna,"* she declares, explaining her name through the pun mentioned earlier (*"amne perenne latens..."*).

At these words, joy breaks out; people run, feast, and drink deeply and long.

*
* *

It is hardly likely, a priori, that Ovid — or the learned author responsible for this Aeneid-inspired tale — completely ignored the popular Lavinian traditions surrounding Anna Perenna in composing his narrative. Nevertheless, the distortions are considerable: Anna no longer bears any nourishing or maternal character, and the rustic feast by which the Lavinians, like the Romans, celebrated her festival finds no echo in the story itself.

Furthermore, Aeneas has brought along his usual entourage into this legend: it is clear that the figures of Lavinia and Achates are present solely because they are inseparable from him in literary tradition.

We may therefore, without imprudence, identify the essential elements of the Ambrosia cycle that one must look for beneath the surface of the story of Anna Soror.

1. Anna (formerly the *anna perenna*) demanded from Battus (= a sea spirit).

In the Indo-European episode, a god comes to demand from a sea-being, in the middle of the ocean, the delivery of an instrument necessary for the preparation of ambrosia — and that instrument is the sea itself. Here, since Anna (the ambrosia) has been personified, it is she, and not a cauldron or any other tool, that Pygmalion comes to demand from Battus, who has himself become a man rather than a marine spirit.

Likewise, in the Indo-European episode, the sea-being yields — too weak or defeated — to the god's demands; here, Battus is too weak, unable to resist Pygmalion. But if he were to surrender Anna immediately, the rest of the cycle would vanish; and since the Latins knew the story did not end there, there was only one possible solution: Battus returns Anna to the sea before having to surrender her.

This is a natural consequence of the personification of Ambrosia. Yet Battus, thus casting Anna back into the sea and inaugurating the maritime adventures of the fugitive, remains a transparent remnant of the marine god opening the sea for the operations from which ambrosia will be born.

That Battus represents a sea god is evident from a curious feature in Ovid's account: Battus reigns at Melite (Malta), on a rock lost in the open sea. Yet tradition consistently attributed to Battus the founding of Cyrene in Libya, and later Silius Italicus, repeating Ovid, felt obliged to correct his model and return to the traditional account.

The island of Malta thus seems to be a compromise between the traditional Libyan setting and the mythic dwelling of a water-spirit — a midpoint that preserves both Battus' terrestrial kingship and his older, divine, marine character.

2. After a thousand hardships, Anna (that is, the *anna perenna*) rises from the waters.

Anna's sea wanderings clearly belong to the Aeneid-inspired framework of the story. In the older Lavinian tale, however, the goddess must simply have emerged from a nearby body of water — most likely the Numicius River, since it was there that she was believed to dwell in hiding.

Her appearance from the water would then have naturally

followed upon the aquatic duel, of which the demand made by Pygmalion to Battus in Ovid's narrative represents an Aeneid-style transformation or reworking of the older mythic motif.

3. Aeneas receives Anna upon her landing (= a demon seizes the *anna perenna* upon her appearance).

The entire final part of the story is steeped in Aeneas and his legend. Though portrayed as gentle, just, and noble, he has in this version taken the place of an older demonic abductor. The learned adaptor, however, has softened the theme: there is no longer an actual abduction, despite Anna's initial fright. The literary memory of Dido, cleverly inserted, turns the "seizure of Anna" into an act of kindness.

Aeneas "welcomes" the one whom his demonic predecessor would once have "carried off." As for Lavinia and Achates, they seem to be present merely for form's sake, and it would be pointless to look for any counterparts to them in the Ambrosia cycle.

4. A feminine form takes back Anna (= the *anna perenna*) from Aeneas (= from the demon).

The ghost of Dido may well be the final transformation of that feminine figure who once, in the older myth, reclaimed the ambrosia. But in this version — because Anna is personified, because she is portrayed as Dido's sister, and because Lavinia's jealousy is central — it is now Anna herself whom the feminine form urges to flee.

Thus, the warning and rescue once addressed to the ambrosia's possessor are, in this softened Roman retelling, directed to the ambrosia itself, now embodied as Anna Perenna.

This transformation of the "false goddess" into a spectre or apparition is no stranger than certain similar evolutions — such as, in India, into *Māyā*. It is noteworthy that here, as in the cycle of the old woman of Bovillae, the "false goddess" is, so to speak, female in essence rather than male: whether as an old woman in disguise or as the ghost of Dido, no male element intervenes in either case.

Perhaps this represents a common Latin trait, which, as we have seen, corresponds to a parallel Greek pattern (Pandora, Athena) and possibly to one of the Indo-Iranian variants (Vāc, the Djahi).

As for the river god Numicius, his presence is easily explained by topography: the Lavinians gathered on his banks just as the Romans did by the Tiber. The need to justify the etymology of Anna Perenna (*amne perenne latens …*) must have aided in preserving his place in the Aeneid-shaped legend.

But what was his original role? Did he, like Mars in the Roman cycle, play the part that Aeneas would later assume — the role of abductor? Or was he the one who brought forth the *anna perenna*?

In the current state of knowledge, these questions have no definite answer.

In any case, the popular revelry celebrating Anna's rediscovery corresponds perfectly to the expected episode in the Ambrosia Cycle—that of the gods' banquet.

⁂

Such is the Lavinian cycle. In some respects, despite its literary adaptation, it is better preserved than the cycle of Anna of Bovillae; yet, like the latter, it has lost both the episode of the demon among the gods and that of the final battle, though it still preserves the expedition to the aquatic god.

The versions that have come down to us — Roman and Lavinian, relatively late in date — do not allow us to reconstruct with certainty the original Latin form of the cycle. Nevertheless, several notable points of agreement can be observed:

1. The personification of the *anna perenna* as a woman, accompanied by the almost complete loss of the notion of immortality.

2. The disappearance of the two episodes of "the demon among the gods" and "the battle between gods and demons."

3. The female, not male, nature of the "false goddess."

4. The cult of Anna associated with a river, whether the Tiber or the Numicius, preserving the memory of her aquatic origins.

⁂

As for the rites of the festival, judging from the final verses that

Ovid devotes to the story of Anna Soror, the celebrations at Lavinium must have closely resembled those at Rome: there too, people feasted and drank deeply:

*"Straightaway, in merry wandering, they feast in the fields,
And celebrate both the day and themselves with generous wine."*
(*Protinus erratis læti vescuntur in agris
Et celebrant largo seque diemque mero.*)
(*Fasti* III, 677–678)

This single detail is enough to show that the sad Carthaginian (Anna, sister of Dido) at Lavinium had come to replace an older goddess — no less a provider of sustenance and no less a deity of the common folk — than the Roman Anna Perenna herself.

⁂

Other cities of Latium must also have known similar festivals and legends, but their memory has since been lost. Perhaps, however, something of Anna's popularity survives in the many Roman and Latin family names — generally plebeian — that begin with Anna- and have been preserved in inscriptions (as noted in the Thesaurus Linguae Latinae):

Annāvos, Annāva, Anna; Annaenus; Annaienus; Annālenus, Annālenius; Annaius; Annaiedius, Annedius; Anneiarius...
(cf. Annius, Annidius, etc.).

These remnants in personal names may well be echoes of

devotion to the old nourishing goddess Anna, once venerated throughout Latium before her myth faded beneath literary reinterpretations and Christian transformation.

⁎⁎⁎

III. The Legend of Saint Petronilla

A version of the legend of Anna Perenna, quite close to the specifically Roman form that we studied first, is preserved in the Christian legend of Saint Petronilla. We saw earlier that, in the area around Lavinium, an ancient sanctuary of Anna Perenna had, by the Christian era, become a sanctuary of Anna Petronilla — and, thanks to this transformation, it continued to receive the devotion of the faithful.

Now, we know the hagiographic story of this Petronilla — better known, moreover, under the popular names Perronelle, Pernelle, or Perine (compare Anna Perenna). Here it is, taken from the *Golden Legend* of Jacob of Voragine (chapter LXXVI): one easily recognises within it the two essential scenes of the legend of Anna Perenna. As for her name, it probably comes from the belief that she was the daughter of Saint Peter.

1. Stricken with fever and confined to her bed, she is first healed temporarily by Saint Peter, so that one day she may rise and serve him and his disciples at table. Later, she recovers her health completely, *"when she begins to be perfect in the love of God."* Beneath this Christian retelling, one can undoubtedly sense an older pagan

episode, quite similar to the first episode of the Roman cycle of Anna Perenna: Anna coming to bring food to the Romans, then being deified. In any case, this scene preserves the double aspect of Anna — as both a nourishing goddess and a goddess of health.

2. *"Then a nobleman named Flaccus, struck by her beauty, came to ask her hand in marriage. And she replied: 'If you wish to wed me, send young maidens to lead me to your house!' When they arrived, Petronilla began to fast and pray, received communion, lay down upon her bed, and after three days, gave her soul to God."*

Here we can clearly recognise, in a slightly altered form of the Roman version, the episode of the enamoured and deceived demon.

3. The *Golden Legend* actually preserves a second version of this episode, very similar to the first, which it places directly beside it. This version ends with another ambrosial episode — that of the thief of ambrosia expelled, scourged, and killed (an episode we will later find again in the Sabine cycle, with the scourging and expulsion of Mamurius):

"Then Flaccus, seeing himself deceived, turned to one of Petronilla's companions named Felicula, and demanded that she either marry him or sacrifice to the idols. When the young woman refused to do either, Flaccus had her thrown into prison, where she remained seven days without food or drink. Then he ordered her to be tortured on the rack and for her body to be thrown onto the refuse heap. Saint Nicodemus took up her remains and buried them; for this he was in turn imprisoned, beaten with leaded whips, and cast into the Tiber..."

This passage clearly mirrors, under Christianised form, the ancient pattern of the punished or banished "thief of ambrosia" — a mythic figure whose rebellion against divine order ends in scourging and death, now transposed into the martyrdom of the saints.

The pagan lineage here is unmistakable: the name and the legendary themes coincide perfectly. Then, through the sanctuary at Lavinium, we can directly observe — in a specific, historical location — the transference of the goddess's powers to the saint. Finally, even though the feast of the Virgin Petronilla does not fall, like that of Anna Perenna, on March 15, it nevertheless remains a spring festival, celebrated on May 31.

IV. Mars and Nerio–Minerva. The "Cista" of Praeneste

Outside the Anna–Perenna–Petronilla cycle, the struggle between the "fatal fiancée" and the "recalcitrant bride" is also attested in other regions of the Latin world, appearing in related forms that the Indo-European theme helps to clarify. Thus, scholars have long noted the close analogy between the episode of Mars deceived by Anna Perenna (cf. Flaccus disappointed by Petronilla) and the nuptial combat between Mars and Nerio–Minerva.

"In the month of March," says Porphyrion (*on Horace, Epistles II, 2, 209*), *"it is impious to marry, because during this month Minerva defeated Mars in a combat he had undertaken to win her as his wife (… et item Martio, in quo de nuptiis habita certamine a Minerva Mars victus est). Having victoriously defended her virginity, Minerva received the*

name Neriene (... et obtenta virginitate Minerva Neriene est appellata)."

Johannes Lydus notes that on March 23, the day of the tubilustrium, a sacrifice was celebrated in honor of Ares and Nerinē, a goddess so called in the Sabine language, in which she represented both Minerva and Venus:

"τιμαὶ Ἄρεος καὶ Νερίνης, θεᾶς οὕτω τῇ Σαβίνων γλώσσῃ προσαγορευομένης, ἣν ἠξίουν εἶναι τὴν Ἀθηνᾶν καὶ Ἀφροδίτην."

Ovid, likewise, mentions for the same day a sacrifice to the *fortis dea* (*Fasti* III, 850). This *fortis dea* was, in Roman understanding, the meaning of the Sabine word Nerio — a feminine form derived from the masculine Sabine Nero, meaning "strong" or "vigorous" (fortis, strenuus). The word goes back to the Indo-European root *nr-*, *nara-* (Sanskrit), *anēr* (Greek), *ner* (Umbrian, plural *nerf*), all meaning "male." The Romans generally translated Nerio as *virilis*, "the manly woman," and that is indeed how Ovid and his contemporaries understood it.

But — since we now know the ancient story of the deceived god, are we not tempted to recognise, in this Nerio of hybrid name, this "Man-Woman," a memory of the god disguised as a goddess, who deceived and defeated the demon? It was probably only later — when that etymology no longer matched the legend — that the name Nerio was reinterpreted through the myth of a virile goddess victorious over Mars. Logically, the name itself must be older than both that goddess and her supposed triumph.

⁂

The tale of Mars and Nerio has come down to us in isolation, without any connection to a food or drink cycle derived from the Ambrosia cycle.

Yet such a cycle must once have existed. We have indirect but explicit evidence of it in a figurative representation of their combat — specifically, the famous casket of Praeneste (*cista* Praenestina), described by Fr. Marx (*Archäologische Zeitung*, 1885, p. 169 ff.), reproduced in Roscher's *Lexikon* (s.v. Mars, col. 2399).

On this casket appears a most curious image of the duel between Mars and Minerva. Roscher already sensed its great significance, but only the Indo-European Ambrosia cycle allows us to interpret all the elements of the scene. Conversely, this casket proves that the duel between Mars and Minerva did not concern merely the goddess's *virginitas*, but, as in the Indo-European tradition, the recovery of a vessel and a marvellous liquid.

One sees Minerva (Menerva), unarmed, winning the victory (a small winged Victory accompanies the goddess) over the god Mars, who is defending a large *dolium* — a great jar or vat — in which, according to Roscher, *"there is either blazing fire or boiling water."*

Neither, we would reply — but rather a fermenting drink, some faithful substitute for ambrosia.

The Cerberus that dominates the scene, says Roscher, indicates

that the action takes place in the underworld — which, in turn, underscores the demonic role of Mars.

People have tried to interpret this scene as a depiction of the birth of Mars, but no such legend exists in Latin mythology. And isn't it clear that we are instead dealing with a variant of the combat between Mars and Minerva?

This version, however, reflects a much more archaic stage of the legend than the one reported by Porphyrion, since the *dolium* and its marvellous liquid are still present, and since Minerva — clearly shown unarmed — appears to win by means quite other than martial ones.

It is, rather, the scene of seduction found in the Indo-European cycle or in the tale of Pandora, than the *certamen* ("contest") of which Porphyrion speaks.

The image is, moreover, surrounded by all the great gods — Juno, Jupiter, Mercury, Hercules, Apollo, and Liber — as befits, in the words of Miss Jane Harrison (*Themis*, p. 199), *"a scene of great solemnity and significance."*

Just so, in the Indo-European legend, the gods awaited anxiously the outcome of the expedition of "the fatal bride."

V. The Feast of the Salians and the Feast of Ambrosia. The Ancile

We have just said that the Sabine legend of the combat between Mars and Nerio has reached us in isolation, no longer connected with any known "alimentary" (sacred food) cycle. Yet this may not always have been the case.

The religious prohibition of marriages in March, which Porphyrion explained as a remembrance of the Sabine duel between Mars and Nerio, is instead connected by Ovid — though without serious justification — to the story of Mamurius and the *ancile* (*Fastes* III, vv. 393–394).

The prominent role attributed to Numa, as well as the form Mamurius (compare the Sabine Mamers, according to Varro, *De Lingua Latina*, V.10.73) of the name of Mars, indicate that this legend belonged to the Sabine element of Rome's population.

On the other hand, we have seen that the cycle of Petronilla included, in addition to the episodes found in the Ovidian cycle of Perenna, one episode — the scourging and execution of Nicodemus — which elsewhere is commonly connected with the story of Mamurius and the *ancile*.

There are, between the cycle of ambrosia and that of the *ancile*, two curious points of contact; moreover, the analogy between the two cycles themselves is no less striking. Here, in a few lines, are the legends of the *ancile*:

The Romans under Numa are threatened with death by an epidemic — a λοιμώδης νόσος (according to Plutarkhos, *Life of Numa*, ch. XIII) — or, according to Ovid (*Fasti* III, v. 289), they are overwhelmed by a thunderbolt, which they do not know how to appease (*piare fulmen*).

Following the instructions of Egeria, Numa fights near their spring against the spirits Faunus and Picus; then, on the advice of these spirits, he engages in a famous contest of cunning with Jupiter. The god, defeated, promises to give him the *ancile*.

Indeed, the next day at noon, in the presence of the assembled Romans, the *ancile* falls from the sky. To reduce the risk of theft — for the *ancile* guarantees the perpetuity of Rome, serving as a *pignus imperii* (pledge of empire) — Numa has eleven identical copies made by a figure recognised as a humanised Mars, the smith Mamurius Veturius, who is at first rewarded and celebrated (Ovid, *Fasti* III, v. 259–398).

But soon, after misfortunes befall the Romans because they can no longer distinguish the true *ancile* (or, in this later version, the true *ancilia*) from the copies, the smith Mamurius is driven from the city with rods. Each year, on the Ides of March, in memory of this event, a man dressed in skins, called Mamurius, is paraded and flogged through the streets of Rome (John Lydus, *De mensibus*, IV, 36).

Servius (*ad Aen.*, VII, 188) mentions the same rite but provides an explanation of obviously little value: "... *Cui (Mamurio) et diem consecrarunt, quo pellem virgis feriunt ad artis similitudinem.*" ("... *To whom they dedicated the day on which they beat a hide with rods, in imitation of his craft.*")

Finally, we have already seen this same rite transposed into legend in the cycle of Petronilla–Perenna, through the scourging of Nicodemus.

In this cycle of the *ancile*, we can clearly recognise the characteristic themes of the cycle of ambrosia — except for the episode of the fatal bride, which, as we have seen, survives separately in the Sabine story of the duel between Mars and Nerio.

Here, just as in the story of Anna Perenna, the gods have been replaced by Romans within a quasi-historical framework: the

Romans, like the gods in the Indo-European myth, are threatened by death — whether by plague or lightning.

A god-hero figure (Numa) confronts spirits or demons (Faunus, Picus) near a sacred spring; victorious, he wins a round, hollow object — the *ancile* — which protects his people from destruction and ensures their continuity.

Then appears a demon-smith figure (Mamurius) — reminiscent of the demonic artisan of the ambrosia cycle. Welcomed among the gods, he helps them in their use of the sacred object. But soon, as in the older myth where the demon is expelled after the recovery of the ambrosia, Mamurius is violently driven out and flogged by those he had aided.

This sequence — divine peril, sacred duel, acquisition of a life-giving object, collaboration with a demonic craftsman, and his ritual expulsion — reproduces almost point for point the structure of the Indo-European ambrosia myth, though transposed into the Roman-Sabine religious setting.

There is, however, one important difference: Ovid's account bears no connection either with food or with a banquet. Yet we shall attempt to show, from various traces, that before the historical period, the *ancile* used in the festivals (and consequently in the legends) must originally have been a kitchen vessel — a dish or cauldron — serving in ritual meals, and thus playing a role in food-related myths.

It will then remain for us to determine under what influences the forgotten *ancile*-cauldron could have been transformed into the *ancile*-shield known to the classical Romans.

⁂

At Rome, it is well known that the numerous festivals of the month of March almost all feature as their main participants the two colleges of Salii, guardians of the *ancilia*: the Salii Palatini, descended from the Latin colonies of the Palatine and Cermalus, and servants of Mars Gradivus; and the Salii Quirinales or Collini, descended from the Sabine populations of the hill, and servants of Mars Quirinus (see the references in Daremberg and Saglio, *Dictionnaire,* article Salii).

Now, among these festivals, those that consist of a solemn procession of the *ancilia* include, alongside the dance rites (which perhaps gave the performers their name — at least, according to traditional etymology), unmistakable alimentary rites, which, to an unprejudiced observer, form the very core of the ceremony.

The final halt of the Salii at the *mansio* — the endpoint of each procession — is marked by two ceremonies: A sacrifice to all the Salian divinities (see Cirilli, *Les Prêtres danseurs à Rome,* Paris, 1913, p. 114 ff.) and banquet, proverbial for its magnificence (ibid., p. 121): *Epulati essemus saliarem in modum,* writes Cicero to Atticus (Ad Att., V, 9, 1).

Suetonius (*Claudius,* XXXI) tells that one day the emperor Claudius, catching from afar the aroma of the meal being prepared by the Salii in the Temple of Mars in the Forum of Augustus, left the tribunal to dine with them.

The people, who rarely err in such matters, knew perfectly well that it was these sacrificial and banquet rites, and not the dances, that constituted the true ritual centre of the ceremony. Hence the proverb that immortalised the fame of the Salian feast.

We understand very little of the chant of the Salii, and even the Salii themselves no longer understood it (Quintilian, I, VI, 40).

However, the fragment preserved by Varro (*De Lingua Latina*, VII, 26), as interpreted by Corssen, seems to contain an invitation to a feast addressed to Janus. It begins with three words that scholars agree to read as: *Cozeulo dori eso,* which Corssen translates as: *In coculum dare esum* — that is, "to put the sacred food into the cooking pot (where the offerings were being boiled)."

It does indeed seem difficult to interpret *Cozeulo* as anything other than *coculo* ("in the pot") and *eso* as anything other than *esum* ("food") (see Cirilli, op. cit., p. 107 ff.).

The *axamenta*, those verses addressed to all the Salian gods, were thus — in the literal sense of the word — invitations (from the frequentative form of the Indo-European root *ag-*) to the feast that was being prepared, to the sacred nourishment that was cooking in the cauldron.

The Salii were supposed to strike their shields in rhythm, but the relief of Anagnia, where M. Bendorf recognised Salii, shows warriors holding a rod ending in a ball, much like the *hasta pura* type reproduced on a denarius of the *gens* Arria. The *hasta*, therefore, resembles more a pestle than a spear.

As for the *ancile*, the ancient etymologies are well known. According to Ovid, the word means *ab omni parte recisum* ("cut off on every side," that is, "without angles"), from *angulus omnis abest*. Varro gives a different explanation: *ancile* comes *ab ambecisu*, because its form was *ab utraque parte incisa* ("cut in on both sides"). Others connected it to Greek ἄγκυλος or ἀγκύλη ("curved").

On coins, the *ancilia* sometimes appear as shields without notches, sometimes with two indentations, as described by Varro (see Roscher, *Lexikon*, s.v. *ancile*). Some have suggested that the two colleges of Salii (Palatine and Quirinal) carried different forms. But this is not necessary: the iconography may have followed the etymology rather than inspired it, and it is perhaps the dubious etymology *am(b)* — *cid/le* that gave rise to the notched *ancilia* or to later depictions of them.

Modern scholars have not hesitated to see in the *ancile* something other than a shield. Jane Harrison, in *Themis* (p. 198), gives it a lunar character, since it was crescent-shaped. A. Reinach, who calls this interpretation "frivolous" (*Revue de l'Histoire des Religions*, 1914, I, p. 342 n.1), does not seem to believe in the *ancile*-shield either. Commenting on K. Latte's dissertation (*De saltationibus Graecorum capita* V, 1913), he recalls (R.H.R., 1913, II, p. 369) Thiersch's opinion that the bronze disks known as the "shields" of Ida or Dicte were in reality sacred cymbals.

So what, then, was the *ancile*? A shield, a lunar symbol, a cymbal? Likely all three at once, by the historical period, when even the priests no longer understood the words they chanted (Quintilian I, VI, 40). The Salii carried in procession twelve shields, symbols of the months, which they struck rhythmically.

But was that the primitive meaning of the *ancile*? The banquet toward which the Salii hastened, and the culinary sense of their chants, suggest a very different interpretation — that the *ancile* was originally a cooking vessel, not a shield.

If the ancient etymologies are correct, there is still no reason to see in the "angle-less object" or in the "object with two notches" a shield. Yet it is difficult to accept either Varro's derivation, or Ovid's, or still less the Greek hypotheses.

The word *ancile* belongs to the same morphological family as *cubile* and *sedile* — words denoting the instrument or object in which an action takes place: the thing on which one lies, the thing on which one sits. What root, then, does the first part *anc-* represent?

The passage from Quintilian cited earlier seems to attribute to the chants of the Salii the very archaic word *escanclare*, "to draw (liquid)." Moreover, among the rare words preserved by Festus and his abridger Paul the Deacon, which, following Corssen, Cirilli (op. cit., p. 119) regards as specifically related to Salian ceremonies, appears, alongside *escanclare*, the word *anclabris, anclabria*, explained as follows (Festus, Ep. P., 77, s.v. Escariae):

"Escariae mensae quadratae vocantur in quibus homines epulantur.
Anclabris ea quae in sacrificando diis anclatur, quod est hauritur ministraturque."

and again (ibid. 11, s.v. Anclabris):

"Anclabris: mensa ministeriis divinis aptata.
Vasa quoque in ea quibus sacerdotes utuntur, anclabria appellantur."

From this it follows that *anclabris* means either "the sacred vessels in which food is offered to the gods" or "the table on which these vessels are placed," while *anclare* means "to draw out (liquid) for serving."

Anclabris clearly derives from *anclare*, which is related to the Oscan *anglaf* ("servant of the gods" or "prophetic priestess"). But whence comes *anclare* itself?

The *Thesaurus Linguae Latinae*, following a text of Festus (a*nclare haurire a Graeco descendit)*, accepts a Greek derivation from ἀντλεῖν ("to draw water"), but that seems highly improbable for so archaic and ritually specific a Latin word. Another traditional explanation, also from Festus, confuses *anclare* with *anculare*, "to serve," yet since *anculare* depends on *anculus* — itself derived from the Indo-European root **am(bh)* — *quolo-* (Greek ἀμφίπολος, Sanskrit *abhicara*) — this etymology seems equally unlikely.

Thus, the origin of *anclare* and *anclabris* remains unknown — as does that of *ancile*. However, the convergence of these three words, all sharing the same root and all belonging to the Salian ritual vocabulary, combined with the culinary and sacrificial character of the chants and rites of the Salii, suggests a plausible interpretation:

Ancile originally meant "the vessel in which food was served to the gods."

The *ancile* was, in all likelihood, simply the vessel (compare the *carmen saliare*: *Cozeulo–coculum*) that the Salii carried in procession to the place where they would prepare, upon the *anclabria*, the feast of the gods and of themselves — something like the Holy Grail of Welsh legend, which presides over the mystical banquet of the faithful, and which, like the Grail, had by then lost its original practical function.

The *ancile* that Numa won from Jupiter (and, in earlier versions, from Picus) in order to guarantee the permanence of Rome, was originally, it seems, the ancient cauldron of ambrosia — the vessel won by a god from a water spirit to secure immortality for the gods.

Nonetheless, it remains certain that, for all of classical antiquity, the *ancile* was regarded as a shield. How this transformation occurred, we do not claim to explain fully here — yet a few remarks may help make it intelligible.

We have already observed, in discussing Prometheus, that the myths of the Scandinavian Loki and the ale of the Æsir, of the Irish Goibniu and the ale of the Tuatha Dé Danann, of the Greek Prometheus and the *píthos* of immortality, and finally of the Latin Mamurius and the *ancile*, all suggest that even among the Indo-Europeans, a god or demonic smith took part either in the preparation of the ambrosia, or in its theft, or in both episodes.

The original meaning of this intervention is not entirely clear. Perhaps it meant simply that, in order to boil their immense cauldron, the gods had to appeal to the possessor of the greatest fire — the divine or demonic smith — and (in the demonic case) that this smith sought to appropriate part or all of the food prepared in common. However that may be, once the ambrosia itself was forgotten (as we have seen, this is a common Italic and even Mediterranean development), and once therefore the Cauldron in which it was prepared lost its immediate function, the presence in the story of the smith Mamurius naturally caused the myth to shift in a "metalworking" direction.

His task was no longer to brew in the *ancile* a now-forgotten drink, but — since the *ancile* had acquired importance in itself — to forge eleven false *ancilia* to protect against theft. Yet the *ancile* still had to be something recognisable; and since Mamurius is a figure of Mars, a war-god from the earliest Italic history, the *ancile* came to be conceived as a weapon, a shield.

A similar phenomenon can be seen in Ireland, where Goibniu, in later (Christianised) versions of the mythic cycle, ensures the victory and supremacy of the gods not as a cupbearer but as a smith.

M. Cirilli, following many others, has proposed to derive the Salii and their "arms" from sacred guilds of smiths and from the magical shields found in abundance in antiquity along the coasts of the Aegean Sea. But this derivation, based on a superficial analogy, is implausible for clear historical and geographical reasons: it would require close relations between the Pelasgians of the Aegean and the conquering peoples of northern and central Italy, for which there is no other evidence.

We have, moreover, already shown that the Salian festivals, even in their evolved form, retain food-related elements and are in no sense festivals of smiths. The mere fact of striking metallic objects is far too general to serve as a basis for classifying festivals or for positing a lineage from a Kretan festival to a Sabine one.

Still, while this hypothesis seems implausible for prehistory, the Aegean (Hellenic) theory regains much of its relevance for the historical period.

As Adolphe Reinach showed in his remarkable study on Llanos et l'inventio scuti ("The Invention of the Shield"), devoted to primitive hoplolatry — the worship of weapons — in Greece (*Revue d'Histoire des Religions*, 1909, vol. 60, pp. 160–190, 309–351), there was a wide and well-attested cult in Greece surrounding sacred shields (*palladia*), fallen from the sky and believed to protect men and cities against lightning (ibid., pp. 335–336).

The Latin scholars, long before Ovid, must have known these Greek legends of celestial shields, as well as the tale of the multiple Palladia of Troy, forged to make theft more difficult. All this could have led them to reinterpret, as shields, the ritual vessels of ancient origin whose original, alimentary (sacrificial) meaning they no longer understood.

Even the bilobed form of the *ancile* — encouraged by etymology, though not the only one represented in iconography — may have been borrowed from these sacred Greek shields, which appear on certain vases (Reinach, loc. cit.). For this cannot have been the *ancile*'s primitive form. The earliest *ancile*-cauldrons, if our reconstruction is correct, were hemispherical, footless cauldrons, designed to be hung rather than set down, like those discovered across the Celtic world (Déchelette, *Archéologie celtique*, vol. II, p. 1420 ff., and plates).

The round *ancilia* without notches, depicted on coins alongside the notched type (Cohen, *Méd. impér.* 12 476, 72; Marquardt, *Staatsverw.* III, 431), match these Celtic cauldrons, and Schumacher (*Beschreibung der Sammlung antiker Bronzen*, Karlsruhe, 1890, pl. VIII) reproduces Italo-Greek cauldrons of the same shape.

Once the ancient beverage once brewed in them was forgotten — a general fact among Indo-European peoples who had adopted wine — what remained to do with these vessels? During the banquet, they became empty ritual objects, "presiding" over the meal (like the Celtic Grail); during the procession, they turned into barbaric musical instruments — or, at best, barbaric dance accessories.

⁎⁎⁎

Thus, the entire legend of the *ancile* in the Fasti seems to be the result of a compromise between an ancient native legend of the *ancile*-cauldron, corresponding to the *ancile* of the Salians' feast, and the Greek traditions concerning the shield fallen from the sky, the false *palladia*, etc.

There is even a point at which we can observe this process taking place, a point where the contamination remains clumsily unfinished: it is the double duel that Numa first wages against the aquatic spirits Faunus and Picus, and then against Jupiter.

If we are right, the ancient *ancile*-cauldron cannot have been connected with lightning or with Jupiter. Like that of Anna, the cycle of the *ancile* must have begun with a famine among the Romans of Numa. To avert this famine, to prepare the meal later commemorated by the feast of the Salians, Numa went to win from an aquatic spirit, through some kind of duel, the *coculum* (cf. *cozeulo* in the Salian chant) or *ancile*, the necessary vessel.

But when, owing to the forgetting of the ancient ritual food (or drink) and under the influence of Greek legends, the *ancile* came to be regarded as a shield, as a talisman fallen from the sky, it had to be linked with lightning, with Jupiter (cf. τὸ διυπετὲς Παλλάδιον). The ancient duel with the aquatic spirit was not so easily forgotten, and in the *Fasti* we have a story composed as follows:

1. Egeria advises Numa to address himself, near their spring on the Aventine, to Picus and Faunus. Numa chains the spirits while they sleep; they try in vain to free themselves by metamorphoses, then resign themselves — not to giving Numa what he needs (to appease the lightning), but to summoning for him Jupiter, the only one competent in the matter.

2. Between Jupiter and Numa, it is quite a different kind of duel. Numa asks Jupiter for the information he has come to seek: *"Give me sure means to appease the lightning."* Jupiter replies, *"Cut off a head."*

"Agreed, I shall obey," answers the king; *"I will cut the head of an onion from my garden!"*

"But I require something human," says the god.

"Then — the tip of the hair," replies Numa.

"But something living."

"A fish," says Numa.

Jupiter, disarmed, laughs — and it is then that he promises Numa the *certa pignora imperii*, that is to say, the *ancile*.

In the fragment of Valerius Antias preserved for us by Arnobius (*Adversus Gentes*, V, 1), Jupiter is not only disarmed by laughter — he is truly vanquished, like the Indo-European possessor of the Cauldron: *"Since, however, your cunning has outwitted me, have your will in this matter..."* says he to Numa.

It has long been recognised that the first duel (Faunus and Picus chained...) is a literary copy of Greek tales where Herakles chains Nereus, or Menelaus, Proteus. By contrast, the scene of argument, of rustic bargaining in which Numa triumphs over Jupiter, clearly bears the Italian stamp.

But why these two duels, when only one has ancient substance and the other must have borrowed its content from Greece? Our hypothesis perfectly explains this clumsy conflation: originally, there was only one duel, at the spring, between Numa and the water spirit (Faunus, Picus, or both — compare the metamorphoses of the sea-spirit in the Ambrosia cycle). This duel took the form of the bargaining scene that, in Ovid's text, is attributed to the Numa–Jupiter encounter.

In that primitive tale, Jupiter did not intervene; it was Picus himself who handed over the *ancile*-cauldron to the king. Do we not see, moreover, in the *Aeneid* (VII, 188), Picus bearing the *ancile* on his arm, as a unique privilege — and is that not proof that ancient legends made him the possessor and giver of this divine object?

But when the *ancile* became, under Greek influence, the magical shield fallen from heaven, Jupiter had to be brought in — while keeping the traditional figures of Picus and Faunus, and the setting of their spring. Hence the coexistence of the two duels: the one (Numa–Picus) serving only to prepare the other (Numa–Jupiter).

Yet these two duels, awkwardly juxtaposed, required two separate plots. The Numa–Jupiter duel retained the substance of the old Italian legend (the bargaining scene); what was left, then, for the Numa–Picus duel? Nothing — and that is why Ovid, or the author he followed, borrowed from Greek mythology (already responsible for transforming the *ancile* into a sky-fallen *palladium*) a new motif.

Thus was born this hybrid and redundant tale, half popular, half learned, which brings together Picus–Faunus and a Jupiter Elicius belonging to a wholly different divine sphere, and which makes the *ancile* fall from the heavens while preserving, through the spring of the two spirits, the memory of its aquatic origins.

For the other parts of the legend, the blending was better done: Mamurius, who was no doubt at first expelled for having tried to steal a share of the *ancile* feast, is no longer expelled — according to the later testimony of Lydus — except as a result of rather vague δυσχερῆ, of misfortunes that befell the Romans concerning the false *ancilia* forged by him.

⁂

We do not claim to have clarified the origins of the *ancile* legend. Too many elements are missing, and the role of hypothesis is too large: it is, for example, impossible to measure how much influence Greek legends had on the formation of the classical version of the story as it already appears in Ovid.

But our conjecture accounts for the alimentary aspect of the rites — and no doubt of the songs of the Salii — and for the curious correspondences that the legendary cycle of the *ancile* presents with the Ambrosia cycle. Celtic evidence, particularly the legends of the Grail, will soon shed light on what may still remain obscure in this conception of the confraternity, the festivals, and the legends of the Salii.

Conclusion on the Latin Legends Derived from the Cycle of Ambrosia

Thus, we have rediscovered — without even speaking of the *cista* of Praeneste or the story of Petronilla — two, and perhaps three, forms of the cycle, simultaneously collected and adopted by the Romans.

The essential fact to retain is the constant transformation of ancient religious legends into historical tales: the devotion of Anna of Bovillae, the dialogue between Numa and Jupiter, the expulsion of the blacksmith Mamurius — these are "humanisations" of former mythological episodes.

It therefore seems that the history of Rome's earliest times contains many elements which, elsewhere — among a less practical and more imaginative people, such as the Greeks — would appear in mythological form. There are, in this, more than a few interesting discoveries yet to be made.

Let us also note this juxtaposition, at Rome, within the same month of March, of two festivals connected to two cycles that seem to have the same ambrosian origin: one of these cycles is purely Roman — the cycle of Anna Perenna; the other is Sabine — the cycle of the *ancile*.

Now, the festival of Anna Perenna is popular, plebeian, without official pomp, without priests: apart from its political character, it closely resembles our "May Day," with the exodus of Parisian workers to the woods outside the city.

The festival of the *ancile*, or rather the festivals of the *ancile*, are, on the contrary, official and patrician — they have their priests, their ritual, their processions...

It would perhaps be rash to generalise from a single example, but this case allows us to glimpse that, in the formation of the national religion — and doubtless in the political organisation of Rome — the part played by the Sabines was not the least important: the city is no less the daughter of Tatius than of Romulus.

Chapter Six

The Cycle of the Ambrosia among the Celts

With the Celtic world, we come to a part of the Indo-European mythological domain which — despite its richness — only late drew the attention of comparative scholars.

The school of Max Müller, fully confident in the authority of the Vedas, completely neglected Celtic legends as well as Slavic ones; even the Germanic myths were rarely called to testify. More often than not, they were simply "illuminated," at the end of the analysis, by the light of Indra or of Herakles.

Celtic scholars, for their part, were not always as well equipped as would have been necessary to undertake the comparison. The book by d'Arbois de Jubainville, *La Civilisation des Celtes et celle de l'épopée homérique* (*Cours de Littérature celtique*, vol. VI, 1899), is full of ingenious observations but does not go to the heart of the matter; the analogies that the same author noted, in his other works, between Irish traditions and certain Greek myths — for example between the legend of Lug and that of Perseus, or between the tales of the *Togail* (Invasions) and the myth of the Achaeans — are likewise superficial.

When Grimm or Rhys compare the Welsh Gwydion with the Wodan-Odin of the Germanic peoples, it is scarcely more than a matter of two names — whose identity, moreover, is not proven.

The main difficulty, of course, comes from the recent date of the available evidence: everything we know about the Gaulish gods is fragmentary and uncertain. In this respect, as in so many others, the Druids' prohibition of writing — whatever its motive — has inflicted an irreparable loss on science and on the history of the human mind.

As for the insular Celts, apart from the Irish, they have transmitted to us only very late, highly developed legends, disfigured by an excessive Christianity. The point of departure for Celtic studies — in religion as in linguistics or in law — remains, and will remain, Ireland.

Here again, all the testimonies are from the Christian era. But the Irish monks of the Middle Ages — whose essential, truly "European" role is well known — were able, through a well-understood nationalism, to unite in their zeal as scholars and devotees the dogma received from Rome and the historical or religious traditions inherited from their pagan ancestors.

All the usual compromises are found here: gods and heroes became saints, or lent certain traits of their legends to genuine saints (such as Saint Patrick and Saint Brigid); the struggles of gods and demons were "humanised" and incorporated into the battles of the Races (the Fomorians and the Tuatha Dé Danann); pagan festivals were given new attire (such as Lugnasad).

Yet it may be said that, beneath a Christian varnish that can often be stripped away, we still possess the essential core of Irish paganism. The texts — ever more numerous each year — published in the journals of both the island and the continent, together with the general and specialised studies that, from d'Arbois de Jubainville to M. Thurneysen, have succeeded one another in France, England, Ireland, and Germany, provide a record to which nothing truly important is likely still missing.

We shall therefore first ask Irish mythology what it has made of the Indo-European cycle of the Ambrosia — and there our inquiry will be fruitful. Then, by examining the Welsh traditions, we shall see that the core of the strange Christian legend of the Grail — whose origin had been unknown — faithfully reproduces all the episodes of the cycle of the Ambrosia and of the Cauldron.

Finally, we shall look in the Gaulish monuments for scattered traces of our legends. This cannot, any more than in the case of the Greek legends, be an exhaustive monographic study.

For the Grail in particular, we do not feel sufficiently equipped to enter into the discussions that arise at every turn in the texts: we shall simply set ourselves before a small central group of unexplained legends and observe the agreement between those legends and the Indo-European cycle of the Ambrosia.

Our study therefore aims only to provide a new element of

explanation to be brought into the debates among Celtic and Romance scholars.

⁂

I. The Cycle of Ambrosia Among the Irish. The Ale of Goibniu and the Battle of Mag Tured

Irish mythology, in the form in which it has come down to us, consists essentially of a series of wars waged between the successive Races that inhabited the island. Among these wars, there is one in which scholars have long recognised the ancient Indo-European struggle between the demons and the gods: that which sets the Fomorians (Fomóire) against the Tuatha Dé Danann.

Under the pens of medieval euhemerists, the Fomóire were confused with pirates — especially with the Vikings who ravaged the coasts of Ireland (Giraldus Cambrensis, *Topographia Hibernica*, distinction III, chapter 3, ed. Dimock, p. 143) — and the learned men, in their biblical obsession, made them the descendants of Ham.

But the oldest texts say nothing yet of these scholarly origins: The *Book of Invasions* merely recounts that the Fomóire arrived by sea (*Book of Leinster*, p. 6, col. 1, lines 39, 40, 46, 47). A more important point — attested by both Giraldus Cambrensis (*Topographia Hibernica.*, dist. III, c. 2, ed. Dimock, p. 141) and the *Book of Invasions* (*Book of Leinster*, p. 5, c. 1, l. 20–22) — is that the Fomóire were regarded as giants, demons with human form

(*Chronicum Scoticum*, 12th cent., ed. Hennessy, p. 6). Among them were said to be monsters with only one hand or one foot (*Book of Leinster*, p. 5, c. 1, l. 22–23).

Originally, the conception of the Fomóire was even simpler. D'Arbois de Jubainville (*Le Cycle mythologique irlandais*, pp. 91–99) established that, for pagan Irish, the Fomóire were the gods (or demons) of Death and of Night. No primitive legend related their arrival; they had always been in the island, by right — like the Thurses in Scandinavia, or the Giants in Greek lands. It was only later, when pseudo-Christian historians sought to make them one of the successive races of settlers, that they were imagined — like Partholon and the Fir-Bolg — to have come through a "migration."

The same thing happened to the Tuatha Dé Danann. Originally, this name — which means "the people of the goddess Danu" — designated simply the Gods, the heirs of the Indo-European **deivo-*.

The word *dé* (or *dee*) that it contains is the genitive of a feminine form of *dia*, "god," whose use in Irish is limited to a few expressions (see H. Hubert, preface to Czarnowski, *Le Culte des Héros...*, p. XIX, p. 3).

According to Celtic belief, these gods of Life and Light are also — and above all — the gods of druidic knowledge and of the poetic science of the *fili* (bards). The Christian monks, determined to give Ireland a history modelled on the biblical genealogies, strove to make them descend from Adam; yet there are many texts in which the Tuatha Dé Danann descend directly from Heaven (see d'Arbois de Jubainville, *Le Cycle mythologique...*, pp. 140–142).

As for the goddess Dana, or Danu (genitive Danann), who here gives her name to the clan of the gods, she is the heir of a great goddess whose existence is attested throughout the Celtic world. In Ireland, she is more particularly the mother of three gods — Brian, Iuchar, and Iucharba — called Tri Dée Danann, "the three gods of Danu," and they are the gods of literary and artistic inspiration.

In Wales, we likewise encounter several gods called "sons of Dôn," notably the great god of wisdom, Gwydion, and the smith Govannon, whom we shall soon meet again (Rhys, *The Hibbert Lectures*, 1886, p. 90).

Among the Gauls, Caesar mentions a "Minerva," goddess of crafts and arts (*Minervam operum atque artificiorum initia tradere*).

Another pan-Celtic name of the goddess has had no less fortune: Danu is sometimes called Brigit among the Irish. Now, four inscriptions from Britain reveal a goddess Brigantia, who also appears in a Gaulish inscription as Brigindo. This name, which curiously echoes the Vedic Brhatī and the Avestan Bərəzaitī, is linked to the Indo-European root **brgh-* meaning "high, elevated."

By a special destiny, the Irish Danu survived the end of paganism under this other name: she became Saint Brigit. We shall have to see whether, beneath the legends of Saint Brigit, there still survive other traces of her pagan personality.

A fortunate accident has preserved for us a direct ambrosial tradition concerning the Tuatha Dé Danann of the pagan era: what granted these gods immortality was the "feast" prepared for them by one among their number — the smith Goibniu (d'Arbois de Jubainville, *Le Cycle mythologique...*, p. 308).

O'Curry, in the *Atlantis* (vol. III, p. 389), brought together two texts relating to this belief. "The expression used by these texts," says d'Arbois de Jubainville (ibid., note 2), *"is fled Goibnenn, 'the feast of Goibniu'; but at this feast one was occupied mainly with drinking (ic ol); what was consumed there was a drink (deoch); it was a drink that made one immortal. It is therefore a question of beer, find or cuirm, which is mentioned in other texts."*

Indeed, a twelfth-century text describing the underground dwelling of the Tuatha Dé Danann Oengus says that one sees there, beside three trees always bearing fruit and two pigs — one always alive and the other always cooked and ready to be eaten — a vessel containing excellent beer. *"There,"* adds the text, *"no one ever dies."* (d'Arbois de Jubainville, op. cit., p. 275.)

And another text, describing the mysterious abode of immortality *"where youth never grows old,"* expresses it thus: "*The beer of Ireland intoxicates, but the beer of the Great Land is far more intoxicating.*" (d'Arbois de Jubainville, op. cit., p. 317.)

It is therefore a feast of beer — beer of immortality — that the Irish gods received from the smith Goibniu (genitive Goibnenn). Goibniu long retained his reputation as a god of cookery: the *St. Gall manuscript* (8th or 9th century) contains an invocation meant to preserve butter, in which the name of Goibniu is invoked three times:

"Fiss Goibnenn, aird Goibnenn, renaird Goibnenn!"

that is, *"Knowledge of Goibniu, of the great Goibniu, of the very great Goibniu!"*

By reaction, the clergy of Ireland came to distrust smiths. The prayer that the Book of Hymns attributes to Saint Patrick asks for God's protection *"against the spells of women, of smiths, and of druids — against every science that ruins the soul of man."*

And among those condemned sciences is included the knowledge of Goibniu, invoked in the St. Gall charm of the 8th or 9th century — that is, the knowledge of the divine smith who preserved the butter of his human worshippers, and who, by his feast, granted the gods immortality. *"It is a diabolical science,"* says d'Arbois de Jubainville, *"and one that the holy apostle of Ireland regarded as an enemy."* (*Le Cycle mythologique irlandais*, p. 308.)

D'Arbois de Jubainville already noted, concerning the smith Goibniu, the parallel with the Greek Hephaistos, cupbearer of the gods. We can now add to this correspondence the smith Loki and the smith Mamurius Veturius — both closely connected, though in different ways, to two cycles derived from the cycle of Ambrosia. There is here, very probably, an Indo-European trait — its meaning obscure, but its form clear.

In the Celtic world, the smith Goibniu is not alone: among the Welsh gods whose mother is the goddess Dôn appears the smith

Govannon, whom we have already mentioned and who, as we shall soon see, is the hero of an "ambrosial" adventure also known to Goibniu. Finally, O'Donovan rediscovered Goibniu in a popular tale — likewise of ambrosial origin — still alive in the nineteenth century, under the name Gavida. All these names evidently derive from the Celtic root that produced the Irish *goba* (gen. *gobann*), "the smith" (pronounced today *gava*).

Unfortunately, although we know the drink and the cupbearer of the ancient Irish gods during the pagan era — when they were still gods — this is only an isolated piece of information. No direct evidence reveals what had by then become of the Ambrosia cycle. We must wait until the Christian era, the time when the gods appear only in humanised form, to find its first redaction in the tale of the Battle of Mag Tured.

But there, ambrosia — the privilege of the gods — has vanished; and although many details, and even the sequence of episodes themselves, can only be understood as deriving from an earlier ambrosial version, we are nonetheless dealing with a very evolved text, laden with elements of entirely different origin and marked throughout by a persistent euhemeristic tendency.

It will therefore not be useless to reconstruct briefly — by comparing the Indo-European facts and the few ancient Irish data we have just gathered — the form that the Ambrosia Cycle must have taken in Ireland during the first centuries of the Middle Ages.

A. Preparation of the Beer of Immortality

(a) The gods, children of Dana, are threatened by famine or death;

(b) They gather in council;

(c) One of them goes to a sea-dwelling being to seize a vast Cauldron;

(d) In this Cauldron, the smith Goibniu brews the beer of immortality and serves the feast to the gods;

(e) War breaks out between the gods and the Fomorians.

B. The Fomorian among the Gods

(a) A Fomorian comes to Goibniu's feast and demands his share;

(b) (Well received at first?), he provokes Goibniu, who kills him.

C. The False Woman

(a) A Fomorian has stolen the beer of immortality;

(b) Goibniu (or another), disguised as a woman, goes to punish the Fomorian.

D. General Battle

(a) (Various episodes.)

(b) The gods overwhelm the Fomorians.

*
* *

Except for one episode, it is this very outline that lies at the origin of a well-known text — the tale of the Battle of Mag Tured, which recounts the victory of the Tuatha Dé Danann over the Fomorians.

D'Arbois de Jubainville has shown (*Le Cycle mythologique...*, p. 150–152) that, of the two battles of Mag Tured known to Irish monks as early as the 11th century, only the second preserves an ancient tradition; and it is this one alone that clearly appears as a continuation of the Cycle of the Ambrosia.

The most explicit text we have comes from a 15th-century manuscript (*Harleian 5280*, British Museum), though it is based on a much earlier version. It was published by Whitley Stokes in the *Revue Celtique* (XII, p. 52–130) with an English translation and extensive commentary. D'Arbois de Jubainville produced a French version in his *Épopée Celtique en Irlande* (p. 393–448), carefully marking the passages that clearly show later interpolations.

The beginning of the tale emphasises the familial and social ties that unite the two enemy clans. Over the Tuatha Dé Danann reigns Bress, whose father is king among the Fomorians; the god Lug is born of a god, Cían or Dagda, but through his mother he is the grandson of one of the Fomorian chiefs, Balar.

There is nothing surprising in this: in India, in Greece, and even in Rome, we have seen that the ambrosian legends begin with a state of harmony between the rival clans — and it is not forgotten that the sons of Iapetos and Kronos, the Asuras and the Devas, are brothers or first cousins.

We will now follow, step by step, the account of the rivalry between the Tuatha Dé Danann and the Fomorians, eliminating only the obvious interpolations according to d'Arbois de Jubainville. It will be seen that, although the Ambrosia — the beer of immortality — has disappeared, the alimentary origin and significance of the conflict, the personality of the smith–cupbearer Goibniu, and the preoccupation with overcoming death have been faithfully preserved.

Certain episodes, such as the god's expedition in search of the immense Cauldron, have lost their purpose — since there is no longer any beer to brew — but survive awkwardly, inexplicable in the current state of the tale. Others have quite naturally been transformed: in Goibniu, people saw less and less the cupbearer, and it is as a smith of miraculous weapons that he secures the gods' triumph and arouses the jealousy of the Fomorians.

Finally, if the episode of the False Goddess does not appear in this tale, we shall soon see that it has survived into the nineteenth century in popular tradition, attached to a doublet of Goibniu, the smith Gavida.

A. Origin of the Conflict and Preparation of the Gods' Triumph by Goibniu (Formerly: Preparation of the Beer of Immortality by Goibniu)

(a) Famine among the Tuatha Dé Danann.

The king of the Tuatha Dé Danann, Bress, was miserly: *"Great murmurs rose around him; the chiefs of the Tuatha Dé Danann were* discontented, for Bress did not grease their knives. However often they came to see Bress, their breath did not smell of beer..." (§36).

They were literally dying of starvation: Ogmé, the Irish Hercules, had been ordered to supply the firewood for the fortress. *"Each day he brought from the islands of Mod a bundle of wood, but every time the sea carried away two-thirds of it, for he was without strength, for lack of food."* (§37)

One recognises here the same theme that opens both the cycle of the Beer of the Æsir and that of Anna Perenna. Having forgotten immortality, the Germans, Latins, and Celts depict the gods — or the men who, in the story, have taken the gods' place — as simply threatened by famine. They no longer seek a food of immortality, but food of any kind.

This miserliness of Bress ends badly: cursed by a poet to whom he had served only *"three little dry loaves,"* Bress is driven out by his people and goes to ask for help from his father, king of the Fomorians. There is clearly a recent, pseudo-historical invention here, devised to explain the quarrel between the Tuatha Dé Danann and the Fomorians. Originally, this quarrel broke out only later, once Goibniu's beer was ready. Hence, in the Irish narrative, a certain inconsistency arises: the war, declared too early, drags on through several episodes.

(b) The Council of the Tuatha Dé Danann.

The council of the gods also changes its purpose: since the expulsion of Bress is enough to end the famine, this is no longer the ambrosial consultation, but a war council.

The text gives a lengthy description of the assembly, as well as the arrival of Lug, who will be a powerful ally to the gods. These are recent developments, consistent with the Celtic taste for assemblies and deliberation.

(c) The god's expedition toward the Cauldron.

The council of the gods sends a god on an expedition. But it is no longer to bring back the Cauldron, nor to visit a marine being who is "neutral," so to speak, between gods and demons: instead, he is sent to the Fomorians "to gain time."

And it is during this strange mission, by chance, that he encounters the immense Cauldron, which must have played an essential role in the ancient pagan versions of the legend:

"*Lug sent the Dagda to see what the Fomorians were doing and to make them lose time until the warriors of the goddess Dana were ready to fight.*" (§88)

The Dagda went to the camp of the Fomorians and asked them for a truce; he obtained it. The Fomorians prepared a porridge for him — it was meant to mock him, for he was very fond of porridge. They filled for him the king's cauldron, which was as deep as five men's fists — fists of gigantic men, like the Fomorians themselves, explains d'Arbois de Jubainville.

They poured into it eighty pots of milk, a proportional quantity of flour and fat; then goats, sheep, and pigs, which were cooked with the rest. Finally, they poured this porridge into a hole dug in the earth.

"*If you do not eat it all,*" said Indech, one of the Fomorian chiefs, "*you will be put to death. We wish you to have no complaint against us; therefore you must be satisfied.*" (§89)

The Dagda took a spoon so large that in its hollow a man and a woman could lie together as in a bed, and devoured everything. Then he returned to the gods, stumbling, his belly swollen, dragging his club along the ground and cutting a deep furrow in the soil.

It seems clear that in this episode there survives a precise, material trace of the Drink and Feast of Immortality.

One will notice how strange is the threat, the challenge, that Indech hurls at the Dagda: "*If you do not eat everything, you shall be put to death.*" Yet the Dagda is an ambassador, one with whom a truce has just been negotiated. Nothing could be more contrary to the Celtic spirit than the idea of such a murder.

Everything becomes clear if we remember that in the gigantic Cauldron there once brewed a food such that whoever ate of it would not die. The Irish tale, humanised and stripped of its marvels, still preserves the bare framework of the ancient pagan myth.

As for the mocking challenge that the Fomorian throws at the

Dagda, it surely descends from the contest or struggle that the spirit, possessor of the Cauldron, once imposed upon the god. Thus this episode of the Cauldron — whose connection to the rest of the tale has become so tenuous — preserves within itself the most exact ambrosial memories: by anticipation, where the Indo-Europeans spoke only of the conquest of the Cauldron, it already shows us the preparation and the very consumption of the feast.

Finally, the Dagda dragging his club heavily along the ground recalls the final part of the Hymiskviða, where Thor leaves Hymir's house bent beneath the weight of the Cauldron he is carrying back to the gods. Such must indeed once have been the burden of the Dagda, in the time when the mission entrusted to him by the gods was still "ambrosial."

The irreverent monks, however, have shifted the load from his shoulders to his belly: *"His belly,"* they explain, *"was larger than the great cauldrons kept in people's houses..."*

(d) Preparations of the Tuatha Dé Danann: Goibniu forges marvellous weapons.

At this point in the cycle, where the gods once prepared the ambrosia in the Cauldron they had won, the Irish text — forgetful of Goibniu's Beer — has found convenient substitutes: the gods, preparing for battle, secure for themselves a number of magical artifices.

In this endless enumeration, so typical of Celtic taste, a few elements still retain something ambrosial:

"When one of our warriors has been wounded," explains the physician of the gods, Dian Cécht, "unless his head has been cut off, or a membrane of his brain or his spinal cord severed, I shall heal him completely..." (§99)

"We shall give the Fomorians, say the divine cupbearers, a terrible thirst, and they will find nothing to drink to quench it..." (§111)

But the leading role, as we might expect, belongs to Goibniu — no longer as cupbearer, but as forger:

"With the spears made by me, never does a warrior miss his blow, and the flesh that this blow strikes will forever cease to enjoy the sweetness of life. Dulb, the forger of the Fomorians, cannot say as much. The blows struck by my spears will decide the outcome of the battle..." (§97)

And, aided by the bronzesmith Creidné and the carpenter Luchtiné, Goibniu sets to work; in three strokes, each spear is finished, and soon all the divine warriors are equipped with a marvellous weapon. The *ancilia* of Mamurius had, in the same way within the cycle, taken the place of the ambrosia.

(e) The war breaks out between the Tuatha Dé Danann and the Fomorians.

The battle, awkwardly delayed until now, finally begins — exactly at the point where it began in the ambrosial cycle. The Fomorians are terrified to see that the weapons of the Tuatha Dé Danann are always in perfect condition. Even more, a new substitute for ambrosia appears in favour of the gods:

"The warriors who had been slain regained the fire of life, and the next day they were more splendid than ever. This was the reason: Dian Cécht (the physician of the gods), his two sons Oc-Trial and Miach, and his daughter Airmed, pronounced incantations over the well called the Spring of Health. They cast their wounded into it — even those who were dead — and these wounded came out alive. However severe their wounds, they were healed by the power of the incantation spoken by the four physicians around the spring..." (§123)

The connection between ambrosia (or its substitute, the reviving water) and a "physician of the gods" is a natural one: Brahmanic India had the same inspiration when it represented Dhanvantari bringing to the Devas the vessel of *amṛta*.

One should also note the intimate union between the notion of immortality and a spring — elsewhere, a lake (§125). We shall return to this point when we study the rites of the ambrosial head.

B. The Fomorian Among the Gods

We recall the ambrosial episode that appears at this point in the cycle: a demon slips in among the gods to partake of the wondrous drink. Welcomed at first (according to the Germanic, Greek, and likely Latin traditions), he then provokes the gods, who punish him with a cruel torment.

In the Irish version, from which the ambrosia has vanished, the structure remains transparent: the Fomorians send one of their own, Ruadan, among the Tuatha Dé Danann with the mission to kill Goibniu, hoping that at the next battle they will no longer be able to replace their broken or lost weapons.

Well received, Ruadan asks the smith to give him one of his marvellous spears, those that never miss their mark. Goibniu agrees; but as soon as he is armed, the Fomorian turns the weapon against the god. Goibniu, wounded, in turn pierces Ruadan, and then goes to heal himself in the Spring of Health.

As for Ruadan, he drags himself to the assembly of the Fomorians, where he dies.

"Brig, his mother, came and wept for her son. First she uttered a piercing cry, then she broke into lamentations; it was then, for the first time in Ireland, that one heard wailing and cries of sorrow..." (§§124–125)

It is probable that in an age when the combatants were not yet humanised, Ruadan's punishment did not end so swiftly. His mother Brig, in any case, plays a role beside him similar to that of Loki's wife beside her tormented husband. Finally, the text says nothing of the "earthquakes" which, among the Germans, Greeks, Hindus, and — as we shall soon see — among other Celts and Slavs, found their explanation in this very episode.

The antiquity of the tradition is, moreover, not in doubt: the murder of the demon Ruadan by the "god-smith of Dana, Goibniu," has its parallel in a Welsh tale, where we see the smith Govannon (cf. Irish genitive Goibnenn) slay the demon Dylan (see Rhys, *The Hibbert Lectures*, 1886, p. 386).

By a curious evolution, in this Welsh legend, which we know only imperfectly, the killing of Dylan is lamented as one of the three crimes of the Island of Britain, and Govannon no longer appears as a just avenger but as a murderer. Rhys plausibly conjectures an earlier state of the myth, in which the death of the Welsh Dylan, like that of the Irish Ruadan, was only an episode in the great battle between the gods and the demons — represented here by the Tuatha Dé Danann, brothers of Goibniu, and by the Fomorians who mourn over Ruadan's corpse; and there, by the sons of Dôn, among whom figures Govannon, and by the "Waves," which, after rocking Dylan's frolics before the duel, lament at the sight of his death.

C. The False Goddess

The version of the Battle of Mag Tured that we possess does not contain this episode. However, it reappears — well preserved — in a modern legend that is merely a doublet of one scene from that battle, just as its hero, Gavida, is a doublet of the smith Goibniu. We will soon encounter this legend again.

D. General Melee

The battle, almost entirely humanised, is described at great length. Fomorian chiefs strike down chiefs of the Tuatha Dé Danann and in turn fall themselves. Finally, the Fomorians, in rout, retreat and flee to a mysterious land beyond the ocean — that is, to the land of the dead, the object of so many Celtic dreams.

The duels that fill the battle are, for the most part, doubtless of recent invention — a theme that, in all literatures, is renewed endlessly. There is, however, one duel that perhaps preserves an ancient feature, and of which we shall soon find a curious variant.

One of the Fomorian chiefs, Balar "of the mighty blows," habitually keeps one of his two eyes closed. When he opens it, he strikes men dead. Yet he eventually falls beneath the blows of Lug.

For a long time, this Balar has been compared to the Greek Gorgon; and this remark takes on full value if one remembers that, according to a variant, it is during the Gigantomakhy that Athena kills the monster.

Whether the Greek detail and the Irish detail arose independently, they are in any case both a more precise form of the malevolence and destructive power that the Indo-European cycle attributed to demons — which, in India for instance, expressed itself in the ecliptic legend of Rāhu devouring the sun.

Such is the tale of the Battle of Mag Tured.

It ends with a scene that bears a certain analogy to the episode of the False Goddess, and which likely took its place: the Fomorians, in retreat, have stolen Dagda's harp. Immediately, Dagda, Lug, and Ogma set out in pursuit.

They enter a hall where the Fomorians have stopped to rest. The harp comes of its own accord into the hands of its rightful owner, who, with magical sounds, puts the Fomorians to sleep and returns safely, harp in hand, to the Tuatha Dé Danann.

It thus seems that the Irish still remembered that an episode involving the theft and recovery (by ruse) of a divine object belonged in the final part of the cycle. Similarly, the Germans tell — in place of the theft and recovery of the beer — the theft and recovery of Thor's hammer.

But here the essential motif of the Indo-European episode — the god disguised as a woman — is missing; there is therefore no direct filiation from the Indo-European theme to the Irish one, but only a simple substitution of two themes that, in their general structure, presented a certain analogy.

*_**

Such a complete correspondence can hardly be accidental: the account of the Battle of Mag Tured so closely parallels the Indo-European cycle of ambrosia that it must be derived from it.

It represents the stage of evolution the cycle had reached at a time when, through the influence of Christian monks, the pagan gods and demons had become humanised and secularised, and attention was directed chiefly to their conflicts.

The ambrosia, or its substitute, the beer of immortality, disappeared along with the divine character of the heroes. Yet we hope to have shown that at every turn it left its trace in the legends it abandoned: the famine at the beginning, the gigantic Cauldron, the broth drunk by Dagda, the central role of the smith–cupbearer Goibniu, the Well of Health, the immortality of the divine warriors.

All these details gain their full meaning, or any meaning at all, only if the ancient ambrosial framework is assumed.

Moreover, at the end of the tale, as if to underscore its alimentary significance, Bress, the dethroned king of the Tuatha Dé Danann, now the captive of his former subjects, saves his life by promising that *"the cows of Ireland shall always give milk, and that the Irish shall have a harvest in every season,"* and by revealing a formula — false, in fact — for ploughing, sowing, and reaping (§§ 149–161).

We shall soon see that the Feast of Ambrosia, of which this cycle is only the legendary translation, was essentially a springtime and communion festival; and then we will better understand how fitting these promises of Bress are in this context.

⁂

C. The False Goddess

Returning for a moment to an earlier point, we shall observe in Irish oral tradition the survival of the only ambrosial episode that the story of the Battle of Mag Tured forgot: that of the False Goddess — the god disguised as a goddess who, by means of a mock marriage, went to punish a demon who had stolen the ambrosia.

This tradition was collected by O'Donovan and cited by him in a note to his *Annals of the Four Masters* (1851, vol. I, pp. 18–21). It was studied by d'Arbois de Jubainville, who focused mainly on the elements analogous to the myth of Perseus (*Le Cycle mythologique*, pp. 208–218), and by Rhys, who sought in Welsh folklore traces of related legends (*The Hibbert Lectures*, 1886, pp. 314–320).

It connects to the Battle of Mag Tured both through the character of Gavida, who is none other than the smith-cupbearer Goibniu, and through Balar, the Fomorian with the evil eye, whose death it recounts differently: Balar is called Balor; Lug, his slayer, is unnamed but recognisable by his feat, and other figures reappear under scarcely altered names.

As for the story itself, it presents a combination of the Persean theme — the grandfather killed by a grandson whom he had tried to destroy — and the ambrosial theme of the demon-thief punished by a god disguised as a goddess. Two distinct tales have merged here: that of Balor's death, still independent in the twelfth century, and that of the god-smith disguised as a woman.

Balor is a bandit king who lives on Tory Island, off the northwest coast of Ireland. On the Irish mainland opposite Tory Island live three brothers — Gavida the Smith, Mac Samhtain, and Mac Kineely.

D'Arbois de Jubainville showed that these three brothers are the heirs of the three craftsmen who ensured victory for the Tuatha Dé Danann during the Battle of Mag Tured — namely Goibniu, Creidné, and Luchtiné — and, beyond these artisans, they are the heirs of the Tuatha Dé Danann themselves and the cousins of the "Sons of Dôn" in Welsh mythology.

The very name Gavida is a popular corruption of the same root that produced Goibniu (Irish) and Govannon (Welsh).

Mac Kineely, brother and counterpart of Gavida, possesses something extremely precious, known as *Glas Gaivlen* (which Rhys, d'Arbois de Jubainville, and all other scholars agree is a modern form of *Glas Goibnenn*), that is, "the *Blue of the Smith*."

In the version collected by O'Donovan, this is described as a cow, *"whose milk was so abundant that all the neighbours were jealous."* Thus appears in the story the well-known theme of the "stolen cow."

However, given the identity of Goibniu, the ancient brewer of Ambrosia, the strangely elliptical name of the cow, and especially the content of the tale that follows, it is highly likely that — at a time when Goibniu's Beer (*Fled Goibnenn, lind Goibnenn;* see above) was not yet forgotten — the expression *Glas Goibnenn* actually referred to that immortal beverage itself.

One day Balor steals the Glas Gaivlen. Mac Kineely swears to take revenge; a druid identifies the thief. Now, a fearful prophecy threatens Balor: the son born of his daughter Ethné will one day be his killer. To avert fate, Balor has locked his daughter in a tower on a precipitous rock on Tory Island; he has given her female guardians, charged with preventing Ethné from even learning of the existence of the opposite sex.

A fairy friend reveals to Mac Kineely the weak point of Balor. Immediately, Mac Kineely disguises himself as a woman and, with the fairy, is transported through the air to Ethné's tower. The fairy knocks at the door:

"*I am,*" she says, "*accompanied by a noble lady whom I have just rescued from the hands of a man as cruel as he is bold, who had carried her off from her family. I come to beg you to grant her refuge.*"

Despite their orders, Ethné's guardians, moved by pity, welcome the supplicants, who spend the night in the tower and then disappear by magic. But nine months later, Ethné gives birth to three sons, one of whom, after many adventures that have nothing to do with our cycle, kills the bandit Balor — it is no doubt, although not named, the famous god Lug.

Thus, collected in the nineteenth century, we have a true counterpart to the *Þrymskviða*, to the story of Pandora, and to the legend of Anna Perenna. It has reached us with differences of detail, with added complications, yet remains perfectly recognisable. Finally, it completes the group of legends derived from the Irish cycle of Ambrosia, which it has not been our fortune to know in a fully pagan version.

⁂

We cannot leave Ireland without raising an important question for which, unfortunately, there is a great lack of documentation: we will show, in the third part of this work, that the Indo-European cycle of Ambrosia corresponded to a festival celebrated at the beginning of spring. The Latin festival of Anna Perenna already allows us to understand this correspondence.

However, the Irish who composed the story of the Battle of Mag Tured, having forgotten Ambrosia and having transformed the ancient gods and demons into heroes, quite naturally lost awareness of this connection between their story and a springtime date. By the eleventh century, two separate battles were even distinguished: one lasting from June 5 to 9, the other beginning, twenty-seven years later, on November 1. Thus, all ritual correspondence with spring had disappeared.

Now, of the four great pagan festivals adopted by Irish Christianity, that of spring — early fixed, moreover, on February 1st — must, according to our hypothesis, once have corresponded in its rites to the themes of Ambrosia. Unfortunately, it is very poorly known, since, at least in Christian times — and perhaps precisely because of its too openly pagan character — it quickly declined in favour of the summer festival. But the little we do know of it fully confirms our expectations.

It so happens that February 1st became, in Christian times, the feast day of Saint Brigit. We know, moreover, that this saint is none other than the goddess Brigit, whose name appears, in similar forms, on Latin inscriptions from Great Britain, and who, in Ireland, merges with the great mother-goddess of the gods, Dana. The hagiographic legend of Brigit, linked to February 1st, to the ancient spring festival, must therefore reproduce Ambrosian themes.

Now we know only one episode of it, which corresponds precisely to one of the episodes of the cycle of Ambrosia:

Sent by Brigit, a diver descends into an underwater chapel and brings back from it the rules of the Brotherhood that Brigit founds. A Christian disguise still transparently revealing the expedition of the envoy of the gods to the marine spirit, to conquer the Vessel necessary for the preparation of Ambrosia: here it is a moral Ambrosia, a monastic recipe capable of granting Salvation.

The Welsh legend of the Grail will soon show us a very similar evolution.

II. The Cycle of Ambrosia Among the Welsh. The Holy Grail

We have already, in discussing the Irish material, mentioned a few Welsh themes, such as the duel between the smith Govannon and the demon Dylan. It has been seen that these themes are extremely evolved and no longer connected to any recognisable form of the cycle: the version they sporadically bear witness to — where Govannon must have played the role of divine nourisher comparable to that of Goibniu — has irretrievably disappeared. We will not attempt to find, in the pagan tales of Wales, traces of other redactions of the cycle.

Is there something Ambrosian in the story of Ceridwen's cauldron? Ceridwen, personification of nature and inspirer of poetry, prepares in a cauldron the brew of inspiration. She assigns its guard to a blind servant named Mordaw (cf. the blind diver of Saint Brigit) and the dwarf Gwion, while she herself goes to gather the magical herbs. The cauldron must boil for a whole year; but before the time has elapsed, three drops of the precious potion fall on Gwion's fingers, and when he licks them, he immediately acquires perfect knowledge. He flees, leaving the cauldron ready to burst from the pressure of the liquid.

Ceridwen pursues him, and there follows a "battle of transformations", at the end of which Ceridwen, changed into a hen, swallows Gwion, who has taken refuge as a grain of wheat. Nine months later, Ceridwen gives birth to a son who will become the celebrated Taliesin, the great master of sacred and profane wisdom, true incarnation of legendary druidism and of the historical bardic tradition of the Welsh. (Rhys, *The Hibbert Lectures*, p. 544 ff., after Guest, *Mabinogion*, III, 321–6, 356–61; Stephen, *Literature of the Kymry*[2], p. 425; on Ceridwen, Cyridwen, Caridwan, cf. W. F. Skene, *The Four Ancient Books of Wales*, 2 vols., Edinburgh, 1868, II, p. 324.)

It is not impossible that there is here, among elements of wholly different origin, the Ambrosian story of the cooperation and subsequent rupture between gods and demons during the preparation of a marvellous drink. The pair Ceridwen and Gwion (Taliesin) corresponds well, in the attributes of the characters, to the pair Dôn–Dana–Brigit and Govannon–Goibniu. Ceridwen, in particular, plays here the same role as Saint Brigit just now, and the role once played, in the Celtic version of the cycle, by that goddess who, in Ireland as in Wales, survives only as a name — the banner under which the other gods act: Dôn, Dana.

But the episode of the Cauldron is too evolved; it carries within itself conceptions that are too specifically Welsh for it to be pressed any further.

⁂

The Welsh version that seems to have preserved the most faithful and complete form of the Ambrosian cycle is the one that, though heavily laden with Christian elements and surrounded by later inventions of every kind, lies at the centre of the legend of the Holy Grail.

This Grail, which Breton churches almost turned for a time into a doctrinal weapon against the authority of the Church of Rome, is the marvellous Vessel which, after having served at the Last Supper, received the blood of Christ when the centurion pierced his side with a lance — the Vessel which Joseph of Arimathea, through a thousand adventures, brought to Celtic lands along with the Christian faith — the Vessel which finally presided over the mystical feast of the faithful.

A strange, heretical, and dangerous legend indeed, since it eliminates from the Eucharistic tradition the mediation of the Gospels, the Apostles, and especially of Saint Peter.

The origin of this conception of the Grail is as complex as the legend itself. As Edmond Wechssler shows in his excellent study (*Die Sage vom heiligen Gral in ihrer Entwicklung bis auf Richard Wagners Parsifal*, Halle, 1898, p. 12 ff.), the Grail legend arose from the fusion of several medieval beliefs and traditions about sacred vessels. Many sanctuaries claimed to possess either the cup that received Christ's blood on the Cross, or the dish or chalice of the

Last Supper — beliefs no stranger than those surrounding the nails or wood fragments of the True Cross.

Yet nowhere else did such beliefs give rise to such a rich flowering of "romances" as around the Grail. Why? Because in this case, they overlaid a pre-existing body of pagan Celtic legend, already organised and celebrated, which served as a nucleus for the later Christian elaborations.

This pagan core, as Wechssler rightly emphasises (p. 20), comes unmistakably from Wales. The *Graal* or *Gradal* — that vast cup or luxurious vessel — is first and foremost a talisman, a magical container that grants its possessor food and drink at will. To this pre-Christian conception attaches the cluster of legends we have been discussing — preserved in several medieval redactions, all clothed in a thin Christian veil, beneath which one can still clearly recognise the Indo-European cycle of Ambrosia and its vessel.

In the synoptic chart appended to his book (op. cit., p. 213), Wechssler arranged these variants in probable chronological order, and it turns out that the oldest versions are also those most closely parallel to the Ambrosian cycle. They concern the first meal provided by the Grail to the famished faithful, and the marvels that followed.

The oldest surviving account of these traditions is found in the romance of Joseph of Arimathea, written in verse by Robert de Boron. Though dating from the late twelfth century, the text was likely revised in the early thirteenth (see Paulin Paris, *Les Romans de la Table Ronde*, vol. I, Introduction, p. 115).

The Judeo-Christian elements dominate the opening of the story, but the pagan nucleus emerges once Joseph of Arimathea, followed by the company of early Christians, leaves Judea and settles "in distant lands," where the people devote themselves to agriculture — the unmistakable sign of the Grail's transformation from a sacred chalice of Christ into the Celtic vessel of abundance, heir to the cauldrons of Ceridwen and the beer of Goibniu.

A. Preparation of the Holy Grail Meal

(a) The Famine of the First Christians.

"At first, everything went as they wished; everything prospered among them. But a time came when God seemed to grow weary of favouring them; nothing responded any longer to their hopes. The wheat withered before it ripened, and the trees ceased to bear fruit. It was the punishment for the sin of impurity to which several among them had abandoned themselves." (Paulin Paris, Les Romans de la Table Ronde, vol. I, p. 140–141.)

Here we recognise the familiar opening theme of famine.

(b) Council of the Christians and of the Holy Spirit.

"In their affliction, they turned to Bron, Joseph's brother-in-law, and begged him to ask Joseph to reveal whether their misfortune came from their own sins or from his. Joseph then had recourse to the holy vessel. He knelt down in tears and, after a short prayer, implored the Holy Spirit to teach him the cause of their common adversity."

The Holy Spirit answered him: *"I will teach you how to separate the good from the wicked... In imitation of the Last Supper, you shall set a table; you shall command Bron, the husband of your sister, to go fishing in the nearby river and to bring back what he catches. You shall place the fish before the vessel, covered with a cloth, exactly in the middle of the table. When that is done, you shall call your people..."*

He also told him to leave an empty seat at his right hand, in remembrance of Judas's seat, and to tell the Christians *"that if they have kept their Faith, and followed the commandments, they may come take their place and share in the grace that Our Lord reserves for His friends."* (P. Paris, op. cit., p. 141–142.)

It is evident that the sin of lust here belongs to the Christian adaptation of the legend. The ancient pagan version knew only gods and demons, the privileged and the unprivileged, whereas we are now about to encounter saints and sinners.

(c) Nourishing expedition of a Christian to the river.

"Bron went to fish, and returned with a fish that Joseph placed on the table beside the holy vessel." (P. Paris, op. cit., p. 142.)

This is the sacrificed episode: in the ancient pagan legend, the purpose of the expedition must still have been the conquest of the vessel — the future Grail — necessary for the preparation of the feast. But in the Christian version, the Grail is already given in advance; it has a completely different origin, coming from Jerusalem; and the nourishing expedition of the Christian Bron to the river, rather strange in this eucharistic scene where the fish has no ritual role to play, becomes an ordinary fishing scene.

There is, however, a trace of the former importance of the episode: Bron receives for life the glorious title of the "Rich Fisher."

Finally, in a variant supplied by the *Prose Romance of the Grail* (P. Paris, op. cit., p. 306), it is not Bron who is sent to fish, but his son Alain: *"It is he whom the tale will henceforth call the Rich Fisher, as well as all those who after him were touched by the Grail and bore the crown... Let us add that the fishpond in which the great fish was caught received, from that day forth, the name of the Pond of Alain."*

These are further proofs that the episode was once far more meaningful than in the form we know it: originally, Bron was not meant to receive the Grail from Joseph's hands, but to bring it back from his aquatic expedition. Thus his surname is explained.

Furthermore, since the Grail no longer served to brew a communal drink, the preparation of the feast, like Bron's expedition, is reduced to its simplest form.

(d) The Feast. Separation of the Saints and the Sinners.

Joseph sat down, and Bron as well, leaving between them, according to the command of the Spirit, an empty seat.

"All the others approached the table — some to sit, others to regret that they could find no place there. Soon those who were seated were filled with an ineffable sweetness that made them forget everything. One among

them, however, named Petrus, asked those who had remained standing whether they felt anything of the blessings with which he himself was filled. 'Nothing at all,' they replied. 'Apparently,' said Petrus, 'you are stained by the vile sin for which Our Lord wills that you receive punishment.' Then, covered in shame, they left the house..."

"Those who had left the house refused to believe in this grace which filled the hearts of the others with such sweetness: 'What is it that you feel?' they said as they drew near. 'What is this grace of which you speak? This vessel whose virtues you praise—we have not seen it.' — 'Because it cannot strike the eyes of sinners.' — 'Then we shall leave your company; but what shall we say to those who ask why we departed from you?' — 'You will say that we have remained in possession of the grace of God, Father, Son, and Holy Spirit.' — 'But how shall we name the vessel which seems to please you so greatly?' — 'By its true name,' replied Petrus, 'you shall call it Grail, for it will never be granted to anyone to see it without finding favour in it...'" (P. Paris, op. cit., p. 142–143.)

Through this Christianised version, we can clearly recognise the ambrosial feast, which originally did not bestow "bliss of the soul" but immortality of the body, and from which the demons were excluded.

B. The sinner at the table of the Saints. His Punishment

(a) The sinner at the table of the Saints.

We find here, well preserved, the expected ambrosial episode: the demon who sneaks in among the gods to partake in their feast, and who is punished by a torment that tradition associated with earthquakes.

When the sinners left the hall of the feast, one remained behind — a man named Moses.

"Moses, who had not wished to separate himself from the other good Christians, though filled with malice and hypocrisy, deceived the people by his pious appearance and feigned sorrow. Moses begged Joseph earnestly to allow him to take a place at the table. 'It is not I,' said Joseph, 'who grants grace. God denies it to those who are unworthy of it. If Moses seeks to deceive us, woe to him!' 'Ah, sire,' said the others, 'he shows such grief at not being among us that we should believe him.' 'Well then,' said Joseph, 'I will ask for you.' He knelt before the Grail and prayed for the favour to be granted to Moses. 'Joseph,' answered the Holy Spirit, 'the time has come for the trial of the seat placed between you and Bron. Tell Moses that, if he is truly what he claims to be, he may count on grace and sit with you.' Joseph relayed the divine message to Moses, who replied that he feared nothing now. 'Joseph sat down, Bron and each of the others in their accustomed place. Then Moses looked about, went around the table, and stopped before the empty seat on Joseph's right. He stepped forward...'" (P. Paris, op. cit., p. 144–145.)

(b) The sinner punished.

"...He had only to sit down: immediately the seat and he vanished as if they had never been, without the divine service being interrupted..."

The *Prose Romance* (P. Paris, op. cit., p. 304) is more explicit: *"Those who were seated then saw three hands emerge from a white cloud; one of the hands seized Moses by the hair, the other two by the arms; thus he was lifted up high. Then, suddenly, surrounded by devouring flames, he was carried far from the sight of the company. The story says that he was taken to the forest of Amantes, and that his body remained there amid the flames, without being consumed."*

A Christian adaptation of a punishment whose original pagan form must have been somewhat different—perhaps involving a kind of engulfment, and possibly still connected, as in other Indo-European myths, with earthquake phenomena.

In any case, the *"tomb of burning stone"* of Moses (op. cit., p. 312) will later find a curious counterpart among the Slavs, where similar mythic imagery links divine punishment, fire, and the underworld — a reminder that this Christianised vision of damnation still preserves traces of its older mythological roots in the cycle of ambrosia and its cosmic retribution motifs.

C. Struggle Between the Saints and the Sinners. The Sinners Defeated and Buried

The verse romance of Joseph of Arimathea says nothing further; but immediately after the episode of Moses, the *Prose Romance* recounts the following (P. Paris, op. cit., p. 313 ff.):

Among Joseph's companions there were still two great sinners, Simeon and Canaan. Now, at the table of the Grail the next day, *"all were abundantly filled, except for Canaan and Simeon."* From this they conceived the desire *"to take hateful vengeance upon their brothers."*

During the night, *"when Canaan believed his twelve brothers plunged into their first sleep, he approached, holding in his hand a knife with a curved point. All twelve were struck down and put to death."* Meanwhile Simeon tried to kill a saint named Peter. But Peter was able to call for help, and Simeon and then Canaan were seized. They were condemned to be buried alive in the very place where the crime had been committed, and twelve graves were dug all around them for their victims.

Here we have the remnant of that great battle between gods and demons in which, after victories shared on both sides, the demons were at last defeated and buried alive beneath mountains or islands.

As in the Indo-European cycle, we perhaps still find here, in this scene from the Grail, the memory of a seismic interpretation: the tomb of Canaan gives off flames, *"as a dry log would if thrown upon a blazing fire."*

D. The False Woman

Robert de Boron's poem, which breaks off abruptly after the first Grail feast, knows nothing of this episode. But the *Prose Romance of the Grail* contains two consecutive variants of it.

First Variant (P. Paris, op. cit., p. 200 ff.)

The first version is connected to Mordrain. Mordrain, one of the main characters of the romance, is none other than the African king Evalac, baptised under this name by Joseph on the eve of the first mystical meal. Thus, this former "demon" takes on the virtuous role in the episode.

Immediately after the departure of Joseph and his companions, Mordrain was magically transported to a sharp rock that rose *"in the middle of the sea, on the line that leads directly from the land of Egypt to Ireland,"* a place that had once served as a den of brigands.

There, after receiving a visit from Christ in the form of a handsome young man, he saw another ship approach and come ashore; a woman rose from it, *"whose beauty seemed to him most marvellous."* She tried every form of seduction to draw him away from his Christian faith, then disappeared. But she soon returned, and Mordrain's heart was deeply troubled.

"The next day, Mordrain, exhausted by hunger and weariness, saw near him a piece of black bread, which he hastened to seize." But as he greedily lifted it to his lips, a marvellous bird, sent from heaven, snatched it from him. And Christ himself came to explain to Mordrain that the Beautiful Woman he had seen was nothing but a form assumed by a devil. Finally, though he had not eaten, Mordrain found himself filled and satisfied.

One recognises here the substance of the episode of the False Goddess, evolved — *mutatis mutandis* — in the same way as the episode of Pandora: Mordrain, now the possessor of Christian grace, has taken the place of the demon thief of ambrosia, yet still plays the "sympathetic" role, just as the thief of the *píthos* of happiness and immortality, Prometheus, once did.

The devil disguised as a woman, who seeks to steal Grace from

Mordrain, corresponds to Pandora, created by the Olympians to deprive the Titan of the blessings of the *píthos*; in both cases, the roles are reversed, and the tempter bears the inglorious part.

Apart from that, the lineage of the details is clear, and the alimentative element at the end — the bread snatched from Mordrain — retains something of the ancient meaning of the episode.

Finally, in the setting, one notes a close kinship between this story and the Irish episode that corresponds to it: Mac Kineely, disguised as a woman, goes to punish the demon-brigand Balor, who dwells on a sea rock off the coast of Ireland. Likewise, the devil disguised as a woman goes to chastise Mordrain, new possessor of Christian grace, who lives "between Egypt and Ireland" on a sea rock, once the den of a brigand. Perhaps already, in pagan times, there existed a shared staging of the episode among the insular Celts.

Second Variant (P. Paris, op. cit., p. 276)

The second version takes place during the voyage that is to bring Mordrain — finally rediscovered — and his companions to Brittany.

"The Castellan of the Coine (Iconium), who was part of the fleet, had long nourished a guilty love for the Duchess Flégétine; but he knew her to be too virtuous to be tempted. A demon offered to make the duchess favourable to him if he would make a pact with him. The castellan renounced God and paid homage to the evil spirit, who, immediately

taking on the appearance of Flégétine, allowed the castellan to satisfy his sinful passion. Then a violent storm arose at sea and threatened to engulf the entire fleet; a holy hermit, warned by a dream, advised the king to sprinkle holy water upon the ship carrying the castellan. At once, the false duchess was seen dragging the castellan of the Coine down into the abyss, crying out: 'I take with me what is mine!'"

Here we recognise a form of the episode very close to the one encountered in Italy: Mars, despairing of conquering Minerva's virtue, turns to Anna, who takes on the goddess's appearance. This variant preserves the erotic element that the preceding one had omitted, but in return it no longer contains any alimentary detail: all that the false Flégétine takes from the castellan is his grace and his life.

✸✸✸

Except for this last episode, which — at least logically — does not connect very closely with the others, the Christian cycle of the Holy Grail allows us to perceive, with remarkable fidelity, the general features and several characteristic details of the pagan cycle from which it arose: the Cycle of Ambrosia, in which the Vessel of divine nourishment gained importance at the expense of the nourishment itself.

Yet the Grail itself became a form of nourishment, or at least a talisman against hunger: it bestows special graces, but above all it intervenes when its possessor is threatened with starvation. Thus, in the land of Norgalles, thanks to the presence of the Grail, the

Christian captives believe, during the forty days of their imprisonment, "that all the finest spices are abundantly served to them." (P. Paris, op. cit., p. 257.)

Accordingly, the author of the prologue to the *Prose Romance* remains fully within the Indo-European tradition when he recounts that, on the day when the books he transcribes were miraculously revealed to him, voices praised the Lord in these words:

"Honour and glory to the Conqueror of Death, to the Source of everlasting life." (P. Paris, op. cit., p. 159.)

Indeed, it is thanks to this shared life-giving power that the vessel which had held the blood of Christ was able to gather around itself an entire body of legends that had originally referred to the vessel of Ambrosia.

When we later study the rites of the ambrosial head, we shall better understand how the Eucharistic meal was able to inherit their symbolism among the Welsh at the close of paganism, and how, by Christianising in turn the pagan legends that explained these rites, the Welsh monks could so faithfully preserve for us the Indo-European cycle.

III. The Cycle of Ambrosia Among the Gauls: Sucellus, Nantosvelta, The Wolf, and Little Red Riding Hood

In the fascinating domain of Gaul, literary texts are lacking. Thus, it is impossible to look for even an incomplete version of the cycle here. We can only turn to monuments — bas-reliefs or statues

— for fragmentary clues.

The Cycle of Ambrosia explains the enigmatic figure that appears on so many monuments, known as the "God with the Mallet." The Gauls called him Sucellus, which probably means "the good striker."

Here is what M. Dottin says about him (*Les Religions de la Gaule avant le Christianisme*, p. 253 ff.; see the illustrations):

"*Among the Gaulish gods, there are few whose worship was as widespread throughout Roman Gaul, and the museums of France contain a great number of his representations, either in bronze or in stone. The god is generally depicted standing, holding in one hand a small vase (olla), and leaning on the long-handled mallet, his characteristic attribute, with the other. Almost always bearded, with long hair, he wears tight-fitting trousers, sometimes replaced by bands winding up the legs like gaiters, and the Gaulish saie (cloak)... Over the tunic, he sometimes wears, thrown across the shoulders, a wolf skin, or a kind of pointed hood covering the back of his head... Sometimes he is shown with a dog or a wolf... once a serpent winds itself around the shaft of his mallet...*"

This Sucellus is not always alone:

"*The consort of the God with the Mallet,*" says M. Dottin, "*the goddess called Nantosvelta (that is to say, 'she who shines through valour') also appears on several monuments... The two deities are represented seated; the goddess has as attributes a patera and a cornucopia. The bearded god is dressed in the sagum; the left hand, with the mallet, survives only on one of the monuments; the right hand is stretched out over a two-handled vase (altar of Dijon) or grasps the hilt of a short sword (altar of Alise)."*

*
* *

We recall the role of Dagda during the preliminaries of the Battle of Mag Tured — that is to say, in earlier times, at the beginning of the ambrosial quarrel between the Irish gods and demons. He is the heir of the Indo-European god who went forth to conquer the Cauldron necessary for brewing the Drink of Immortality.

Now, d'Arbois de Jubainville, who did not yet know the ambrosial origin of the Irish cycle, had already wondered whether this Dagda *"might not be the archaeologists' God with the Mallet."* (*L'Épopée celtique en Irlande*, p. 448.) He based this idea on the similarity of attributes between Dagda and Sucellus: Dagda too possesses a cauldron, which explains his taste for soup; he is of gigantic stature and carries a club or mace.

It is indeed likely that the god bearing the *olla* (pot) represented on Gaulish monuments is none other than the Indo-European deity who conquered the ambrosial vessel. We need not be surprised to find beside him a goddess "brilliant in courage" — for among the Irish, Dana–Brigit, and among the Welsh, Dôn, perhaps even Cerridwen, have already shown us that, in the Celtic version of the cycle, the great mother-goddess played a role difficult to define, but certainly an important one.

The attributes of the god and goddess — the two-handled vase, the urn, the pot, the *patera* — are but varied representations of the ancient Indo-European Cauldron, just as the Grail (compare the Latinized Gaulish *Gradale*) of the Welsh legends and the cauldron of the Irish Dagda are later forms of the same primordial vessel.

We can therefore easily interpret the attributes that the monuments assign to Sucellus: the hood that sometimes covers his head, the wolfskin he wears, and the wolf or dog (sometimes the serpent, cf. Renel, op. cit., p. 255) that often accompanies him.

Are these not traces of the animal transformations of the god — or of his adversary — during the duel fought for possession of the ambrosial Cauldron? The Hindus and the Germans could just as well have depicted Viṣṇu beside a turtle, or Thor beside a black ox or a serpent (cf. the *Amṛtamanthana* and the *Hymiskviða*).

Finally, even the episode of the god disguised as a woman may perhaps find a place here. At least, this is suggested by a famous fairy tale, *Little Red Riding Hood*.

Indeed, this tale — though extremely evolved, and where one of the characters, by a common law of the genre, has become a little girl instead of an adult — seems to us nothing more than a popular reinterpretation of the Gaulish images under discussion. Yet it is not at all an arbitrary one: it still retains several echoes of the ambrosial cycle.

That little girl who carries "a small pot of butter," the wolf who tries to steal it from her during a first encounter, the same wolf who then disguises himself as a woman and succeeds in seizing the pot of butter — these are all characteristic details that recall both the representations of Sucellus and Nantosvelta, and certain episodes of the ambrosial myth-cycle.

No doubt, it would be futile to ask here whether the wolf represents a god or a demon; yet since it is he who dons the female disguise, he seems to play the role of the Indo-European god in disguise. The tale is, of course, too far evolved for any firm conclusion. But it is at least plausible that Perrault's Little Red Riding Hood preserves a final echo of the Gaulish version — or of a variant — of the ancient cycle of Ambrosia.

Conclusion on the Celtic Legends Derived from the Cycle of Ambrosia

Is it possible, then, to identify some characteristic correspondences among the Irish, Welsh, and Gaulish forms of the cycle — features that might help us define its common Celtic structure?

We have already noted one such correspondence: the prominent role of the Great Goddess, attested under various names by classical historians and found again in Dana–Brigit, Dôn, Cerridwen, and Nantosvelta. Nowhere else — not even in Greece — is this trait so clearly emphasised, except perhaps in the Sabine cycle, where Nerio–Minerva, "the virile one," closely recalls, even in name, Nantosvelta. This coincidence gains full significance when we remember that in Celtic lands — specifically in Helvetia — an inscription reveals the goddess Naria, meaning "the virile one" (see

Dottin, *Les Religions de la Gaule*, alphabetical list of divine names, p. 401). It is not surprising to find such close kinship between Italic and Celtic mythic traditions.

The legend of the Grail, the monuments of Sucellus, and the earliest tales of Goibniu all show that, until a relatively recent period, the ambrosial feast and its sacred vessels were still familiar, tangible elements of Celtic religious practice. In this, the Celts proved more conservative than their Latin cousins who, if our reconstruction is correct, had so far forgotten the meaning of the *ancile* — the vessel of the Salians' sacred feast, the ancient Ambrosia-Cauldron — that they mistook it for a shield. The Celts, on the contrary, align more closely with the Germans, among whom we shall later encounter ritual drinking ceremonies that preserve analogous meanings.

We shall later explain why this northern preservation contrasts with the southern alteration of the rite. It is surely no accident that, among both Germans and Celts, the earthly counterpart of Ambrosia is beer.

The most important consequence of this continuity of the ambrosial vessel is that, in the Celtic world, the cycle remained unified: the battle between the Fomorians and the Tuatha Dé Danann, and above all, the romance of the Grail, reproduce faithfully — and in the expected sequence — all the essential episodes of the ancient Indo-European myth.

What valuable insight we would gain from a true Gaulish version of the cycle! But the Druids, jealous guardians of their sacred science, ensured that no such version has reached us.

Chapter Seven

The Cycle of the Ambrosia among the Slavs

No part of the Indo-European world has been so barren that we have not found, in fairly good condition, traces of the cycle of Ambrosia. Will it be the same in Slavic lands? The Slav, no doubt, is an extremely conservative people — linguists and sociologists alike can attest to this. But the documents available to us are either very brief or very recent: very brief for the Western tribes, whose beliefs and ceremonies were written down by monks and travellers only toward the end of the Middle Ages; very recent for the Russian tribes, whose epic songs were not collected until the eighteenth century.

Moreover, the origins of these traditions are far from clear. Russia, in particular, has served as a battlefield for so many rival nations, as a gathering ground for so many invaders, and, since the most ancient times, has maintained political and economic relations with such diverse worlds, that one may — without being wholly right or wholly wrong — claim that the motifs of its poems came from the shores of Lake Baikal, the plateaus of Iran, the Finnish forests, and even the manuscripts of Byzantium. Nowhere — not even in Greece — have we encountered conditions of study so difficult.

⁂

I. The Cycle of Ambrosia and the Western Slavs. The Goddesses Živa (Živena) and Marena

We cannot hope to find, among the few remnants of Polish or Czech paganism preserved in Latin chronicles, any continuous traces of the ambrosial cycle. What we know of it relates to festivals rather than legends.

There is, however, a goddess whose name and rites deserve attention here: a goddess of Life (or "the Life-Giver") who is the heroine of springtime and lake festivals that have long been compared to the celebrations of Anna Perenna along the banks of the Tiber and the Numicius (Usener, *Italische Mythen, Rheinisches Museum*, N. F., XXX, p. 182–229). Here is what M. Léger says of her (*Revue d'Histoire des Religions*, 1900, I, p. 149):

"*Helmold (I, 52) cites, alongside Prove, the god of Altenburg, and Radigast, the god of the Obotrites, Siva, the goddess of the Polabians. This Siva became well-known. She was taken up by the forger of the Mater Verborum, who interprets her as dea frumenti... Siva also appears among the false Obotrite deities.*

"*The Czechs interpreted Siva as Živa (Life, the Living); the Czech dictionary of Kott gives us an entry Živa, Živena, goddess of human and natural life and the name of the planet Ceres. All these fantasies came from the text of Helmold. Yet it is not even certain that one should read Siva. Certain manuscripts give Sinna.*

"The interpretation Siva–Živa, 'the Living One,' seems more plausible. M. Maretić supposes it is an abbreviation of a compound name, Dabyzyva! 'May you live!' A Slavonic text from the fifteenth century, originating from Novgorod (cited by Krek, p. 384), mentions a goddess Diva. Długosz claimed to have rediscovered among the ancient Poles the cult of Diana under the name Dzevana. On the other hand, a god of life is also mentioned, called Żywie."

It therefore seems that the very imposture of the Mater Verborum and of the lists of Obotrite divinities is not without foundation. The agreement between the Czech Živena and the Polish Dziewana (Żywana? cf. Żywie, Żywy, "living," Żywić, "to nourish," Żywność, "food") indicates that the Western Slavs knew a nourishing goddess whom they called "the Life-Giver," analogous to the one whom the Latins called "the Everlasting Nourisher," Anna Perenna.

This goddess, associated with a Marena (Czechs), or Marzana (Poles), presided over spring festivals, of which, in the fifteenth century, the Cracovian Jan Długosz, in his *Historia Poloniae* (I. II, p. 94, Frankfurt, 1711), briefly described some rites. He relates that the first Christian king of the country, Mieszko, had forbidden all his villages to celebrate the festivals of March 7, during which effigies of the goddesses Marzana and Dziewana were solemnly plunged into swamps or lakes and then stoned (see Mannhardt, *Der Baumkultus...*, pp. 413–414).

The rite of immersion immediately recalls the Lavinian legend of Anna, where the ancient nourishing goddess falls into the river Numicius, where the water spirit holds her, and where she receives each year, on March 15, the joyful homage of the peasants. As for the rite of stoning, we would expect to find it separate from the previous one, applied to an effigy other than that of Žyvana, and representing a demon (cf. the flogging and expulsion of Mamurius alongside the river honours to Anna).

Perhaps there was a confusion of two distinct rites, the second (stoning) having originally belonged to Marzana. Indeed, this Marzana is found among other Western Slavs under the names Marena, Muriena, Mamurienda, or again under the characteristic name Śmierć, Smrt, meaning "Death." And the folk songs quoted by Mannhardt (ibid.) speak of "driving Muriena out of the village," of "chasing Mamurienda away"; it thus seems that Marena–Marzana was originally, in contrast to Živena–Dziewana, a malevolent divinity, comparable to the Russian Marina, whose sad exploits and exemplary punishment some byliny recount (see Rambaud, *La Russie épique*, pp. 88–91; cf. the Russian Maria of whom we shall speak later).

But nothing more, in Długosz's text, allows us to oppose Dziewana and Marzana: they appear as strict doubles, and Długosz can attribute to Marzana a feature we would expect rather from Dziewana:

"Ceres, moreover, the mother and goddess of the crops — which the region greatly needed — was called Marzana among them, and was held

in the highest honour and veneration." ("Ceres autem mater et Dea frugum, quarum satis regio indigebat, Marzana vocata apud eos in praecipuo cultu et veneratione habita fuit.")

Is there not, in this explanation — undoubtedly born of popular traditions, and in any case quite strange for a region famous for its agricultural wealth — the memory of alimentary themes comparable to those that open the story of Anna Perenna and several other ambrosial versions: a shortage, a famine threatening mankind, and a goddess "of enduring life" arriving in time to nourish them?

I. The Cycle of Ambrosia among the Russians: The Byliny of Mikhailo Potyk

All those who have tried to apply a single system of explanation to the entirety of the *byliny* have gone astray. The wisest course is to accept a little from each hypothesis: to recognise the borrowings of Russian traditions from Iranian, Germanic, or Mongolian legends, and to take into account the historical memories, the local concerns — religious or political — that contributed to shaping the texts that have come down to us.

But among all these hypotheses, there is one above all that it would be unwise to dismiss, though its use is delicate: it is the hypothesis which sees, in several *byliny*, a humanised and Christianised form of the mythological tales of the ancient Russians.

In 1876, in his *La Russie épique,* A. Rambaud wrote these lines, in which only his conception of Indo-European mythology has since aged:

> "The heroes, even those whose names appear in chronicles, seem to have taken the place of very mysterious figures whose origin goes back to universal mythology. The enemies they must fight have scarcely any definite form: they are monstrous embryos barely emerged from the universal matrix, still half-engaged in the pantheistic chaos. Soloveï the brigand is almost impossible to describe in precise traits; the Serpent of the Mountain can hardly be distinguished from the confused mass of the cloud or the mist...

> "In giving Vladimir the epithet of Fair Sun, the Russian song itself opens the way to mythological explanations. This immobile Vladimir of the byliny, who recalls so little the tireless Vladimir of history, is indeed the sun. These monsters that assault the royal city of Kiev are the dark or hostile forces of nature — sinister personifications of the night that banishes the sun, of the cloud that eclipses it, of the winter that makes it pale. The Fair Sun is the principle of light, but a motionless, passive, non-militant principle. To fight the spirit of darkness, another luminous, active, and warlike force is needed. It is then that Ilia of Murom attacks Soloveï, Dobrynia the Serpent of the Mountain, Alyosha Popovich the monster Tugarin, Dioule Stepanovich the giant Charles. Like Indra, tamer of the serpent Ahi; like Sigurd, conqueror of the dragon Fafnir; like Bellerophon and Perseus, Apollo and Hercules of the Greek traditions; like Saint George of the Christian legends — they strike the enemy with their blazing swords, inflict terrible blows, open wide wounds in his sides, and make streams of his blood flow, a fertile wave that will restore to the earth its fruitfulness and to the sun its splendour." (pp. 108–109)

Today we distrust this poetic mythology of clouds and suns; we rather seek in divine legends a social origin — the idea that men imagine the other world after the model of their own. But from that point of view, Rambaud's observation retains its full value: these heroes who leave only reluctantly the sumptuous table and the ever-full cups of Vladimir-the-Sun to confront the most marvellous adventures are the "natural gods" of that race of drinkers and knights which the Russians have been throughout their history. And for our particular purpose, we must expect to find, in a corner of the *byliny* of the Vladimir cycle, near that "feast of heroes," the echo of ambrosial adventures.

The mythic elements are, moreover, less humanised here than in the pseudo-historical tales of the Romans or in the Celtic legends of the Middle Ages. Rambaud noted the somewhat disparate aspect of the heroes of the *byliny*:

"In any song taken at random, one finds superimposed archaic fragments belonging to very diverse periods of poetic genesis. One sees at once Ilia identified with nature itself and asleep in the winter slumber, then as the god of thunder wielding the club of Perun, the bow of Apollo, the hammer of Thor, then as a Russian hero running from Murom through Chernigov to the aid of the prince of Kiev, then as a Christian knight protecting orphans and building churches to Saint Nicholas...

"But already for the popular singers of the Middle Ages, Ilia is truly a bogatyr (knight), just as Soloveï is truly a brigand. What they admire, what they glorify, is the living, human Ilia, and not the mythic Ilia. It is the same with the other heroes of the Kiev cycle." (p. 113)

⁂

Finally, on the vast Russian land, as much as elsewhere, various local doublets of the cycle — linked to different heroes and developed in different modes — must have coexisted in popular tradition. It is therefore not impossible a priori that the *byliny* have preserved several versions of it. In fact, however, it seems that apart from those of Mikhailo Potyk, the cycle does not appear anywhere else with its characteristic structure.

No doubt, the story of Ilia of Murom contains several variants of a kind of "alimentary quarrel" that recalls — with a different conclusion — the Indo-European scene of the demon at the table of the gods, and more particularly the Scandinavian form of that scene, the *Lokasenna*: Prince Vladimir, unaware that Ilia is in Kiev, has not invited him to a banquet; Ilia comes anyway, but under a false name, and Vladimir, not recognising him, assigns him an unworthy seat. Ilia becomes angry, insults the prince and the knights; a superhuman brawl ensues, and Ilia leaves Kiev forever.

Another time — again forgotten when the prince's invitations are sent — Ilia gathers all the beggars, all the hungry of Kiev; then, with his bow, he shoots down the golden domes of all the buildings, sells the treasures thus obtained, and with the money buys wine to intoxicate his new companions. For three days, Kiev is full of unheard-of scandals. Vladimir then invites Ilia to a second banquet, to which Ilia comes — but with his beggars... Everything ends in a monstrous drunken feast: the taverns of the city remain open for three days at the prince's expense.

No doubt, in this second variant, Ilia with his hungry followers and Vladimir with his guests stand opposed as, in the Indo-European cycle, the demons greedy for ambrosia and the feasting gods, or as in the Greek feast of Mekone, Prometheus with his protégés and Zeus with his companions. And surely, too, Ilia destroying with his fiery arrows all the golden cupolas of Kiev, and those beggars ravaging the city, seem almost mythological forms of demons attacking the dwelling of the gods.

But apart from the fact that its conclusion is entirely different from that of the Indo-European episode, the Russian episode of Ilia at Vladimir's table appears isolated: the story of Ilia contains nothing that corresponds even remotely to the other characteristic themes of the cycle — no marine conquest of a nourishing object related to immortality; no avenging expedition of a god disguised as a goddess; no petrification or crushing under rocks of the drinker demon.

⁎⁎⁎

The Byliny of Mikhailo Potyk and the Indo-European Cycle of Ambrosia

The only Russian cycle in which the themes of the Indo-European cycle of Ambrosia are found again, with their original meaning and in their ancient sequence, is the cycle of Mikhailo Potyk, another of the heroes serving Vladimir-the-Sun.

The story of Mikhailo is told in several *byliny*, collected at different times and in various places, and showing notable variations. As early as the beginning of the 19th century, Kirsha Danilov recorded the first part of it (*Drevnya Rossiiskiya Stikhotvoreniya — Ancient Russian Poems*, Moscow, 1818; reissued in 1878: *Bylina* XXII, p. 147 ff.). Later, Rybnikov collected seven versions (*Songs, Moscow*, 1861, vol. I, songs 36, 37, 38; vol. II, songs 15, 16, 17, 18), the most interesting being the first (I, 36), transcribed from the singer Riabinin; the second (I, 37), dictated by a ninety-year-old man; and the fourth (II, 15), from the village of Krasnyia Liagi.

Finally, one can find a fairly faithful French adaptation, drawn mainly from Rybnikov's versions (I, 37 and II, 15), in *Francisque d'Armaide, Héros légendaires de la Russie* (ch. IX, pp. 68–85, Milcaïlo Potik).

Russian scholars naturally examined these texts closely. Stasov, according to his usual method, claimed to have found for them improbable originals from India to Tibet (*L'Est Européen*, Feb. 1868, pp. 671–677). Finally, in his great work on Ilia de Mourom, Oreste Miller devoted a long analysis to the episodes and variants of the cycle of Mikhailo Potyk. Following the scholarly fashion of his time, Miller's mythological interpretations derive from storm myths and solar symbolism; yet he organised and critically examined the folklore materials gathered by his predecessors, and clearly brought out the distinctive features of our *byliny* (*Ilia Muromets i Bogatyrstvo Kievskoe: Ilia of Murom and the Heroes of the Kievan Cycle*, St. Petersburg, 1869, pp. 387–414; cf. pp. 463–473, 487, 502–509, 534–542).

The development of the story of Mikhailo corresponds exactly to that of the cycle of Ambrosia.

A. The Feast of Vladimir-the-Sun, The "Discovery" of the Immortal Maria

In all these variants, the evolution of the story has taken a course similar to what we have already seen in Italy with Anna Perenna, in Greece with the Oceanid Ambrosia, and probably also among the Western Slavs with the goddess Zywena: the ambrosia, which no longer had any place at the human table of Vladimir and his knights, has been personified, incarnated in a young woman who presents herself as immortal and who is seen emerging from the waters, from the sea. The material notion of nourishment — the idea of the divine feast — has been sacrificed in this transformation. It is absent from all the *byliny* collected by Rybnikov, in which Mikhailo Potyk, sent by Vladimir on a purely diplomatic or military mission, happens by chance to encounter Maria on a lake.

Only the *bylina* of Kirsha Danilov, whose form was fixed by the end of the eighteenth century, still remembers that the expedition for which Vladimir has mobilised Mikhailo is an alimentary expedition; Mikhailo has gone over the sea to fetch nourishment for the heroes' feast. Here is the entire beginning, important for our analysis: the gracious prince offers a banquet in his capital of Kiev — not, however, to all the heroes, but only *"to the three brothers, the three mighty Russian heroes,"* that is, Mikhailo Potyk (or Potok, as this variant calls him), Dobrynia Nikitich, and Alyosha Popovich:

Vo stol'nom gorod vo Kïevè
U laskova kniaza Vladimira
Bylo pirovanie, potchestnoï pir
Na tri brattsa nazvannye
Svetorusskie mogutchie bogatyri...

"In the stately city of Kiev,
with the gracious Prince Vladimir,
there was a great feast, an honourable banquet,
for the three brothers,
the three mighty heroes of holy Russia..."

Then Vladimir asks Mikhailo to perform a service for him: to go to the blue sea and kill some geese, white swans, and ducks, to provide food for the princely table:

A i ty, goï esi, Potyk Mikhaïlo Ivanovitch,
Sosluji mnè slujbu zaotchnuïu:
S'èzdi ty po moriu sinemu
Na teplyia tikhi zavodi
Nastrèliaï mnè guseï, bèlykh lebedeï,
Pereletnykh malykh utotchek
K moemu stolu Kniajenetskomu ...

"And you, hail to you, Potyk Mikhailo Ivanovich,
Do me this distant service:
Ride across the blue sea,
To the warm and quiet inlets,
Shoot for me some geese, white swans,
And little migratory ducks,

For my princely table..."

And so Mikhailo sets out. He will kill nothing, but he will triumphantly bring back to Kiev the White Swan par excellence — the beautiful Maria, Mar'ya Belaya Lebed'.

Here we find, scarcely altered from the *Edda*, the Indo-European theme of the divine nourisher sent by his peers across the ocean on a quest for sustenance. Yet even in this old text from Kirsha Danilov we can already see the beginnings of the evolution that led to Rybnikov's versions — an evolution quite comparable to that of the Latin tale of Anna Perenna and Aeneas. The nourishment that Vladimir charges Potyk to obtain is a simple kind of food — birds flying over the sea.

Why these birds, and especially why this Swan-Woman whom the hero brings back to Kiev, and whose capture is celebrated with a joyful wedding feast? There is a double explanation. First, whenever nourishment is mentioned, the *byliny* immediately think of such birds: Volkh Vseslavievich already feeds his company with geese, white swans, and little gray ducks:

Poletèl on daletche na sine more
A b' ët on guseï, bèlykh lebedeï
A u sèrym, malym utkam spusku nèt ,.
A poïl-kormil drujinuchku khorobruïu ...

"He flew far out over the blue sea,
And he struck down geese, white swans,
And for the small gray ducks he showed no mercy;

He gave drink and food to his brave company..."

The White Swan has, moreover, remained by tradition the most delicate dish a sovereign could offer to his guests: at the coronation of the last Tsar, Nicholas Alexandrovich, in 1896, the white swan was served — adorned with its own feathers — at the banquet table. We can better understand, then, how in the "secularised" legends of Mikhailo Potyk, Ambrosia, the rare and precious food above all others, could have been transformed into the white swan.

Furthermore, the personification of Ambrosia as a woman could only have helped introduce this detail into the legend. It is well known — and even Miller, following Buslaev and Afanasiev, has shown it — that the figure of the Swan-Woman, a sorceress, a fairy, and the treacherous wife of heroes, is a commonplace throughout the folklore of Central, Southern, and Eastern Europe (Miller, op. cit., p. 388). Ambrosia, personified among the Slavs as among the Greeks and Italians, quite naturally entered into this class of female spirits; and we shall soon see that she borrowed from them their most common traits — treachery and perversity — thus introducing into the ancient cycle folkloric themes of an entirely different origin.

We can therefore easily understand how this first episode, having lost all nutritional significance, took on the forms we find in the *byliny* collected by Rybnikov.

In one of them, for instance, Mikhailo, sent by Vladimir to collect tribute in Podolia, pitches his tent near a lake. The king's daughter, Maria — a "cunning" creature (Lukavaya Mar'ya) —

comes wandering around the hero's tent as he sleeps. Awakened by his horse, Mikhailo looks out and sees a flock of swans on the lake. He is about to shoot when one of the swans swoops down toward him and takes on human form — it is the king's daughter, who says to him bluntly:

Primëm my s toboï zoloty vèntsy
I stanem my s toboï jit' da byt'
Jit' da byt', dèteï svodit' ...

"Marry me,
And we shall wear golden crowns,
And live together,
And raise children..."

Moreover, all these *byliny* — the most modern as well as the oldest — have preserved the memory that Maria, the White Swan, was somehow connected with Enduring Life, with Immortality.

Since Ambrosia itself had been forgotten, these notions found another material support in popular belief, and Maria was given a "life-giving" adventure — one known among many peoples, already present in Apollodoros' *Bibliotheka* (the resurrection of Glaucus, son of Minos): dead, her husband brings her back to life by means of a Living Water (*zhivaya voda*), which he forces a serpent to fetch for him.

This theme is not, strictly speaking, ambrosial, but it clearly entered popular tradition to explain the enduring vitality attributed to Maria — a trait left without justification once the memory of

Ambrosia was lost. She is, in essence, the spirit of life, the immortal woman. One *bylina* even preserves the characteristic words uttered after Maria's resurrection:

"The people marvelled, and the rumour spread that she must be immortal." (D'Armade, op. cit., p. 76.)

Thus, beneath the layer of foreign themes drawn in by the analogy of certain ideas — Ambrosia and the Life-Giving Water, the Resurrected Woman and the Immortal Woman — we rediscover a very ancient pattern, one without parallel in ordinary folklore, which closely recalls the Roman, and especially the Lavinian, story of Anna Perenna: the nurturing goddess, the woman become immortal, the woman carried off by the hero Aeneas from the riverbank where the sea had cast her.

Mikhailo, sent on a food-gathering expedition for the heroes at Vladimir's table, conquers from the sea a feminine spirit who — after an adventure involving the life-giving water — comes to be regarded as Immortal.

It is remarkable that in Russia, as late as the eighteenth century, we find such precise memories of the most delicate part of the cycle — one that the Greeks had almost completely forgotten, even in their oldest testimonies, and which the Latins had profoundly altered. Yet it is the following episodes that show most clearly how extraordinarily conservative these Slavic legends are.

B. The False Bride

The episode of the false bride is preserved even more faithfully than in the Latin cycle of Anna Perenna. As among the Latins, since Ambrosia had disappeared as a drink and had, in a sense, been personified in the Immortal Maria, a natural confusion arose between the drink and the woman whom the demons in turn stole or demanded. More precisely, there is no longer any theft: the "gods" have lost nothing and have nothing to recover; the "demons" simply demand from the beginning, without reason, that Maria be handed over to them (Rybnikov, I, ch. 37, and II, ch. 15).

1. Forty *tsars*, forty *tsareviches*, forty kings, and forty sons of kings demand that Vladimir hand over Maria.

And behold, upon the mountains of Sorotchinsk appeared forty *tsars*, forty *tsareviches*, forty kings, and forty sons of kings, who sent ambassadors to Kiev, to Prince Vladimir, Brightness of the Sun.

"We wish," they said, "that the prince surrender to us the beauty whose fame is universal; if he will not give her up of his own free will, we shall destroy the whole city of Kiev."

A ne otdast s dobra, Ves' Kïev grad povyrubim!

"And if he will not yield her willingly, we shall cut down all Kiev!"

Vladimir, dismayed, is ready to give Maria up:

"Is it possible that an entire empire should perish for a single woman?"

he explains to Mikhailo:

Aï je ty duchetchka Mikhaïlo Potyk Ivanovitch!
Dlia odnoï baby ne pogubat' tsèlomu tsarstvu...

"Ah, dear little soul Mikhailo Potyk Ivanovich!
For one woman, shall we let a whole kingdom perish?"

For the life of the entire court of Kiev is at stake; and in this, the episode joins the Scandinavian *Þrymskviða*, to which it often bears resemblance in detail: the Æsir, to avoid their own ruin, were likewise ready to send Freyja to the demon Thrym in exchange for Thor's stolen hammer.

2. Mikhailo Potyk disguises himself as a woman and goes to the *tsars*, the *tsareviches*, etc.

Mikhailo flies into a rage and refuses to hand Maria over. He answers Vladimir: "Give, if you wish, your princess Opraksia, but I will not give my wife willingly."

Otdaï svoïu bogatyrslcu Kniaginu Opraksiiu,
A ia ne otdam jeny s dobra!

"Give your heroic princess Knyaginya Opraksia,
But I will not give my wife willingly!"

He puts on a woman's dress over his armour and rides toward the Sorotchinski Mountains; there, taking his bow and quiver, he goes to the place where the *tsars* and the *tsareviches* are encamped...

He greets them and presents himself: *"I am Maria... but which one of you shall I choose for a husband? ... Here is what I propose: I will shoot the arrows from my quiver into that meadow, and the first who brings me one of them will be the one to whom I shall belong."*

3. Mikhailo Potyk kills the *tsars*, the *tsareviches*, etc.

The *tsars*, the *tsareviches*, and the others successively bring him the arrows; and to each, he cuts off the head.

Zatchal po tchistu poliu poèzjivat',
Zatchal golovuchku otvertyvat',
Otvertèl im vsè golovuchki...

"He began to ride over the open field,
He began to twist off their heads,
And he twisted off all their heads..."

Then he returns to Kiev.

We have just recalled the *Þrymskviða*: O. Miller (op. cit., p. 411) already mentioned, regarding Mikhailo disguised as a woman, the feminine disguise of "Loki," forgetting that Loki is, in the *Þrymskviða*, merely the "maidservant" of Thor, the "bride" of Thrym. The reader may easily compare the details for himself. The Russian version is, all in all, more faithful than the Latin version of Anna's expedition or the Greek version of Pandora's expedition. The only alteration it shows is minor — and even then, it aligns with the episode in the Hindu epic (Viṣṇu disguised as a woman among the demons): it is not a single suitor who demands the fair

Maria, but forty — or a hundred and sixty — "demons" who take part; that is to say, all of them.

B. Mikhailo Turned to Stone for Drinking Maria's Potion

The entire third part of Mikhailo's story, like the first, is filled with themes that are not Ambrosian. Among them is the theme of the woman's betrayal — a motif common in the *byliny*, and well known among the Serbs and Bulgarians in the following form: a woman (or a mother), carried off by a stranger, aids her abductor against her husband (or her son) who pursues them; she binds her husband to a tree so that her abductor may kill him; in the end, the husband, freed by a passerby, kills both his rival and his wife.

(Among the Russians: *Ivan Godinovich, Nastasya, and the pagan tsar* — Rambaud, op. cit., p. 92; among the Serbs: *John, his mother, and the leader of the brigands* — A. Al. Yakchitch, *National Poems of the Serbian People*, 1918, pp. 28–38; among the Bulgarians: *Iskren, his wife Militza, and the voivode Pervan* — Dozon, *Bulgarian Folk Songs*, 1875, pp. 55–60 and 226–232.)

Stasov, Benfey, and O. Miller have also gathered and studied a large number of Eastern tales more or less corresponding to this pattern (see O. Miller, op. cit., p. 400 ff.). This is the tale that concludes the story of Mikhailo Potyk. It contains nothing Ambrosian; even Maria is no longer "the immortal" Maria. Yet it is introduced and prepared by a scene which, appearing neither among the Serbs, nor among the Bulgarians, nor in any other bylina, and which corresponds exactly to the expected Ambrosian theme of the "demon who drinks and is turned to stone," must here be retained.

While Mikhailo was slaying the *tsars*, the kings, the sons of kings, and the *tsareviches*, the King of Volhynia carried off Maria. The hero sets out in pursuit of the fugitives. Seeing her husband drawing near, Maria, armed with a cup of green wine — a magical, narcotic drink — goes out to greet him.

"Let us drink," she says, *"and return to Kiev."*

Scarcely has he drunk when Mikhailo falls asleep... Then Maria, throwing the body of her husband over her shoulder, cries out:

"Wherever Mikhailo shall fall, let a burning stone arise! And when three years have passed, let that same stone sink down into the bosom of the nurturing earth!"

The wished-for transformation is fulfilled.

Here we recognise the Ambrosian theme of the punished demon: this man, drinking the potion offered to him by the Immortal Maria and immediately falling victim to a seismic metamorphosis, is undoubtedly the heir of the Indo-European demon who, for having taken a single sip of ambrosia, was turned to stone by the gods or crushed beneath a mountain.

This figure, moreover, was not originally meant to be Mikhailo, but rather a stranger, an abductor — a "demon." Yet the theme of the woman betraying her husband is so dear to the authors of the *byliny*, the pattern so natural to them, that Maria could only be placed among these faithless women, and Mikhailo, her husband, made the hero of this sorrowful tale.

But it must be strongly emphasized that this artificial ending, added onto the Ambrosian episode of the petrified demon, contradicts everything previously known of the Immortal Maria. For Maria, to take her place among the unfaithful and the punished, had to become entirely human — and cease, in any sense, to embody ambrosia.

As for Mikhailo's final petrification, it corresponds precisely to the Indo-European punishment of the "drinking demon." Perhaps, moreover, there is a memory of the ancient battle between gods and demons in the independent tale of the struggle waged by the Russian champions — Ilia Muromets, Alyosha Popovich, Dobrynia Nikitich, and four other valiant knights — against a mysterious, ever-growing legion, in which they finally recognise the army of angels.

Terrified, they flee into the mountains and hide deep within dark caves. But there the expected fate overtakes them:

"As soon as one of them reached the mountain, he was immediately transformed into stone... They were all turned into burning rocks." (G. d'Armade, op. cit., pp. 287–292)

Were not these burning rocks, at their origin, a faithful expression of the seismic punishment of the demons?

⁎⁎⁎

It would be futile, as we have said, to claim a general method for explaining the *byliny*. We shall simply note, then, that in this particular case, a group of *byliny* from the cycle of Vladimir still recounts — humanised and embellished, yet recognisable — the ancient fabulous story of ambrosia. They allow us to glimpse a fragment of the pagan mythology of the Slavs, of which only a few divine names and a few more or less attested rites had hitherto given no living idea.

The Cycle among the Balts?

Alone among the Indo-European family, the Baltic peoples are missing from the record. Neither the Lithuanians nor the Letts have given us their version of the cycle. This fact, though much to be regretted, is hardly surprising: we know very little of ancient Baltic mythology, and what we do know relates almost exclusively to solar myths, the core of the popular songs or Dainos (see Mannhardt, "Die lettischen Sonnenmythen," *Zeitschrift für Ethnologie*, 1875, VII, pp. 73–104, 209–244, 261–330).

We can nevertheless glimpse, alongside the famed Perkūnas, the figures and setting that must have given the Baltic cycle its distinctive character. It has already been noted (by Louis Herbert Gray in *The Mythology of All Races*, vol. III, Slavic, part V, "*Baltic Mythology*," p. 329) that the tales concerning the "Daughters of the Sun" (*Saulės duktelė*) often speak of a "sea," of a "silver sea," which some have sought to identify with the so-called atmospheric ocean of the Indo-Iranians.

The Letts likewise know of the "Great Water," the Daugawa, which they equate with the river Dvina. Now, upon the shore of this sea — or of the Daugawa — dwells the divine Smith, who forges spurs and belts for the "Sons of God" (*Dêvo sunélei*), and for the "Daughters of the Sun," crowns and rings. Mannhardt (op. cit., pp. 319–324) compares this figure to the Greek Hephaistos and the Finnish Ilmarinen. Louis Herbert Gray (op. cit., p. 330) considers him even closer to the Vedic Tvaṣṭṛ, who forges the cup in which rests the drink of the gods.

Thus, between this "Great Water," this divine Smith, and these Daughters of the Sun, we can easily imagine what form the Indo-European cycle of ambrosia might have taken among the Balts — but no trace of it has come down to us.

Chapter Eight

The Cycle of the Ambrosia among the Armenians

I. Armenian Mythology

We do not know the paganism of ancient Armenia. The scattered testimonies in literature do not allow even an approximate reconstruction of it. Yet, since 1874, thanks to the efforts of Bishop Servantzian and his successors, Armenian folklore has entered the realm of scholarship.

And, as Manuk Abeghian observed in 1899, in his inaugural dissertation at Jena on *"Armenian Popular Beliefs"* (*Der Armenische Volksglaube*), a people who, until our own time, have remained strangers to all scholastic culture and have lived in contact with completely illiterate nomads, must have preserved a considerable portion of their ancient national traditions.

These popular beliefs, as presented by Abeghian, appear under a Christian guise. But if one sets aside this final metamorphosis, what strikes one at first glance is the considerable influence that ancient Iranian ideas and myths have exerted on Armenian religious thought.

The dominant idea — here as in Iran — is the opposition of two principles: the good Light and the evil Darkness, each served by angels and demons, who preside respectively over Life, Day, and Happiness on the one hand, and over Death, Darkness, and Disease on the other.

The God with a Christian countenance intervenes but rarely; those who most readily concern themselves with human affairs — akin to the Iranian *yazatas* — are the saints and angels, Christ, the Virgin, and the very important archangel Gabriel.

In detail, at every turn, Iranian influence is evident: the conception of Hell and Paradise, the narrow bridge that the souls of the dead attempt to cross, from which the wicked fall into the flames, dragged down by the weight of their sins — all this comes directly from Persia. We shall soon encounter, in connection with our legends, borrowings just as characteristic.

It has also been known, since Hübschmann, that the later development of the cult of Mithra profoundly affected Armenia, and that the language itself bears more than one trace of it.

Yet many popular traditions — whether tinged with Iranian elements or not — rest upon a native foundation. And we shall see, in connection with ambrosia, that alongside certain metaphysical beliefs of clearly Iranian origin, Armenia still preserves the cycle of Indo-European legends.

If it has survived at all — and we shall better understand this circumstance when we come, in the third part, to the Feast of Ambrosia — it is because the games and rejoicings that were its ritual expression have endured to our own time: Armenian peasants still re-enact, once a year, the principal and most characteristic episodes of the cycle.

Just as we know the legends of Anna Perenna, for instance, only through her festival and the explanations that Ovid felt compelled to provide, so too here we know the Armenian form of these same legends only through the festival — closely akin to the revelries of the Roman plebs — which once a year translates them into human gesture. Yet this testimony, thanks to the meticulous care of Manuk Abeghian who recorded it, is remarkably detailed, and despite its late date, it remains one of the clearest surviving traces of the ancient state of things.

We shall now examine in turn the Iranian borrowings and the Armenian festival, and we shall soon see that the two intersect at least at one essential point.

II. Legends Borrowed from the Iranian World

In Paradise, at the disposal of the elect and the angels, the Armenian places the "Fountain of Immortality." Likewise, the elect and the angels, seated at the divine table, partake of the *anushak kerakur* — "the food of perpetuity" or "of eternal life."

Here, however, the Iranian borrowing is evident in the very words themselves: Hübschmann has shown (*Armenische Grammatik*, I, p. 99) that the terms *anoish*, *anushak* — meaning "perpetual," "eternal," and consequently, in their only surviving sense in the modern language, "sweet," "fragrant" — derive directly from Persian.

We have already seen, in discussing the Iranian legends, the exquisite dishes that Ōhrmazd has served to the Righteous in Paradise (*Minokhired*, ed. Westergaard, II, 152).

There is more. We recall the twin pair of Ameša Spənta whom Mazdeism made the "patrons" of waters and plants: Haurvatāt and Amərətāt. Now, the Armenians still know today of the two herbs *Haurot* and *Maurot* — herbs of happiness and long life — whose role in popular tradition we shall soon see. Manuk Abeghian is clearly right to associate them with these two Mazdean abstractions and to explain their evolution accordingly:

"Doubtless Haurot and Maurot were originally spirits of the waters and the plants, who now appear only as flowers."

The lineage in both form and meaning is certain.

Moreover, this expansion — already observed in Iran — of the life-giving and immortalising virtue to all plants and all waters is found again in Armenia, where trees and springs are believed to cure every illness and restore youth.

Finally, even the *Gaokerena* has its counterpart here: the Armenian seeks out in his gatherings "the king of plants," the potent *loshdag*.

⁎⁎⁎

III. The Armenian Festival

But it is not merely through Iranian borrowings that we find Ambrosia in Armenia. Ancient popular legends — the legitimate heirs of our Indo-European cycle — became attached to springs and plants, the modern successors of ambrosia; and thanks to these natural associations, they have survived to the present day.

These legends reveal themselves through the rites of a spring festival, which we shall examine according to Manuk Abeghian. At its centre stands a potion — a *philtre* prepared with spring water and certain wondrous plants.

In its present form, the festival is essentially one for young girls or women; all the principal roles are feminine. We shall later ask whether this was always the case; for now, let us simply record the episodes.

1. The Petrified Water Thieves.

On the eve of the festival, while several young girls climb the mountains to gather certain flowers — chiefly the *Haurot* and *Maurot* blossoms — seven other young girls, who officially take the name of "thieves," go to draw water from seven springs (or rivers, or fountains).

The utmost secrecy is required; the thieves must remain unknown to one another and must not allow themselves to be seen. When they have filled their vessels, they must go without ever setting them upon the ground, without speaking, without looking about them.

And yet, they hear the mountains, the valleys, the trees — indeed, all of nature — crying out against them. But if they were to turn around, they would be turned to stone.

Setting aside the feminine nature of the participants, we can clearly recognise here the close fusion of two Ambrosian episodes: first, at the beginning of the cycle, the expedition of a god to the aquatic possessor of the Vessel and the conquest of that Vessel; then, the scene of the demon among the gods. A demon, in great secrecy, goes to steal a portion of the ambrosial liquor; discovered or betrayed by certain natural beings (the Sun and Moon among the Hindus, here the mountains, the trees, and so on), he is bound to a rock or turned to stone.

Indeed, we must assume that in the legendary cycle underlying these rites, the "thief" when caught was in fact punished. What is now, among humans, a mere empty threat must once have corresponded, among the gods, to an actual event.

This fusion of an episode of the preparation of ambrosia (the expedition to the marine being) with an episode of the theft of ambrosia became natural from the moment when the first no longer concerned the conquest of a tool — a Vessel — but rather that of the water itself. In both cases, it was a liquid either won or stolen, and the difference between the unprepared water and the potion later brewed from it was too slight for the episodes connected with one or the other to have remained distinct.

Finally, the conquering god — here merged with the thieving demon — has not only changed sex but has also been multiplied: there are seven thieves. This number, belonging to the ritual cycle, does not prove that the corresponding legendary cycle ever knew several thieves, male or female; we are dealing with a popular game in which there must be amusement for more than one participant, and where the single hero — or heroine — of legend has been multiplied sevenfold.

2. Preparation of the Miraculous Liquor in the Vessel "*Havgir*."

On the evening of the day when the water-thieves and the flower-gatherers have brought their spoils back to the village, everything is poured together into a vessel bearing a special name: *Havgir*. The mixture thus prepared possesses marvellous properties, which we shall consider shortly.

Here we have a very recognisable form of the preparation of ambrosia: in India, for example, Viṣṇu likewise advised the gods to pour all the precious herbs into the water of the Ocean Vessel. As for the *Havgir* vessel, it clearly represents the vast Cauldron we have already encountered.

It is unfortunate that Manuk Abeghian did not record any tradition concerning the origin of this utensil, which surely does not appear ordinary to those who use it, since even today they designate it by a special name.

3. The False Bride.

The mixture obtained is a potion of happiness: all who wish to take part in the game must throw into the *Havgir* vessel a token — some personal belonging. Once the rite is performed, the young girls place two pieces of wood in the form of a cross, dress this rudimentary mannequin in the attire of a bride, and adorn it with pearls and jewels. This figure receives the name *Vicak* ("Fate" or "Lot").

It is fastened to the *Havgir* vessel, and throughout the night the young girls guard both the potion and the mannequin from the boys who try to steal them. The next morning (or, in some places, only after eight or fifteen days) the girls and young women go out at dawn to the outskirts of the village, near a spring or a river, where they set up the mannequin. Then, as in the Latin festival, they share a meal upon the grass.

They then draw the mannequin forth, passing it from hand to hand and covering it with caresses, until it comes to rest with a young girl who sets it before her, receives the name of "Bride," and serves as the interpreter of the *Vicak*. To mark more clearly their shared identity, the girl and the mannequin are covered with the same red veil. Songs are then sung, each stanza foretelling a future event; and after each verse, the "Bride" draws a token from the vessel, allowing the prophecy just pronounced to be applied to one or another of the celebrants — like a new Pandora, emptying before Epimetheus the jar of blessings and of evils, that ancient jar of immortality.

These rites are largely determined by the new meaning of the episode — by the new virtue attributed to the potion in the *Havgir*. It is now a philtre of happiness, and the scene one of fortune-telling, rather than a drink of immortality or healing and a scene of divine banquet. Thus are explained the rite of the tokens, the designation of the little bride who, beneath the red veil, lends her arms to the artificial bride — the mannequin — and, finally, the prophetic songs.

Yet here again we find, as the essential foundation, an episode from the cycle of Ambrosia:

This artificial Bride, whom the "thieves" (the former thieving demons) embrace eagerly, to whom they willingly surrender the precious vessel, and who alone — through the hands of the young girl — is supposed to touch the potion contained within that vessel, is the false bride who, in the Indo-European cycle, went among the demons, bewitched them with love, and took back from them the vessel of ambrosia.

It is a version of the legend closely akin to the Greek one: even more than Viṣṇu, Thor, or the aged Anna donning the veils and charms of Lakṣmī, Freya, or Minerva, the Armenian mannequin recalls Pandora. Like her, all adorn it eagerly; like her, it is but an artificially created doll, not a disguised being; like her, it is bound

— here, in the most literal sense — to the vessel of blessings, if not of evils.

Let us not be surprised to see the same women who, a moment ago, called themselves "thieves" now playing, in dressing the false Bride, the role of the gods. This is not a legend told or recited, but one acted out; and the roles of gods as well as of demons must, on earth, be taken by human beings. Yet it is certain that this necessarily imperfect "casting" casts some obscurity upon the original sequence of themes.

Manuk Abeghian cites a few verses of a song that accompanies, in his native village of Astapat, the making of the false Bride. Let us gather these humble brothers of the ironic stanzas of the *Þrymskviða*, the sumptuous *ślokas* of the *Bhāgavata Purāṇa*, the grave hexameters of Hesiod, and the lively distichs of Ovid. It is moving to rediscover, in a wholly modern oral tradition, the echo of poems which for centuries have delighted or amused the learned.

This song from Astapat has, moreover, the merit of emphasising the ancient, divine — almost cosmic — value of the mannequin scene. Here are the verses, translated from the German version given by Manuk Abeghian:

Go find a great artist,
And have him fashion the bridal gown of my beloved;
Let the sun be its fabric,
Let the moon serve as its lining;
Trim it with clouds,
Unwind from the sea the thread of silk,

String the stars in a row for buttons,
Sew into it all love…

The gods who vied with one another to adorn Epimetheus's fatal bride showed no greater generosity.

4. (Attack and Defense of the Havgir Vessel.)

I recall here only briefly this episode, already included in the preceding one: during the night, the young girls keep watch around the vessel and foil the assaults of the boys. Should we see in this the ritual outcome of the ancient war between gods and demons?

We may now conclude that the monopoly presently held by women over this festival is neither one of its essential nor its original features. It is an evolution explained, on the one hand, by the prominence within the ritual as a whole of the distinctly feminine episode of the false bride, and on the other, by the abundance of songs accompanying the pantomime. It is no coincidence that, in the Roman festival of Anna as described by Ovid, the role of women — especially of young girls — has likewise become predominant.

We need not emphasise the importance of this Armenian testimony: the extremely recent date at which it was collected, and yet the remarkable preservation of the Ambrosian themes it contains — the confusion within it between the motifs of "theft"

and those of "preparation," the close correspondence it confirms between our legendary cycle and a ritual cycle in which humans "perform" the stories of the gods, and finally the transformation of the liquor of immortality into a potion of fortune-telling — all combine to give it, within the gallery we have assembled, a distinctive character and a place of high distinction.

Let us retain above all this lesson: Indo-European comparative mythology must consult the folklore of the belated peoples just as much as the mythological poetry of the precocious ones. Pandora, seven centuries before our era, was already as far from her origins as, today, the *Vicak* of the young Armenian girls.

Chapter Nine

The Cycle of the Ambrosia among the Kucha

A study by M. Sylvain Lévi, published in the *Journal Asiatique* in 1913 (10th series, vol. II, pp. 311–380), has shown that the Indo-European language known as Tocharian B was that of the people of Kucha, about whom the Chinese annals inform us almost continuously from the second century B.C. to the end of the first millennium.

M. Sylvain Lévi brought to light the distinctive civilisation of this distant vanguard of our race and the important role it played in the intellectual and religious relations between China and India. In this corner of Central Asia, around the beginning of the Christian era, there was a flourishing of Buddhist monasteries which, in the realm of texts, doctrine, and philosophical vocabulary, became the great suppliers of learning to China.

It may seem more than daring to seek traces of an Indo-European mythological cycle among a people who, from the earliest known documents, appear already in the full fervour of Buddhism and clearly under Indian influence — above all, among a people known to us only through Chinese accounts.

Yet a fortunate accident of civilisation has preserved for us — not the texts themselves, but the titles, the bare record — of legends that are authentically Kuchean: legends that are neither Indian nor Chinese, born neither of the monastic invasion from the south nor of the military invasion from the east, and which must therefore be linked to that substratum of popular tradition where fallen mythologies long survive.

This fortunate accident of civilisation lies in the universally admired excellence of Kuchean music throughout Asia, and in the existence, since the fourth century, of a Kuchean orchestra at the imperial court of Peking.

M. Courant, in his *Essai historique sur la musique classique des Chinois* (p. 192 ff.), has traced the history of this orchestra through the Chinese texts. First established when Lü Guang destroyed the kingdom of Kucha (384 A.D.), it was suppressed and reconstituted several times, and finally became, in the sixth century, the favoured orchestra of Yang Di of the Sui dynasty, who commissioned Po Ming Da, the master of music, to compose melodies in this style — melodies enumerated in the *Book of the Sui*.

This music, moreover, was cultivated from father to son within a Brahmanic family named Zhao, whose most distinguished representative was Zhao Miao Da, under the Qi dynasty. There thus existed a truly Kuchean tradition, carefully preserved, whose culmination we find in the orchestra's repertoire, as recorded by several witnesses. In his study, M. Sylvain Lévi reproduces the list from the *You Luo Tien* (ch. LXXVI, 3, 17), which itself borrows it from the *Tong Zhe* of Zheng Zhiao (1108–1166).

Some of these titles are strange: "Thrown into a Bottle" (air no. 7), "The Double-Chignon on the Dancing Mat" (air no. 8)... But here are the titles of the three melodies numbered 4, 5, and 6:

"The Jade Woman Passes the Cup."

"The Holy Immortal Detains the Guest."

"The Throwing of Bricks Prolongs Life."

The last concerns a "throwing of bricks," of which we know nothing, except that its result is "to prolong life." In the second, there is mention of an "immortal" being in whose dwelling another character has entered, and who "detains" him. The first speaks of a feminine being called the "Jade Woman" (and we know how commonly jade was used in these regions for the making of artistic objects), who passes around a certain "Cup."

Titles of musical airs, certainly — but of mimed airs, since dancers accompanied the orchestra; airs themselves composed upon popular traditions, jealously preserved within a single family; airs doubtless accompanied by songs. In short, these titles are very probably those of legends that must once have existed alongside their musical interpretation.

The evidence is too scant to allow absolute proof. Yet, for the first two at least, the surviving titles closely correspond to two consecutive episodes of the Indo-European cycle of Ambrosia — precisely the two episodes that, everywhere else, have been the best and most enduringly preserved in both tradition and popular festivals: in Rome, for example, the episode of Anna Perenna nourishing the plebs, and that of Mamurius punished by the Romans; in Armenia, as we have just seen, that of the "fabricated Bride" distributing the "fates" drawn from the Vessel, and that of the "petrified water-thief."

In the Indo-European epoch, these were, as we know, the episodes of the false Bride and of the demon among the gods.

Here then, by way of simple hypothesis — but with a measure of plausibility — is what the stories mentioned under numbers 4 and 5 of the musical repertoire might have contained:

4. A feminine being of surpassing beauty, fashioned (in jade) by the gods, has regained the Cup of Ambrosia that some demon had stolen, and now passes it among the gods (or among the "Saints," to preserve a Buddhist colouring).

5. A demon (that is, a "guest") has come to the dwelling of a god, the rightful possessor of ambrosia (the "Holy Immortal"). He has doubtless attempted to steal the ambrosia, and the god "detains" him in punishment (immobilises and petrifies him, as the Indo-European cycle has it) — unless, indeed, the Kuchean version corresponds to the Germanic, Celtic, or Greek form, in which the gods, possessors of ambrosia, first receive the demon amicably among them, only for him soon to attempt to despoil them.

As for the title of number 6, the "Throwing of Bricks" may perhaps represent a form of popular game — a wholly earthly ritual re-enactment of the ancient mythic bombardment between gods and demons. The terms are obscure; yet it is at least striking that, following the two preceding episodes, the Indo-European cycle itself also includes a highly dramatic scene of battle and of "missile-throwing," whose happy outcome secures for the gods both long life and dominion.

This interpretation may perhaps be thought too bold. Yet the sequence of titles deserves consideration: it would seem that here we have a group of legends related to one another, as is the case, for example, with the *Hymiskviða* and the *Lokasenna* of the *Edda*. Can it, then, be mere chance that these three consecutive titles so naturally encompass three of the four episodes of the Ambrosia cycle?

Chapter Ten

Indo-European Conclusions

We can now answer the questions that, at the end of the first part, the comparison of the Indian and Scandinavian data had left unresolved.

1. The Greek legends (Tantalos, Prometheus, the Titans and the gods), the Latin (Mamurius and Numa), and the Celtic (the Fisher Kings and Saints in the Romance of the Grail) agree with the Indo-Iranian legends in speaking of a cordial understanding, a collaboration between gods and demons at the beginning of the cycle.

2. Like the Scandinavians, the Iranians (Tištrya and Apaoša), the Greeks (Herakles and Nereus…), the Latins (Numa and Picus), and doubtless the Celts (the expedition of Dagda — cf. Sucellus) and the Slavs (Mikhailo and Maria's father from across the sea) tell of a struggle between the possessor of the Vessel and the god charged with conquering it. Originally, this struggle was no doubt a contest of transformations.

3. It is only among the Indo-Iranians that the appearance of ambrosia is accompanied by the birth of certain divine beings. Even

so, it is not certain that this constitutes a fact common to both Indo-Iranian branches.

4. The Indo-Iranians, Greeks, Germans, Celts, and Slavs all agree in placing, at some point in the cycle, an explanation of seismic phenomena — generally at the end of the episode of the punished demon. The form of the punishment varies somewhat: the giant is crushed beneath a mountain or an island, or swallowed up by the earth (Greek giants; the Fisher Kings of the Grail cycle); or bound to a mountain (Prometheus, Ahriman, Loki); or turned to stone (the Armenian Water-Thieves; Mikhailo Potyk); or, in the humanised versions, stoned (the *pharmakós*), or scourged and cast down (Mamurius, Nicodemus). As for the eclipse, the agreement — though obscure — is limited to Indo-Iranian and certain Greek traditions.

5. Certain Greek (Gigantomakhies and Titanomakhies) and Celtic (the Battle of Mag Tured; the slaughter of the Fisher Kings in the Romance of the Grail) accounts confirm the Indo-Iranian testimony regarding the final mêlée of gods and demons. Everywhere else, the conflict remains limited to one god and, especially, to one demon.

We must add, in conclusion, two further features to the outline we have sketched of the cycle:

1. Judging by Greek, Latin, Celtic, and Germanic evidence, a smithing spirit — no doubt more demon than god — took part in the preparation of the ambrosia, and perhaps later sought to steal the liquor.

2. The episode of the Fatal Bride appears in several forms that may be grouped under three headings:

(a) The Fatal Bride is a male being disguised as a woman (Viṣṇu, Thor, Mac Kineely, Mikhailo Potyk...).

(b) The Fatal Bride is a mannequin disguised as a woman — an artificial female (Pandora, Athena?, the Armenian Vicak, perhaps the Kuchean "Jade Woman"...).

(c) The Fatal Bride is a female being, disguised as a man (Vāc, the Djahi, Anna Perenna, Nerio, Athena?).

We shall later attempt to account for this threefold variation.

***

The existence of two opposing classes of superhuman beings is well established, as is the victory of one class over the other. We have called them gods and demons — without regard, moreover, to their relations with humankind — and we have seen, within the cycle, that various "malignant" natural phenomena were regarded as the work of the demons. That is all we can say of them.

Among the gods, it would be difficult to define distinct personalities. There is, to be sure, among the goddesses at least one who stands out — the one with whom the demon thief of ambrosia falls in love. The principal divine hero of the cycle — the one who subdues the marine spirit, who crushes a demon beneath a rock or mountain, and who disguises himself as a goddess to ensnare another demon — was doubtless the great Indo-European luminous god whose existence we otherwise know: in any case, this luminous nature reappears in most of the younger gods who later took his place (Indra or Viṣṇu, Tyr or Thor, Zeus or Herakles).

If the school of Max Müller was wrong to see, in every mythic theme and every divine being, mere translations of natural objects or phenomena, it is nevertheless probable that such mythic transpositions were not unknown to the Indo-Europeans. It was certainly neither earthquakes, nor eclipses, nor storms that gave birth to the Cycle of Ambrosia; yet these were later inserted into it, as interpretations of one or another episode.

What place did the marine spirit — the possessor of the Vessel — occupy between gods and demons? For him, one might be tempted to restore a name, though a rather vague one: Apām Napāt, "the Lord of the Waters," in India; Hymir, that is, Humiaz (*tivaz*), "the god of the winter sea," among the Norse; or Ἅλιος Γέρων ("the Old Man of the Sea") among the Greeks. But it is better to refrain from linguistic speculation and simply to note that the Indo-Europeans recognised at least one marine spirit, a "master of the waters," skilled in metamorphoses, who in springtime was vanquished by the luminous god previously defined.

This marine spirit is properly neither god nor demon; he partakes of both. Indeed, if there is one point beyond doubt, it is the kinship — the cousinship — between gods and demons. From the Vedic testimonies onward, as in the epic, the Devas and Asuras are close relatives, even equals, until the war for *sóma* or *amṛta*; the Titans and the Kronid gods are first cousins; intermarriage has mingled the blood of the Fomorians and the Tuatha Dé Danann, to such a degree that the chief combatants at Mag Tured could almost choose their sides at will; in the Romance of the Grail, the Fisher Kings and the Saints belong to the same social and familial order; Mars and Loki are at once gods and demons.

What separates these beings forever — otherwise so alike by nature — is precisely the possession or the deprivation of ambrosia. Through ambrosia, the gods acquired another nature, an unparalleled privilege that, more than their strength or their form, distinguishes them from mortals — whether demons or men.

Within this notion of ambrosia lay philosophical possibilities that the Indo-Europeans may perhaps have glimpsed, and which explain the vast development given to the cycle.

✦✦

To measure the originality of the Indo-European legends concerning the food of the gods, it is enough to glance at another mythology, comparable in both time and setting. Apart from the highly developed legends of the Tree of Life and the Fountain of Life (see Causse, *Revue de l'Histoire des Religions*, 1920, vol. 81, pp. 289–315), the Semitic world also knew of a true "ambrosia," a divine food about which we are poorly informed and which was perhaps merely the celestial transposition of the substances used in sacrifice.

To this ambrosia is attached a distinctive theme: that of immortality offered by a god (or a goddess) to a mortal — and refused by that mortal.

In Eridu, says a religious text, lives Adapa, the priest-hero of Ea:

"He prepares each day the food and drink of Eridu."

One day he is raised up to the heaven of Anu and appears before the supreme god. Ea had given him this command:

"When you stand in the presence of Anu,
Food of death will be set before you — eat it not.
Waters of death will be offered you — drink them not..."

Now Anu wishes to give him the divine foods—the food of life and the waters of life. But Adapa refuses:

"They offered him the food of life,
And he did not eat.
They offered him the waters of life,
And he did not drink.

Then Anu looked upon him and marvelled, saying:
'Come now, Adapa, why did you not eat, why did you not drink?
You shall not live...
Take him, and return him to his earth.'"

From early on, this text was compared with the beginning of the Epic of Gilgamesh, in which the goddess Ishtar — whose love brings death — falls in love with the hero and vainly offers him superhuman power and destiny. It has also been compared with the episode, probably of Semitic origin, in which Kalypso vainly proposes to Odysseus, in exchange for her love, to make him "immortal and ageless for all days" ("ἀθάνατον καὶ ἀγήραον ἤματα πάντα" *Odyssey* V, 136; cf. ibid., 208).

Here, indeed, we are in the presence of an "ambrosial" theme that seems common throughout the Semitic world, from Chaldea to Phoenicia. Yet is it not precisely the reverse of two well-known Indo-European themes? First, that in which a demon surreptitiously joins the company of the gods to drink ambrosia with them; and second, that in which a (false) goddess, maddening a demon with love, wins back from him the stolen ambrosia.

Here, by contrast, an immortal being vainly invites a mortal to share his feast, and a goddess, mad with love for that mortal, goes so far as to yield the ambrosia to him. It would almost seem, at least for the two themes of theft, that Semites and Indo-Europeans tell the same story, but from opposite points of view — the one giving the noble role to Mortals, the other to Immortals. Let us not hastily conclude from this that the Semites were the demons and the Indo-Europeans the gods.

The true difference lies elsewhere: in the Semitic legends, it is always an isolated mortal who is summoned to partake of the pre-existing food of the immortals — and who refuses. In the primitive Indo-European cycle, on the contrary — and in almost all its derived cycles — it is a matter of two classes of beings, originally equal, between whom inequality arises only after the appearance of ambrosia. The Indo-European cycle (and we shall understand this term more fully at the end of our study) is social; the Semitic cycle remains individual.

Transposed to the human plane, the one would concern the clan or the tribe; the other belongs to those numerous legends in which a solitary figure escapes his mortal destiny by magical means. In spirit as in substance, then, the Indo-European cycle differs from the tales collected by Sir James Frazer in his two volumes on belief in immortality among the peoples of the Pacific (*The Belief in Immortality and the Worship of the Dead*, London, vol. I, 1913; vol. II, 1922); or from those studied by L. R. Farnell in his *Greek Hero Cults and Ideas of Immortality* (Oxford, 1921, ch. XIV, p. 372 ff.: "*Individual Belief in Immortality: The Mysteries and Orphism*"); or again from those analysed by Miss Harrison in chapters X and XI of her *Prolegomena*.

It is only in particular cases, as we shall see, and under the influence of original theologies, that ambrosia has sometimes taken on a moral meaning and thus could appear as an individual reward. Nothing of the kind appears in the primitive cycle.

⁎
⁎

Certainly, among the various Indo-European peoples, the cycle was transformed in a national manner, embodying in its characters the grand or ironic, refined or rough types in which successive generations loved to recognise themselves. But the very notion of ambrosia itself did not evolve in many directions. Through the diversity of details, one may distinguish in all versions of the cycle three or four main lines of development:

1. The rarest case, first of all: for a longer or shorter time, depending on the people, ambrosia remained what it had been among the Indo-Europeans — a drink that freed one from death. Yet, though this meaning still survives in the Hindu *amṛta*, in the ale of the Tuatha Dé Danann, and perhaps in the *phármakon* of immortality in the Gigantomakhies, almost everywhere else this original value has been altered.

2. Often, ambrosia appears only as a drink more pleasant, more nourishing, and so forth, than others — but not essentially different from them. Those who partake of ambrosia and those who are deprived of it no longer stand opposed as "freed from death" and "subject to death," but rather, with varying shades of meaning, as "well-fed" and "poorly fed." This is perhaps already the case with the Homeric ambrosia, of which it is nowhere explicitly said that it confers immortality, and which is distinguished chiefly by its fragrance and its flavour.

It is certainly the case with the ale of the Æsir. The evolution is completely achieved at Rome, where the nourishment that Anna Perenna gives the Romans, or the meal served by Petronilla, like the feast of the Salii, has become wholly human. The same holds true, among the Slavs, for the banquet of Vladimir-the-Sun; among the Greeks, for the feast of Theseus and his companions returning from Crete; and finally, among the French, for the "pot of butter" that the

Wolf and Little Red Riding Hood have doubtless inherited from Sucellus and Nantosuelta, armed by the Gauls with a characteristic *olla*.

3. More rarely, ambrosia has remained a potion of immortality — or, by weakening of meaning, of happiness, of health, and so on — but has ceased to be an actual drink. Thus the contents of Pandora's *píthos* are "the absence of death," and more generally, "the absence of evils." Likewise, the liquor prepared with the *Maurot* and *Haurot* herbs in the vessel *Havgir*, which the mannequin *Vicak* bears as Pandora bore her *píthos*, has become merely a charm for good fortune: one bathes omens or tokens in it, but no longer drinks it.

4. Finally, wherever Ambrosia encountered an organised religion — a theology — it sooner or later assumed, under various forms, a moral value seemingly foreign to its primitive conception: those who partake of ambrosia and those deprived of it are now opposed as "pure" and "impure," "holy" and "sinful."

Without returning to the moral evolution of Orphism, Vedic India, Zoroastrian Persia, and — failing any clear evidence of the Druidic society's views on this point — Christianised Western Europe all display the same development, often with curiously parallel results. Frequently, ambrosia becomes an immaterial principle; yet even when it retains a physical form, this is only secondary. In the Mazdean paradise, Amərətāt provides nourishment for the elect — the righteous. The *Brāhmaṇas* refine endlessly upon the nature and effects of *sóma*'s virtue, which the gods, they say, establish *"within their own inner being"* (cf. above, p.

33).

The feast of the Grail, a spiritual banquet, serves at the same time to discern Saints from sinners. What Saint Brigit's diver wins in the undersea chapel is neither ambrosia nor the Vessel in which ambrosia is to be prepared — it is monastic rule. The work of priests, monks, and theologians is everywhere the same: beneath their skilful hands, ambrosia, like so many other mythic objects, becomes the symbol of new conceptions. What had hitherto possessed only a social or magical role acquires, through them, a moral meaning.

If the adaptation appears too difficult, the ancient notion simply disappears. Alongside the Christianised banquet of the Grail, we see within a few centuries the disappearance, under missionary assault, of the feast and the "craft" of Goibniu. Pure Zoroastrianism, at least as we glimpse it in the *Gāthās*, proscribes *haoma*.

One final transformation of ambrosia deserves consideration: that which turned the drink itself into a feminine spirit. Amərətāt, Ambrosia, Anna Perenna, and doubtless also the Slavic Ziwena and the "White Swan" Maria are, in various forms, personifications of the marvellous nourishment. This is not surprising, since everywhere that a magical force or power of seemingly supernatural kind exists (fire, rivers, and so forth), it is easy to conceive that force or power as a spirit external to the object itself.

Yet in the case of Ambrosia, a particular detail of the cycle may have favoured this transformation: the demons do not merely covet the ambrosia — they also demand a goddess, the one whom the Hindu cycle (where *amṛta* remains an inanimate substance, a drink) represents as being born from the churned ocean at the same time as the *amṛta*. There was therefore a natural solidarity between ambrosia and that goddess; confusion was then easy.

It is worth noting, moreover, that wherever the "Fatal Bride" is truly a woman (and not a disguised man or a mannequin), it is often the personified ambrosia herself who plays this role (Anna Perenna — cf. Maria, at once woman and personified nourishment, claimed by hostile *tsarevitches*...). This is a sign that the personification of Ambrosia is not unrelated to the well-attested presence, in the primitive cycle, of a goddess. Among the Celts, as we have seen, this goddess met with another fate: without becoming one with ambrosia, she took an honoured place within the clan of the gods and appears to preside over the ambrosial battle.

We have now reached the outer limits of legend: if we wish to explain its evolution and discern its origin, it would be unwise to separate it any longer from the rites that accompanied it — and which, at several points, we have already glimpsed.

PART THREE

The Festival of Ambrosia

The Festival of Ambrosia

The Latin and Armenian examples have shown us that the ambrosial legends were not self-sufficient. They were accompanied by rites that translated their themes into action — or, conversely, whose themes translated the rites into words. The examples of the *Fasti* and of Manuk Abeghian's book even suggest that if the ambrosial legends were preserved so long and so faithfully throughout the Indo-European world, it was precisely because they were sustained by a popular celebration — a festival.

The structure of these religious or magico-religious dramas is well known, thanks to the modern testimony of semi-civilised peoples. As one might expect, rites and themes, mimed scenes and recited scenes, continually influenced one another in the course of their evolution, and it would be rash to attempt to interpret the one without regard for the other. Moreover, the importance of ambrosia in the Indo-European legends can only be understood if one mentally reconstructs that spring festival of communion, in which men, while singing of the ambrosial victory of the gods, sought to share for themselves in the eternity and strength of their divine protectors.

Unfortunately, the study of these rites presents special difficulties, which we have not encountered in discussing the legendary themes, and which we do not feel fully equipped to resolve. In many cases, versions of the legendary cycle have come down to us without any record of the festivals that must have accompanied them: thus Hesiod says nothing of the festival of which his Promethean episode seems clearly to have been the poetic translation; the *Amṛtamanthana* likewise appears isolated, an epic fragment without ritual support.

But the reverse accident is no less frequent: in many cases, the ambrosial festival must have survived — with that tenacity peculiar to popular rites — after the properly ambrosial legends had been forgotten. We may therefore encounter it, in certain regions, either detached from any legendary cycle or enriched with new legends. But then, how are we to recognise it? How distinguish what is truly ambrosial from what is not? This is the first difficulty, arising from the divergent evolution of themes and rites.

There is, however, a second difficulty, arising from the very nature of the rites themselves.

A rite, so long as it lives a popular life, tends to preserve itself with remarkable tenacity; but once it becomes the property of specialists — when it enters a liturgical framework—it is exposed to radical alteration. Once fixed in a liturgy, it may indeed remain unchanged for centuries; but it is in that initial passage from popular practice to priestly ritual that its transformation can be most complete. Thus, wherever we encounter religious confraternities — Brahmans, Mazdean priests, Salii, Druids — charged with carrying out ceremonies, we can no longer discern with confidence the ancient, simple outlines of the original popular festival.

Through this process, contaminations, stylisations, changes of perspective, and excesses of theological subtlety arise, masking the original meaning, structure, and even form of the rites. For example, it is highly probable that the great Vedic spring festival of the *sóma*, the great banquet offered to all the gods, took the place of the earlier spring festival of Ambrosia. But in the details — what belongs to the Indo-European past, and what is a Hindu innovation? Mystery. At first glance, the Indo-European elements seem neither the most numerous nor the most apparent.

A third difficulty is peculiar to our spring festival. In two major Indo-European regions — among the Celts and the Germans — or at least among the Irish and Norse, the only branches for which we possess ancient, explicit testimonies, this spring festival is precisely the least well known.

In pagan Ireland, four annual feasts were celebrated: *Samhain* (beginning of winter, November 1), *Beltaine* (beginning of summer, May 1), *Lugnasad* (beginning of autumn, August 1), and *Oimelc* or *Imbolc* (beginning of spring, February 1).

Now, while the documents are detailed for the first three, we know nothing of how the pagans celebrated *Imbolc*, which later became the ecclesiastical and popular feast of Saint Brigid (cf. Czarnowski, *Le Culte des héros*, p. 108). Whether because the date was not truly springlike, or because of a particular hostility from the Christian clergy, *Imbolc* died very early, taking its secret with it.

A similar fate befell the Scandinavian spring rite. A chronicler reports that, after abolishing the sacrificial libations (*blótdrykkjur*), Olaf Tryggvason instituted four great Christianised drinking-feasts (*hátíðardrykkjur*): "*jól ok páskar, Jóansmessu mungat ok haustmál at Míkhjálsmessu*" — that is, Yule and Easter, the feast of St. John, and the autumnal feast of St. Michael (Cahen, *La Libation*, p. 138). These Christian festivals replaced the older pagan seasonal feasts (ibid., pp. 10–11). Yet the spring feast, unlike Yule, had already lost its pagan name in being absorbed by the new religion (*Páskar* = Easter; *veizlur at Páskum*, "the Easter feasts") and then disappeared entirely and very early, leaving us no means to determine its original content.

Thus, the conditions for research are poor. The wisest course is therefore to compare first the two explicit testimonies to ambrosial festivals that we possess — the Latin and the Armenian — and to interpret them in light of a principle that is difficult to dispute: in antiquity, rites and myths must have corresponded exactly. From this comparison, we may at least form an approximate image of the Indo-European Festival of Ambrosia.

※

The Festival Among the Latins and Armenians

1. The Ambrosial Festival was a spring celebration.

For the Latins, the date (March 15) is given with precision. For the Armenians, Manuk Abeghian is not as exact. Yet, if one considers that the rites involve a night spent in the open air, the gathering of flowers in the mountains, and a meal beside a spring or a river, and if one also notes that a "festival of springs and flowers," closely resembling it, is reported by Abeghian as taking place on the day of the Ascension, it becomes clear that we are dealing with a springtime festival.

2. It was celebrated beside a body of water — a spring or a river — near the city or village.

At Rome, it took place by the Tiber; at Lavinium, by the Numicius; in Armenia, by the springs or rivers near the village. The Armenian rite of placing the *Havgir* vessel and the *Vicak* mannequin into the spring or river clearly suggests that these natural "containers" symbolically represented, in the ritual ceremony, the marine Cauldron of the legendary cycle.

Elsewhere — among the Irish, Welsh, and Western Slavs — we shall find lakes fulfilling this role; elsewhere still (among the Alemanni), it is simply a large vat. But the Latin and Armenian evidence alike seem to prove that, from the common Indo-European period onward, ambrosial rites were localised around springs and other natural waters, whose cult, in the Indo-European world, is otherwise well attested.

3. It was a festival of food and communion.

By the Tiber, as at the foot of the Caucasus, one of the essential rites of the festival was a meal taken beside the water. The young Armenian women appear moderate in their libations, whereas the peasants of Rome or Lavinium roll unrestrained beneath their leafy tables. Moreover, the feast of the Salii, whose origin we have seen to be probably ambrosial, still remained the culminating point of the *ancile* liturgy.

4. Women played a considerable part in this festival — almost an exclusive one among the Armenians. In all likelihood, however, at the origin, as among the Latins, the festival must have been mixed, as was fitting for the human representation of mythical events in which both gods and goddesses took part. It was noted earlier, with some reasons for the phenomenon, that even in the Roman festival, women and young girls already held a preeminent role, and that the Armenians merely pushed to the extreme a natural tendency inherent in such rites.

So much for the setting and the participants. What, now, was the content of the festival? The general law governing such magico-religious dramas allows us to suppose that, originally, the rites and the legends corresponded exactly. One could thus propose the following hypothetical outline:

LEGENDS

1. Council of the gods. Conquest of the marine Vat and brewing of the ambrosia.

2. The ambrosia being prepared, a demon comes to mingle with the gods who are about to drink it. Recognised or denounced, he is expelled and punished (petrified? bound to a rock? crushed beneath rocks?).

3. The gods drink the ambrosia.

4. A demon having stolen the cup of ambrosia and being in love with a goddess, a god disguised as a goddess is led to him in a bridal procession, drives him mad with love, and wins back the ambrosia.

5. Battle of the gods and demons. The demons are vanquished.

RITES

1. Preparation of a certain ritual drink in a Vat, near a body of water (scene of an "aquatic duel"?).

2. The ritual drink being prepared, a man representing a demon comes to steal it—or mingles with the men representing the gods who are about to drink it. These seize him, expel him from the place of the feast, and punish him (flogging? originally stoning?).

3. The ritual drink is drunk by the "men-gods."

4. The celebrants parade in procession a man disguised as a woman (or a female-shaped mannequin), carrying a cup filled with the ritual drink. — Sexual rites.

5. Various rites of collective combat, jousts, and the like.

In fact, nowhere — or almost nowhere — is the ambrosial festival found in such a complete form. We have already noted several times, and will return to this point at the end of the study, that the ritual drink corresponding to the mythical ambrosia, probably a fermented beverage similar to beer, had ceased to be used among all the Indo-European peoples who, migrating southward, encountered the vine or the soma.

We have explained, through this transformation, the complete oblivion into which the Greeks and Latins allowed the episodes of preparation to fall — episodes that, moreover, survive in India only in a fantastical form. There is therefore nothing surprising in the fact that the rites of preparation were forgotten among the Latins.

As for the Armenians, although the liquid they prepare in the *Havgir* vat is no longer a true drink, they have, as we have seen, preserved certain preliminary rites in their festival — the conquest of the water, the gathering of the *Haurot* and *Maurot* herbs, and the mixing or brewing.

Conversely, it is reasonable to suppose that, in the ambrosial festivals of the Irish and the Scandinavians, the preparation of the ritual beer closely reflected the mythic themes of fabrication.

Similarly, the episodes of combat and general mêlée are no longer found in Rome. The Armenians may have retained some trace of them in that nocturnal scene where the young girls defend the Vat that the young men try to steal. But this was clearly one of the more vulnerable points of the ritual: as customs softened, calmer, more regulated games must have replaced the scenes of combat.

On the contrary, the three central episodes — the punished demon, the feast of the gods, and the false bride — showed great resistance to erosion. We find them well preserved in Armenia: the expedition of the "Petrified Thieves," the feast beside the water, and the procession of the mannequin-bride.

At Rome, the festival of Anna Perenna consisted essentially of the feast by the Tiber and the mimic performance of the scene of the false Minerva deceiving Mars. As for the episode of the punished demon, the plebs did indeed re-enact it, on the same day as the adventures of Anna — or on the eve of that day (March 15 or 14) — but, as we have seen, they connected it with the story of the *ancile*: a "Mamurius" covered with hides was ceremonially beaten with rods through the streets.

This popular scene is all the more striking because the set of the ancilian festivals otherwise bore an official character; by contrast, the flagellation of Mamurius belonged to the plebeians, as did the feast by the Tiber and Anna's ruse. Moreover, if the festival of Mamurius was celebrated on the same day as that of Anna, it would be arbitrary to separate them; and if, on the other hand, Mamurius was celebrated on the 14th and Anna on the 15th, since two public festivals (*feriae publicae*) never followed one another in Rome without at least one intervening day, we must not separate them either. The first must therefore be regarded as the preparatory festival of the second — the *Voreia* — as Wissowa himself suggests as a possibility (*Religion und Kultus der Römer*, p. 370, note 2).

Finally, we have seen that the Christian story of Petronilla, heir to the pagan story of Perenna and no doubt also covering ancient

Perennian rites, tightly unites the three expected episodes: the feast of Peter and his friends; the "bride" Petronilla deceiving the wicked Flaccus; and Nicodemus, scourged and thrown into the Tiber. There must therefore once have existed more complete traditions than the one Ovid recounts concerning Anna Perenna — traditions in which the "scourged thief" episode was linked with those of the "feast" and the "false bride."

As for the corresponding rites, whatever legends may overlay them — ancilian or Perennian — their temporal union and their common plebeian character make it impossible to dissociate them. Thus we find again, at Rome as in Armenia, the three central scenes of the ambrosial drama.

It is deliberately that we use the word drama: we have seen the fragment, transcribed by Manuk Abeghian, of the Armenian song that accompanies the making of the mannequin. In the same way, we know that during the final amusements of the Latin festival, the young girls, among other lively songs (*obscena; certa probra*), celebrated the expedition of the false Minerva to the demon Mars; and we have preserved a few words from a mime by Laberius on this subject.

In the ambrosial festival, there were the seeds of dramatic art — seeds that the various Indo-European peoples caused to bear fruit in unequal measure.

⁂

Among the Slavs

We have already pointed out the difficulties confronting our study of the Celtic, Germanic, and Slavic domains: spring festivals smothered by Christianity, ambrosial festivals that have long ceased to be ambrosial, and new meanings assigned to ancient rites — so many accidents and transformations among which we risk losing our way. The situation is even more complex than we first stated.

If one leafs through the two dense volumes of Mannhardt on the *Gods of the Woods and Fields,* and on the *Cult of Trees in Central and Eastern Europe,* one finds on nearly every page — among the spring and vegetation rites he describes — scenes that often closely resemble two of the scenes from the ambrosial festival. There appears a mannequin, or a man representing the Spirit of Vegetation, carried beyond the boundaries of the village and then stoned (Mannhardt, *Baumkultus der Germanen*, p. 412). One also finds the procession of the "false woman," under three different forms that correspond precisely to the three variants of the ambrosial theme of the "false bride" (see above): either men dressed in women's clothing are carried in procession; or mannequins dressed in women's clothing take their place; or else real women, similarly disguised and adorned — as in the cases of the "May Bride" or the "Queen of May." (Mannhardt, ibid., pp. 314, 411–412 and note, and ch. V, *Vegetationsgeister: Maibrautschaft*).

In the face of such parallels, several interpretations are possible, each containing some portion of truth.

Either the ancient ambrosial themes were merely a particular, temporary, and accidental interpretation of spring rites that were older than they, and that continue to be found unchanged in regions never touched by the ambrosial cycle. In this case, we must assume that, once ambrosia had taken an important place in Indo-European religious thought, it served to give a new explanation to ancient spring and vegetation rites of entirely different meaning (stoning, disguise, etc.).

Or, conversely, properly ambrosial rites, born with and for the festival of ambrosia, survived the forgetting of ambrosia and acquired a new significance. In this case, we may suppose that several of the vegetation festivals described by Mannhardt are merely distorted remnants of the ambrosial festival.

We shall not attempt to apply these theoretical views here. But to appreciate the difficulty, it is enough to consider the Western Slavic festivals of Ziwena and Marena that Mannhardt (*Baumkultus*, pp. 406–416; *Antike Wald- und Feldkulte*, p. 297) treats — and perhaps rightly so — as simple vegetation festivals, while Usener (*Italische Mythen, Rheinisches Museum*, XXX, 1875, pp. 182–229) compares them to the Roman and Lavinian festivals of Anna Perenna, and which we have tried to show to be of ambrosial descent.

It seems we catch there, in the very act, the fusion of the ambrosial festival and an ordinary vegetation festival—or, rather, the transition from one to the other, once ambrosia was forgotten. This "Life" (Ziwena, "the life-giving one") and this "Death" (Marena, Mamurienda, elsewhere *Smrt, Smierc'*) — originally ambrosial notions — became vegetation spirits.

In the fifteenth century, the Polish chronicler Długosz, who first mentions these rites, wrote: *"Ceres autem mater et Dea frugum quarum satis regio indigebat, Marzana vocata apud eos in praecipuo cultu et veneratione habita fuit."* (*"Ceres, the mother and goddess of the crops, of which the country stood in great need, was among them held in special honour under the name Marzana."*)

And the Czech dictionary of Kott gives, under the article Ziva, Zivena: *"Goddess of human and natural life, and name of the planet Ceres."*

If, as we are led to suppose, the Russian cycle of Mikhailo Potyk once corresponded to a festival, it is easy to imagine what rites — closely resembling those of the Lavinian festival of Anna Perenna — that festival must have included: a feast near a lake or "sea" (= the feast of Vladimir; the aquatic birth of the White Swan); a procession of a man disguised as a woman, or of a female-shaped mannequin (= Mikhailo's expedition disguised as a woman against the forty suitors); and finally, the stoning of that mannequin (= Mikhailo turned to stone for having drunk the magic potion).

What connection there may be between this hypothetical festival and certain spring or late-spring vegetation festivals (*Jarilo, Kostroma*) still observed in modern Russia, we cannot say.

As an example, here is the festival of *Kostroma* as it is celebrated in the district of Murom (Mannhardt, *Baumkultus*, loc. cit.): The peasants dress a straw doll — formerly made of field herbs (*Kostra*,

Kostera = "reed, weed") — in flowers and women's garments, place it on a kind of trough (exactly as the Armenian villagers place the *Vicak* mannequin on the *Havgir* vat), and carry it in procession amid songs to the bank of a lake or river. There, the crowd divides into two opposing groups: one defending the doll Kostroma, the other attacking it. At the end, the victorious attackers throw the doll into the water.

⁎⁎⁎

Among the Germans

Among the ancient Germans, as we have already said, there is a lack of documentation concerning the spring festival. However, M. Cahen (*La Libation...*, Paris, 1921) has shown that in the Germanic world, and particularly among the Scandinavians, the word "festival" is synonymous with "drinking feast." From the earliest texts, all the words that designate a festival (*drykkja, mót,* etc.) are derived from words meaning "to drink" or from the name of a specific drink — namely, beer.

The expression *"gørva drykkju"* (or *rel*) means both "to make beer" and "to prepare the festival."

"A Scandinavian festival," says M. Cahen (p. 121), *"is defined by a certain quantity of beer to be drunk according to specific rites. The festival begins when the woman starts brewing the drink; it ends in the hall where the guests gather for the libation."*

Was it in spring that the apostle to the Germans, Saint Columbanus, found the Alemanni gathered around a huge vat of beer that they were preparing to offer to Wotan?

Reperit eos sacrificium profanum litare velle, vasque magnum, quod vulgo Cupam vocant, quod viginti et sex modios amplius minusve capiebat, cervisia plenum in medio habebant positum ("He found them about to make a profane sacrifice, and in their midst was placed a great vessel, which they commonly call a Cupa, holding more or less twenty-six bushels, filled with beer.") (*Vita S. Columbani*, ch. 53; cited by Cahen, op. cit., p. 20.)

On the other hand, the famous phrase of Tacitus about the long drinking bouts of the Germans — *diem noctemque continuare potando nulli probrum* ("to continue drinking day and night is considered no disgrace by anyone") — which, moreover, did not end without violence (*crede et vulneribus*, "with quarrels and wounds"), raises a question: does this passage refer to a ritual or periodic festival? Could it be a representation of the *Lokasenna* or of some analogous legend? Nothing allows us to say for certain. (See Cahen, op. cit., p. 20.)

⁂

Among the Celts

There is the same absence of evidence regarding the spring assemblies of the Celts. The Irish *Imbolc* is completely unknown to us; and although the little that we do know of the legend of Saint

Brigid — whose Christian feast succeeded *Imbolc* — does indeed preserve a characteristic episode of the ambrosial cycle, we do not know in what way its rites differed from those of the other seasonal festivals.

These other festivals involved banquets, athletic games, recitations by poets and musicians (see Czarnowski, *Saint Patrick*, p. 109), as well as marriages — and very likely temporary marriages lasting one year (see d'Arbois de Jubainville, *Les Assemblées publiques de l'Irlande*, pp. 2 and 12).

The account of the Battle of Mag Tured lays special emphasis on the healing spring:

"It is now called the Lake of Herbs; in Irish, Loch Luibe, because Dian Cécht had placed in it a sample of every herb that grew in Ireland." (§126; d'Arbois de Jubainville, *L'Épopée celtique en Irlande*, p. 434)

Similarly, the romance of the Grail highlights the pond beside which the first spiritual feast was celebrated — the Pond of Alain (Paulin Paris, *Les Romans de la Table Ronde*, vol. I, p. 306).

From this, one may easily conclude that — as in Italy, Armenia, Poland, and elsewhere — the ancient spring festival that once accompanied these legends was celebrated beside a lake or another body of water.

Is there not a trace of an analogous Gallic festival in the account given by Gregory of Tours (*De Gloria Beatorum Confessorum*, II, 6; cited by Renel, *Les Religions de la Gaule avant le Christianisme*, p. 175) describing a curious survival of paganism at the Lake of Saint-Andéol, near Aubrac, in the Cévennes?

"There, at a certain time of year, a multitude of country folk would perform something like libations at this lake. They threw into it pieces of cloth or garments belonging to men, some even fleeces of wool; most of them threw cheeses, cakes of wax, bread, and, according to their wealth, other objects too numerous to mention.

"They came with wagons bringing food and drink, slaughtered animals, and for three days they feasted merrily; on the fourth day, when they were preparing to leave, they were assailed by a storm accompanied by thunder and great flashes of lightning, and such torrential rain and violent hail fell from the sky that each participant barely believed he could escape. Such things happened every year, and superstition held the thoughtless people captive..."

In this account, all the essential features of the ambrosial festival reappear:

1. An annual celebration, held during the fair season and the time of spring squalls — likely March or April.

2. A festival by a lake.

3. A communal feast and sacrificial banquet.

4. A festival involving both men and women.

As for the ritual content, Gregory's simple narrative still lets us glimpse several ritual traits: the throwing of garments and cloths — common in spring festivals; the communal feasting and libations — recalling both the Roman orgy of Lavinium by the river and the meal of the Armenian maidens beside the spring.

Most striking of all, however, is the terrifying storm that, according to Gregory, unfailingly concluded the festival each year, as if arriving "on command." The best explanation for this feature is that it preserves a fragment of the ancient myth that originally explained the rite — awkwardly reinterpreted by Gregory long after both myth and rite had faded. The storm, in this light, would represent the final mythic episode of the Ambrosial Cycle: the battle of gods and demons.

Thus, the festival of the Lake of Saint-Andéol seems to preserve, under a Christianised surface, the Indo-European Festival of Ambrosia.

The testimony of Gregory of Tours is especially valuable in itself, for in the lines that follow this passage, he shows how great and prolonged were the efforts of the Christian clergy to suppress these pagan rites and myths. Similar festivals must once have existed in many parts of ancient Gaul, though their memory has vanished — for want of a Gregory of Tours to record them.

We have even wondered — as noted earlier — whether the Wolf-God with the Mallet (Sucellus) and his consort Nantosvelta, with their symbolic vase, may not be related to these same rites, and whether they might not stand at the origin of later folk tales still alive today, such as that of Little Red Riding Hood.

Conversely, we have seen in the festival and the legends of the Grail the result of a Christian appropriation of earlier pagan rites and themes.

The pagan feast was certainly not purely "spiritual," as it became in the Christian tradition. The cup of the Grail, which nothing material has filled since it was touched by the blood of Christ, must once have contained a "drink of life" — from which the Welsh, imitating their gods, drew strength, health, and youth.

Christian metaphysics, substituting the life of the soul for that of the body, grace for health, and the notion of purity for that of strength, did not, however, remove from the ceremony its external appearance of a feast and communion. The similarity of this rite to the Eucharist undoubtedly helped to preserve its form unchanged.

As for the scenes of the festival — the drama performed beside the body of water, the pond or the lake — they must have corresponded to the major episodes of the legends we have studied: the Fisherman at the table of the saints, the feast of the saints, and the demon disguised as a woman.

To better understand the ritual role of the Grail, which we have compared to the *ancile* presiding over the Salian feast, one should recall the famous Celtic vessel discovered at Gundestrup, in Jutland, in 1891.

This vessel — *"which appears to have been abandoned under circumstances dictated by religious motives"* — depicts Celtic deities, along with Celtic costumes and weapons, yet it also presents features that make it impossible to believe it was manufactured in Gaul or the British Isles.

M. Henri Hubert devoted two series of lectures to it at the École des Hautes Études (1912–13 and 1919–20). He reached conclusions that are highly significant for our study, suggesting that the Gundestrup cauldron was connected with a ceremonial of ambrosial origin.

The best way to convey this is simply to reproduce the few lines summarising M. Hubert's course, as printed in the *1920–21 Yearbook of the École des Hautes Études* (*Sciences religieuses*, pp. 50–51).

"Were there still Celts in Jutland at the date of the vase, or had the local Germans by then become sufficiently Celticised? This question of dating has received the most varied answers, and it remains open for further study. In any case, the vase is a central monument of Celtic religion taken as a whole, and it must be interpreted in the light of elements of the Celtic tradition that were — or could have been — shared among its various branches.

"It was a sacred cauldron, comparable to those known in Gaul, Britain, and Ireland, not to mention the Cimbrian cauldron and certain Scandinavian cauldrons. Such ritual vessels had their counterparts in mythology. The ornamentation of the vase is directly related to its religious function. That function was sacrificial. The central panel (the bottom of the vessel) depicts a sacrifice, which is repeated on one of the inner panels. These inner panels appear to represent the unfolding of the ceremonies and their mythic narrative. This sacrifice, presented in the forms of both an

animal sacrifice and a human sacrifice, was analogous to the Indian sóma sacrifice.

"*The outer figures of the vase signify the divine attendance at the rites. It is the assembly of the gods, a representation of the world encircling a ceremony of grave importance. As in Greco-Roman magic and in the religion of the Imperial era, this representation must have been conceived in relation to time. The Gundestrup vase has been compared to the so-called "weekly" vases, adorned with images of the gods of the days of the week. But this hypothesis does not fit — neither with the number of figures, which is eight, nor with the ratio of gods to goddesses, nor with the most plausible date of the vase, which is the La Tène II period.*

"*The external figures of the Gundestrup vase correspond in pairs to the four great festivals of the Celtic year, to its four principal divisions, and individually to the eight half-seasons of forty-five days each — whose memory is preserved in the Irish calendars.*"

We are therefore in the presence of a vessel used in seasonal festivals of communion, particularly during a ceremony of great importance, at which gods and goddesses were present.

If these details are fragmentary, they nonetheless agree perfectly with what one would expect of a Celtic festival — an heir to the Indo-European Festival of Ambrosia — and they illustrate the evolution through which one of the Celtic mythic cycles, namely the Welsh cycle, could give rise to the Christian cycle of the sacred vessel, that of the Grail.

⁎⁎

Among the Hindus

When studying the evolution of the ambrosial legends in India, we observed the following phenomenon: throughout the official literature of Vedic society, the themes of the ambrosial cycle appear only transposed into the language of *sóma*.

However, we were compelled to recognise that — whether among other tribes or within social classes different from those whose thought is reflected in the Vedas — the cycle of ambrosia must have continued to live independently for a long time. Indeed, a few centuries later, after numerous political, territorial, and religious upheavals, epic literature presents us, as one of its favourite themes, with a cycle of the *amṛta* that has been remarkably well preserved.

It is easy to understand why Vedic liturgy contains no truly ambrosial festival, but only a great spring festival of *sóma*, in harmony with the central concerns of the hymns. The change, however, predates the Vedas: the *sóma* ritual, in its essential form, is Indo-Iranian.

Victor Henry, in his study on *sóma* and *haoma*, pointed out the numerous correspondences between these twin rituals and showed that the Vedic ritual, in its broad outlines, can serve as an Indo-Iranian witness. The Avestan ritual, for its part, is known only in a much more developed form and from a much later period.

And if the *Gāthās* — the oldest religious texts of Iran — systematically neglect *haoma*, it is not, as we have seen, out of a desire to restore older ritual elements, but rather in favour of a new moral philosophy, or at least an original one.

The Vedic liturgy recognises a great festival of *sóma*, which surpasses all the more specific ceremonies and displays all the general characteristics of the ambrosia festival:

1. It is an annual festival, very probably springtime in nature.

Oldenberg (*Die Religion des Veda*, p. 451 ff.) notes that this festival is not as closely tied to a specific calendar date or astronomical event as most Vedic ceremonies. However, he gives no real reason to reject the testimony of relatively late sources that clearly describe it as an annual spring festival.

In fact, Oldenberg's reluctance to acknowledge its seasonal character stems from his view that the *sóma* sacrifice is primarily a social act — a gesture of generosity by the wealthy and powerful toward the gods and the priests. But there is no contradiction here: the Indo-European festival of ambrosia was both a seasonal celebration and a festival of communion, and the "generosity" of the rich Hindus simply consisted in financing a communal seasonal rite.

A curious *Brāhmaṇa* text, in which we have already noted a trace of the ambrosial cycle, clearly connects the ideas of death and immortality with those of the year and the end of the year:

"*The gods were afraid of Death, which is the End, which is the Year, which is Prajāpati.*" (Śatapatha Brāhmaṇa X, 4, 3, 3)

2. It is a festival of nourishment, a festival of communion.

"*The sacrifice of sóma,*" says Oldenberg (*Die Religion des Veda*, p. 452), "*is a general drinking feast for the gods and for the priests.*" ("*So ist das Somaopfer ein allgemeines Trinkfest für Götter und Priester.*")

The very notion of a priestly order or sacerdotal college seems particular to Indo-Iranian and Italo-Celtic societies (as noted by Vendryes, *Mémoires de la Société de Linguistique*, XX, p. 265 ff.), and this collective drinking of the priests must have been only a Hindu restriction of what was, among the Indo-Europeans, a still broader communal banquet, meant to reproduce on earth the divine feast of the gods.

It is important to note here that the sacrifice was addressed, in at least one of its three parts, to "all the gods."

The same is true of the *Yasna*, the Avestan sacrifice. This essential feature — a feast for all the gods — corresponds exactly to what we have seen elsewhere in the Indo-European world within the ambrosian festivals, and it is particularly significant since this inclusive character is absent from other Vedic liturgical contexts.

Therefore, since in India there existed, in spring, a festival of communion that represented the banquet of all the gods, and since such a festival also existed, in ambrosian form, at the Indo-

European stage, our hypothesis — that the Hindu *sóma* festival derives from the Indo-European festival of ambrosia — appears at least highly plausible.

3. Women take part in the Soma festival.

On the divine level: the sacrifice is addressed to goddesses as well as gods (Oldenberg, op. cit., p. 461). On the human level: aside from the mixed crowd gathered around the sacred arena, the wife of the man who sponsors the ceremony is seen seated in a place of honour beside her husband (Oldenberg, ibid.). This participation of women was, as we have already seen, a characteristic feature of the Indo-European ambrosial festival.

4. Finally, the proximity of a body of water is again part of the ritual requirements, since the sacrificer, immediately after the ceremony, must bathe "in a quiet cove formed by running water" (Hubert and Mauss, *Mélanges d'Histoire des Religions*, p. 69, note 2).

As for the details of the *sóma* ritual "scenario", if it still contains the outlines of the ambrosian sequence, they have either been magnified and stylised, or submerged within a multitude of secondary rites. One can still clearly recognise the general scene of the feast in that of the three pressings (*trīṇi savanāni*), to which all the gods are invited alongside Indra — one of the high points of the liturgy.

By contrast, the episode of the demon who at first collaborates with the gods in preparing the magical drink, but is then expelled by those same gods — the episode we encountered at Rome, for example, in the form of Mamurius being flogged — has been relegated in the *sóma* ritual to a marginal element of the ceremony.

The Vedas describe the *sóma* merchant as an inferior being, a reprobate, an intruder. He is always a *śūdra*, and we have already seen that, in Vedic thought, the Asura on the divine level corresponds to the *śūdra* on the human level. During the sacrifice, after the *sóma* has been received with all the honours due to a royal guest, there follows a prescribed rite consisting in expelling the vendor, while threatening him with a stick (V. Henry, *Soma et Haoma*, p. 3). That is all.

As for the third scene of the ambrosian drama, the "False Bride", which still lives on in the *Brāhmaṇa* legends, it has no ritual counterpart, no place within the Soma liturgy. Conversely, the rest of the *sóma* ritual is undoubtedly not of ambrosian origin.

One detail, however, deserves our attention: it is the threefold division of the festival, the tripartition of the offering into three pressings — the morning pressing dedicated to all the gods, the midday pressing reserved for Indra alone, and the evening pressing offered to Indra and a few lesser lords. Now, this represents an original form of the festival that corresponds exactly to what we know of the ritual structure of the Scandinavian feasts.

"*The toast,*" writes M. Cahen (*La Libation*, pp. 172–173), "*is the solemn moment of the libation. The ritual of the libation undoubtedly adapted itself to the particular purpose of each feast. The divinities invoked varied according to the prayer to be addressed. But every libation involved the successive invocation of several gods: according to Norse tradition, as fixed by Snorri, there were at least three toasts in the ritual banquets, and this custom survived in the Christian guilds of Denmark and Sweden.*

"This number did not limit the quantity of horns that might be emptied during the libation, but it gave the ceremony a fixed framework. The feast officially began with the first toast and ended with the last. It reached its climax at the moment of the great toast, which was drunk with particular fervour; by the end of the Middle Ages, the guilds would light their candles for this solemn moment. The toast lasted as long as the drinking horn circulated through the assembly."

Now, most often, one of these three toasts was offered to all the gods together, just like one of the *sóma* pressings, or like the banquet that formed one of the three central scenes of the ambrosian drama.

Thus, in the account cited by M. Cahen of the appearance of Saint Martin to Olaf Tryggvason, there is mention of drinking successively to Thor, to Odin, and to the Æsir. Similarly, in the Swedish guild of Saint George, which squared the ancient number to make a total of nine toasts, grouped in threes, the libations of the final triad were offered *"to all the saints, to Saint Gertrude, and to Saint Benedict."*

We know nothing of the ancient ritual which, among the Celts, made use of sacred cauldrons like that of Gundestrup, and which M. Hubert (see above) compares to the *sóma* ritual. However, the ornamentation of the vase depicts a gathering of the gods for a libation, corresponding to what we have already seen among the Hindus and the Scandinavians.

Nor should we forget that, at the table of Joseph or Arthur, the nourishing Grail is passed around three times (see Wechssler, *Die Sage vom heiligen Gral*, synoptic table of variants, p. 213, columns 4, 6, and 14, line 1).

As for the Latins, alongside the popular festivities of the Feast of Anna Perenna, they may have preserved, in the ritual meal of the *ancile*, a more liturgical form of the ambrosian ritual. Now, from what little we know of the chants of the Salians, these appear to be addressed first to all the gods collectively — in the *axamenta* — and then to various gods individually:

"*Axamenta* were the salian hymns sung to all the gods (or semones? or men?) collectively. For each god, separate verses were composed, named from their divine titles — as Janian, Jovian, Junonian, Minervian..." (Paul. p. 3)

Moreover, as we saw earlier in the preserved verses of Janus, these four lines seem clearly to contain an invitation to the god to attend the banquet celebrated at the *mansio* — a distant, prose-like echo of the Brahmanic invitation to Indra and his companions.

Do these parallels establish a feature of the Indo-European ritual as practiced during the spring banquet? It would seem so. The Hindus, Scandinavians, Welsh, and Sabines all appear to have preserved in their liturgies a division into several toasts — probably three — with one dedicated to all the gods. This division, however, was naturally forgotten in the purely popular festivals, in those festivities that had lost their religious significance and become mere rejoicings.

⁂

Among the Greeks

Earlier, we tried to give some idea of the multitude of Greek counterparts to the ambrosian cycle, whose existence is revealed by the most varied testimonies. At the same time, we pointed out that all these legendary groupings probably corresponded to ritual groupings, to festivals themselves derived from the Indo-European feast of ambrosia.

So as not to enlarge unnecessarily the share of hypothesis, we shall refrain from inquiring what the Θεοδαίσιαι of Dionysus at Andros or at Delphi (see *Suidas*, s.v.), or what the Orphic banquet, may owe to the ambrosian ritual, or what was contained in the Dionysian festival called Ambrosia, of which we know only the name (*Etymologicum Magnum*, s.v. Ληναίων; Mommsen, *Heortologie*, p. 340).

We shall consider only two extreme cases: first, that of a festival whose existence is not directly attested, but which it is possible to discern beneath the known legends that cover it — this is the case of the Hesiodic story of Prometheus and Pandora. Then, that of a festival attested by direct testimony, but for which the legends parallel to the rites are very imperfectly known — this is the case of the festival of the Thargelia.

⁂

Nothing has come down to us of the local festival — no doubt a Boeotian one — to which the scenario of the Prometheus story, as told by Hesiod, must have corresponded. But does not the Hesiodic text itself indirectly prove its existence?

Jules Girard, in his book *Le Sentiment religieux d'Homère à Eschyle*, while seeking the first manifestations of dramatic genius in Greece, paused before the episode of Prometheus, so striking in its vividness and its dialogue amid the slow and rather static narratives of the Works and Days.

"We have before our eyes," he wrote (p. 66), *"a true scene, in which the Greek imagination delights in showing actions, gestures, even general expressions of face: such as the care with which Prometheus, patron of men, arranges under the ox's hide the bones covered with fat so that Zeus, deceived by appearances, may choose the worse portion for the gods; and the words exchanged between the two adversaries; and above all the smile that accompanies Prometheus' speech, an expression of cunning drawn directly from the manners of a half-barbaric society; finally, the irony of Zeus, who, out of jealousy and vengeance, pretends to be deceived — all these features are expressive and possess a thoroughly human dramatic quality in which the Greek character shines through."*

Now we have seen how many ambrosian elements this scene of contention contains; it is impossible, when reading it, not to think of the corresponding Scandinavian episode, the *Lokasenna*, the quarrel at the banquet of the gods. If, departing from his usual manner, Hesiod becomes almost a dramatic poet on this occasion — if he inserts into his poem a fully dialogued scene — is it not because the story of Prometheus presented itself to him in a living form, acted, mimed, spoken — a popular drama, like the corresponding episodes of the ambrosian cycle?

If one recalls the Armenian scene of the mannequin, the songs accompanying its making, the ornaments lavished upon it, one will naturally interpret the creation of Pandora, the sending forth of Pandora, even her name, as traits of a popular, springtime, ambrosian play, scarcely altered by their divine transposition. The banquet of Mekone, the punishment of Prometheus, the scene of Pandora and the *píthos*, all no doubt correspond to a festival that Hesiod and his first listeners knew perfectly well.

*
* *

It is precisely these three episodes that constitute the ritual content of a springtime, communal, and mixed festival celebrated in Athens and in many other parts of the Greek world: the *Thargelia*. The documents concerning Athens have been collected by Mommsen (*Feste der Stadt Athen*, p. 468–486), and those for other Greek cities by Nilsson (*Griechische Feste*, p. 105–115).

They have often been studied and interpreted — notably by Mannhardt (*Antike Wald- und Feldkulte*, p. 214–258), by Miss Harrison (*Prolegomena*, p. 78 ff.), and by Sir James Frazer (*The Golden Bough*, 2nd ed., IX, p. 255 ff., 272). These authors recognised, even in the apparently "expiatory" rites, authentic vegetation rituals: the Thargelia, like so many other Greek festivals, are indeed festivals of vegetation.

But had they not once possessed a more precise meaning? Nilsson (op. cit., p. 111–112) already emphasises the serious difficulty one encounters in interpreting this festival: one cannot explain what link connects two of its essential scenes — the expulsion and stoning of the φαρμακός (*pharmakós*) and the procession of the Εἰρεσιώνη (*Eiresiônē*). Nor is it any clearer how the third rite, the banquet, relates to the other two.

Yet, if one does not dismiss the "explanatory legends" that the ancients told about these rites, their common origin and their primitive, ambrosian form begin to emerge. Before becoming a merely ordinary vegetation festival, the spring Thargelia may once have been the festival of a springtime food made from grain — the festival of Ambrosia.

1. First rite: the stoning of the *pharmakós*.

A man (at Athens, two men — one, it is said, burdened with the impurities of the men, the other with those of the women) is solemnly expelled from the city, flogged (at Kolophon), stoned (at Marseilles, at Abdera).

The ancients explain the origin of this rite in various ways: most often, they speak of some vague famine or calamity during which it was instituted — just as the Latins, as we have seen, explained the expulsion and flogging of Mamurius by "misfortunes" that had occurred in connection with the *ancile*. But that does not account for the annual nature of the rite.

Moreover, Harpokration has preserved a testimony from the historian Istros that allows us to recognise the ancient form and meaning of the rite:

"A man named Pharmakós had stolen the sacred cups (ἱεράς φιάλας) of Apollo; seized by Achilles and his companions, he was stoned to death." (Mommsen, op. cit., p. 470, note 2).

In this legend we can recognise a variant of the episode of the demon stealing the cup of ambrosia and being buried beneath rocks by the gods. It is, moreover, indisputable that very early the Greeks themselves associated this "thieving demon" with the ordinary φαρμακοί (*pharmakoí*), the human victims who, in times of grave crisis and outside any fixed date, were sacrificed in many cities to redeem the community from peril.

2. Second rite: The Feast. — This rite is clearly attested only for the city of Miletos (Parthenius, IX, 5):

"...Among the Milesians (here referring to the Milesian troops at Naxos), on the third day after the Thargelia, there was a festival at which they brought in large quantities of unmixed wine and consumed what was most precious." ...τοῖς Μιλησίοις ἑορτὴ μετὰ τρίτην ἡμέραν Θαργήλια ἐπήει, ἐν ᾗ πολύν τε ἄκρατον εἰσφοροῦνται καὶ τὰ πλείστου ἄξια καταναλίσκουσι. (Nilsson, op. cit., p. 110, note 3).

The banqueting of the Milesians recalls the feast of the Latin peasants held on the banks of the Tiber during the festival of Anna Perenna. For both groups alike, the festival seems to have become nothing more than a pretext for purely human rejoicing.

In earlier times, the ritual meaning of this feast must have been more deeply felt. There may even be a trace of it in the Athenian sacrifice offered on the 6th of Thargelion to Demeter Chloë (Mommsen, op. cit., p. 477 ff.). We shall soon see the close links uniting the θάργηλος and the θαλύσιον, and consequently, the Thargelia and the Thalysia.

Now, for the latter we possess Homeric testimony (Iliad II, 534), which proves that originally the Thalysia, the "festivals of the first fruits," were not addressed — as they were later, in the time of Theokritos — solely to Demeter and the agrarian deities, but rather to all the gods and all the goddesses without exception.

Such must also have been the nature of the second episode of the Thargelia: originally, both at Athens and at Miletos, it was a feast of all men and women, representing the banquet of all the gods and goddesses. In historical times, it became reduced to a double sacrifice — male and female — offered to Demeter Chloë on the Akropolis.

Even so, the silence of the texts does not prove that between the 6th and 7th of Thargelion, the Athenian people did not hold their own kind of feast — a celebration in which we hear only of cakes, fruits, and similar offerings. It would indeed be surprising if the participants had completely denied themselves.

Moreover, as we shall see, an Athenian legend explaining the origin of the next rite begins precisely with a communion feast of the ambrosian type.

3. Third rite: The procession of the *Eiresiônē*.

This rite, unlike the preceding one, is attested explicitly only for Athens. But since it is specifically connected with the very word θάργηλος (*thárgēlos*), and since the festival as a whole was commonly known, outside Athens, under the name θαργήλια (*thargêlia*), we can only agree with Nilsson in considering the procession of the *Eiresiônē* as one of the essential and universal elements of the festival.

The *Eiresiônē* is a branch of olive, wrapped in wool (εἶρος), in a garland (στέμμα) of white and red, and adorned with fruits and various foods. During the Pyanepsia and the Thargelia, a child (or children) whose both parents are living (ἀμφιθαλής) carries it at the head of a solemn procession through the city and sets it up before the temple of Apollon. In the same way, each Athenian household places an *Eiresiônē* upon its threshold, which it renews each year. (See the numerous texts collected by Mannhardt, op. cit., notes to pp. 217 ff.)

We must first note, as Miss Harrison (*Prolegomena*, p. 80) has emphasised, that the *Eiresiônē* is not regarded as an object or a mere symbol; it possesses a personality of its own. A ritual prayer is addressed to it, sung by the children of the procession, in which it is said to bring abundance of food and drink:

Εἰρεσιώνη σύκα φέρει καὶ πίονας ἄρτους,
Καὶ μέλιτος κοτύλην καὶ ἔλαιον ἐπικρήσασθαι,
Καὶ κύλικα εὔζωρον ἵνα μεθύουσα καθεύδῃ.

*"The Eiresiônē brings figs and rich loaves,
A cup of honey, and oil to anoint oneself,
And a brimming goblet, that she may drink and sleep."*

The Roman peasants addressed Anna Perenna in similar terms, invoking her likewise as a giver of nourishment and plenty.

But that is not all in this procession: they do not merely lead the *Eiresiônē*. The participants also carry herbs, grains, figs, loaves of bread, round cakes shaped like bowls (χύτρος), and a "pot." They bear the *thárgēlos* and the *thargêlia*, the very objects that gave their name to the festival, and to which we shall return shortly.

According to the *Etymologicum Magnum*, at the moment when the children sing the verses just quoted, they pour over the effigy a cup of mixed wine: καταχύσματα δὲ καὶ κύλικα οἴνου κεκραμένην καταχέοντες αὐτῆς ʼ επιλέγουσιν· "Ειρεσιώνη σύκα φέρει κ.τ.λ... "

"And while they pour libations and a cup of mixed wine over her, they recite: 'Eiresiônē brings figs, etc.'"

(See the relevant texts collected by Mannhardt, op. cit., pp. 217 n. 3; 224 n. 1; 225 nn. 1–2; 226 nn. 1, 3.)

By this feature, this third Thargelian scene is closely related to the Armenian form of the Indo-European rite, in which one sees the effigy *Vicak*, the dispenser of prosperity, fastened to the vat *Havgir* and carried in procession by the young Armenian women.

Here again, the ancient explanatory legends help to illuminate the meaning of the rite. Most often, they speak vaguely of famines that were once averted through this ceremony, thereby emphasising its alimentary character. But Plutarkhos and Pausanias give us more precise information.

According to Plutarkhos, it was Theseus and his companions who instituted the rite upon their return from Krete, in thanksgiving for their victory and deliverance:

"They gathered together what remained of their vegetable provisions, put them all into a single pot, cooked them, and ate the meal together." (συμμῖξαι τὰ περιόντα τῶν σιτίων καὶ μίαν χύτραν κοινὴν ἑψήσαντας συνεστιαθῆναι καὶ συγκαταφαγεῖν ἀλλήλοις — Plutarkhos, *Theseus*, ch. XXII; cf. Mannhardt, op. cit., p. 220, note b).

Pausanias tells a similar story: that Theseus, on his return, in fulfilment of a vow, prepared pots of porridge and vegetable stew, and made the first *Eiresiônē* (Pausanias, in Eustathius on Iliad XXII, p. 1283, 6; cf. Suidas, s.v. Εἰρεσιώνη; Mannhardt, op. cit., p. 219, note 3a*).

Here again, Theseus, like Achilles in the story of the Pharmakós, is clearly a proper name attached somewhat artificially to motifs we can easily recognise: several gods prepare together, in a common cauldron, a sacred vegetable feast, which they solemnly consume, and they create an effigy that they carry in procession — toward a certain destination that we, unlike the Greeks, still know: to the demon-thief who had demanded a goddess as his prize.

However, it is noteworthy that the same Plutarkhos (*Theseus* XXIII), when explaining the closely related rite of the Oskhophoria, gives another etiological story: Theseus, tasked with leading the Athenian maidens due as tribute to the brigand Minotaur, included among them two strong youths, disguised, haired, and dressed as women.

By bringing this passage together with the previous one, we glimpse an entire "Thesian" version of the Ambrosia cycle — comparable to the Promethean form, but humanised. Unfortunately, we know of it only what Plutarch has chosen to tell us.

The Athenians of the fifth century, who celebrated the festival, seem unaware that the *Eiresiônē* had once been a "bride," a "false bride", sent to some demon in order to recover the χύτρα (*khýtra* — cooking pot), or the κύλιξ (*kýlix* — drinking cup), or the διακόνιον (*diakónion* — sweet pastry) that she carries with her procession to the temple of Apollon — exactly as Pandora, in another myth, went to Epimetheus to reclaim the contents of the *píthos*.

However, Miss Harrison, from a completely different perspective, has emphasised the importance of some obscure verses of Hipponax (in Athenaeus IX, 9; cf. Harrison, *Prolegomena*, p. 280), in which Pandora appears to be closely associated with the Thargelia, and seems indeed to play some mischievous trick on someone. Unfortunately, the fragment is too short, the text too uncertain, and the story too fragmentary to allow any firm conclusions to be drawn from it.

Nilsson, moreover, supposes — though without much plausibility — that the Pandora mentioned here is not the mythical one, but merely a woman of that name (Nilsson, op. cit., p. 107).

For the Athenians, *Eiresiônē* is therefore even less than what Anna was for the plebeians of Rome, or what *Vicak* was for the young Armenian women. They no longer believe that this dispenser of prosperity, or her mythic prototype, was once the one who, in some distant past, brought back to the gods the lost cup of ambrosia.

The Latins still knew the story of Mars deceived; the Armenians, for their part, had preserved from the ancient legend only the name "bride", which they gave to their effigy. But in Athens, long before the time of Christ, *Eiresiônē* had lost even that faint trace of her story: she had become nothing more than a shapeless effigy, retaining of her personality only a proper name, of her disguise only a bit of wool, and of her exploit only a cup or a pot.

To understand the evolution by which the scene of the *Eiresiônē* lost its ambrosian character and came to take the form of a purely vegetal rite, nothing is more instructive than to trace the changes in meaning of the word *thárgēlos* (see the texts collected by Mannhardt, op. cit., p. 228 and notes; cf. Miss Harrison, *Prolegomena*, p. 78).

Originally — if we are correct — the term must have designated the vessel containing the cereal-based drink that was ritually consumed at the feast of ambrosia. The earliest attested meaning still lies close to this:

"The *thárgēlos* is a pot full of seeds, a pot in which is cooked, for the gods, the offering of the first fruits." (χύτρος ἀνάπλεως σπερμάτων: Hesychius, s.v.; ἥψουν δ' ἐν αὐτῇ ἀπαρχὰς τῷ θεῷ τῶν πεφηνότων καρπῶν: Suidas, s.v.)

Later, like its synonym θαλύσιον (*thalýsion*), the word came to designate the first loaf made from the year's new wheat (τὸν ἐκ τῆς συγκομιδῆς πρῶτον γενόμενον ἄρτον: Athenaeus, IV, 8).

Finally, it came to mean the ἱκετηρία (*iketēría*), the olive branch adorned with various fruits — the *Eiresiônē* herself (Hesychius, s.v.).

Thus, we can trace a progressive fading of the notion of a container in favour of the notion of the plant itself. It is even possible to go back further into the prehistory of the *thárgēlos*. Miss Harrison (*Themis*, p. 293) has shown the close relationship between the *panspermia* and *pankarpia*, which appear in various festivals (Kernophoria, Liknophoria, Thargelia, etc.); these always involve a mixture of plant products.

Now, Athenaeus, citing the *Exegetikon* of Anticlides, says that in the καδίσκος (*kadískos*) — the vessel used for libations to Zeus Ktêsios — one must pour ambrosia. And he adds: ἡ δ' ἀμβροσία ὕδωρ ἀκραιφνές, ἔλαιον, παγκαρπία — "*Ambrosia consists of pure water, oil, and a pankarpia.*" (Athenaeus, XI, 46; cf. Miss Harrison, *Themis*, p. 299).

This confirms our conception of Indo-European ambrosia as cereal in nature, and helps us understand how the vessel of ambrosia could have become the *thárgēlos*, the vessel of *pankarpia* used in the Thargelia festival.

Beyond the clarifications that our interpretation of the Thargelia brings to several points already noted — the unity of the three episodes of the festival; the origin of the explanatory legends given by the ancients for these episodes; the figure of *Eiresiônē*; the cakes shaped like bowls, the pots, the cooking vessels; and the semantic evolution of *thárgēlos* — it also accounts for two other important features of the celebration.

First, the ἀμφιθαλής (*amphithalês*), "the child whose two parents are alive," is clearly designated to play, in the procession of the false bride, the role of an immortal god, since death is, so to speak, as far from him as possible.

Then, the various gods to whom the rites of the *Pharmakós* and of the *Eiresiônē* are addressed (cf. Miss Harrison, *Prolegomena*, p. 81) are precisely those one would expect in an ambrosian festival: Helios or Apollon, the luminous god who, in the Indo-European cycle, leads the battle against the demons; the *Horai*, the agrarian goddesses who preside, among other seasons, over spring; and finally Artemis, chaste and virile, no less than Pallas herself.

As for Demeter, we have already said that in the second rite of the Thargelia, as in the Thalysia, she seems to have appropriated to herself alone what was once the "feast of all the gods" — the universal banquet that we would naturally expect to occupy that place in the ritual.

Let us repeat, in conclusion, that this interpretation in no way contradicts the traditional interpretations of the Thargelia — those, notably, of Mannhardt, Frazer, or Miss Harrison. We have said repeatedly, and we say once more, that although the rites of the *Thargelia* were ambrosian in origin, they had already become something quite different in the minds of the Greeks who celebrated them by the time of the earliest historical documents.

The *Pharmakós*, as its expiatory and purificatory meaning derived from φαρμακός proves, had ceased first to be simply, and then to be at all, the "demon thief punished by the gods", and had entered instead into another category — that of human scapegoat victims. The *Eiresiônē*, in turn, developing its vegetal skeleton at the expense of its garments and adornments, was on the verge of becoming like the "May-trees" and other spring emblems, thereby losing all individual personality, all trace of a goddess or false goddess. Finally, the *thárgēlos* itself, losing any character of a vessel, became before our very eyes a vegetal cake.

Yet, we hope to have shown that the unity of the various scenes, and within each scene the presence of numerous details, are well explained by the hypothesis of a communal feast that gradually became above all a vegetal celebration — an ambrosian festival detached, step by step, from ambrosia itself. Long before the Christian era, the Thargelia likely show us the beginning of the same evolution which, more advanced among the Germans and the Slavs, has made our investigation into those regions almost impossible.

With ambrosia forgotten, the ambrosian rites survived, but re-entered the most ordinary pattern of vegetal rites. If the demonstration of the ambrosian origin of the Thargelia has not been conclusively achieved, the foregoing comparison has at least brought to light the kinship between the festival of Ambrosia and the general schema of purely vegetal festivals. It is in this sense that we shall now seek the origin of our own rites and of the myths that correspond to them.

Essay on the Interpretation of the Rites and Legends of Ambrosia

It should not surprise us to find ambrosia celebrated in a spring festival: the Indo-Europeans, by a very simple reasoning, associated the spectacle of nature's rebirth with the idea of immortality.

It was not the same, as we know, among other peoples. Before the vegetal phenomena of spring and summer, the Semite does not think of an endless life, but rather of an alternation of lives and deaths, expressed in the cycle of Adonis–Tammuz. For the Chinese, autumn and spring mark the meeting within nature of the two sexual principles — *yin*, the feminine, and *yang*, the masculine — the former ruling over winter and dark places, the latter working in summer, in the full light of day.

The Indo-European, on the contrary, commemorates each year the definitive triumph of life over death, a victory that unfolds without ever knowing reversal. At the springtime banquet, those who drink the ritual beverage do not imagine the life they wish for in their prayers as a succession of rises and falls, of fortune and misfortune, of strength and weakness — but rather as a continuous progress in strength, in happiness, and in health.

Perhaps it was in possessing this simple and optimistic idea that the Indo-Europeans found the inner power to conquer the world.

On this point, one should note the absence of the dead from the spring festivals of the Indo-Europeans. Unless our analysis is seriously incomplete, nowhere — neither in the boisterous feasts of the Latin peasants, nor in the drunken revelries of the Norse warriors, nor in the frolics of the young Armenian women — have we seen the least trace of melancholy, or even of solemn meditation upon the souls of the dead who might be thought to animate the newly awakened vegetation.

Nowhere have we found that "dreamy and voluptuous cult of death" which Renan discerned in the Adonia, nor that impulse to explain what is born by what has disappeared — to link the sources of life with the realm of the dead — that Marcel Granet detected in the springtime beliefs of the ancient Chinese (Granet, *La Vie et la Mort...*, École des Hautes Études, section des sciences religieuses, Annuaire 1920–21, p. 16–18).

But though the principle of interpretation differs, it is crucial to emphasise that among all these peoples, the ritual substance of the spring festival remains the same — proof, no doubt, that this ritual material predates the various legendary cycles that later overlaid it.

The question of whether rites or legends came first cannot, of course, be settled absolutely — since each constantly reacts upon and reshapes the other. Yet it remains of great interest to determine whether, apart from the ambrosian interpretation we know, the springtime rites of the Indo-Europeans might have stood on their own, independent of any doctrine of ambrosia — that is, whether they might originally have expressed more general beliefs, common to other civilisations as well.

And it is precisely to this conclusion that we are led by a comparative study of spring festivals in two societies as different as Indo-European and ancient Chinese. These Chinese festivals, recently reconstructed by Marcel Granet in several works — notably in his *Fêtes et Chansons anciennes de la Chine* (Paris, 1919) — show such striking analogies with certain Indo-European spring feasts, especially that of Anna Perenna, that Granet himself felt compelled to point them out in his notes.

We would like to sketch here a comparison between the two traditions, to show the original independence of the ritual material — which, among the Indo-Europeans, eventually organised itself around the idea of immortality, the drink of immortality.

I. The Festival of Ambrosia and the Spring Rites

We have already indicated, following M. Granet, the meaning that the Chinese attached to their seasonal ceremonies: they celebrated, in spring and in autumn, the meeting of the two sexual principles, *yin* and *yang*.

Thus, the spring festivals were in close relation with those of autumn; both appear, at first glance, as belonging to the same type

— *"festivals of the mountains and waters."*

"I have the impression," writes M. Granet (op. cit., p. 137), *"that the crossing of the waters and the gathering of flowers played a greater role in the spring festivals, whereas in autumn it was rather the climbing of hills and the collection of firewood."*

And a few lines later:

"Spring festivals and autumn festivals do not seem to have had the same importance; spring was surely the season of the principal rejoicings."

1. The Chinese Spring Festivals and the Waters

These spring festivals were celebrated sometimes at the edge of a lake or a pond, sometimes near a ford or a spring, sometimes at the confluence of two rivers (Granet, op. cit., p. 130).

The philosophical explanation is straightforward: spring is the season when the activity of the yang, concentrated deep within the yellow springs, bursts forth and rises to the surface — the season, as the texts say, *"when the sources of water are stirred."* (Granet, La Vie et la Mort, p. 16).

The renewal of life comes from the depths of the northern waters (ibid.). At least, this is how the learned commentators explain it. But the ancient Chinese who, a thousand years before our era, gathered around a body of water probably sought no such metaphysical reasoning. For them, it was enough to see, each spring, the springs swell and the rivers rise, to justify their rite —

the visible sign that life itself was returning.

2. The Chinese Spring Festivals as Feasts of Communion

Around the body of water, the inhabitants of neighbouring villages would gather together.

"Young men went in search of one another and set out in groups; some offered their chariots, others invited themselves along. Upon arriving at the festival grounds, one found great animation; there were doubtless temporary structures, itinerant merchants, a crowd of wagons and boats, and ferrymen calling out to customers... Drinking bouts and communal meals completed the sense of communion. An orgy ended the feast, during which the ancient rhinoceros horn was used: for these solemnities had an august, sacred character." Granet, *Fêtes et Chansons...*, p. 133–137.

Thus, these were not mere rustic gatherings: they were true communal celebrations, binding together the people of the countryside through shared feasting, libations, and ritual intimacy — a moment when the entire community symbolically partook of life renewed.

It is as though one were witnessing, on the banks of the Tiber, the Roman festival of Anna Perenna, or the frolics of the Gauls by Lake Saint-Andéol. To complete the resemblance, here are the prayers for "perennity":

"In this exceptional communal meal, everyone became aware of a kind of intimacy—different from that which founds kinship, less part of daily life, but of a higher nature, since in the intoxication of these feasts the

feeling burst forth with force. On both sides, with a cup made from rhinoceros horn, they drank to one another's health: 'Ten thousand years of life! A life without end!' And all gave thanks together." Granet, *La Religion des Chinois*, p. 15–16

Thus, says Ovid about the feast of Anna:

Invenies illic qui Nestoris ebibat annos,
Quae sit per calices facta Sibylla suos...

"You will find there those who would drink the years of Nestor,
Or the Sibyl who, through her cups, has made herself immortal."

In both cases — among the Romans and the ancient Chinese — the festival meal is a sacrament of longevity, a ritual communion of eternal life shared through the sacred drink.

3. Men and Women Attend the Chinese Spring Festivals

"It is a unique fact in the classical ritual," says M. Granet of these spring festivities (*Fêtes...*, p. 164), *"that a single festival should bring together, in the open countryside, both men and women."*

This joint participation of both sexes — their equal presence and the active, prominent role accorded to women in the ceremonies — is precisely what also characterises the Indo-European festival of ambrosia. In both traditions, the spring feast becomes not only a rite of renewal and communion, but also a moment of sexual and cosmic harmony, when male and female principles unite to affirm the return of life and the continuity of creation.

4. The Chinese spring festivals include, besides the communal feast, sexual rites and rites of competition, of tournament, of combat...

It will be remembered that the ritual core of the ambrosia festival seemed to us to be composed of three scenes: the expulsion and punishment of the "demon" drinker; the feast of the "gods"; the expedition of the false "goddess." In ancient times, rites no doubt corresponded as well to the legends of struggle between gods and demons. Now, the Chinese spring festivals, in which we have just noted an important communal meal, are composed essentially of two series of rites: sexual games and scenes of combat.

(a) Sexual games.

"In these festivals of renewal and youth," says M. Granet (La Religion des Chinois, p. 14), *"sexual communion was the principal rite, and at all times the word spring has meant the idea of love. When could love have had greater effective power than in its fresh newness? ..."*

Thus are explained the numerous sexual rites and games of the Chinese spring festivals, thus are explained the verses of *"those love songs of the Che King"* which M. Granet has made the centre of his study.

Of all these rites, we shall retain only one, which suggests a possible explanation for the Indo-European episode of the amorous demon and the false fiancée:

"The ancient festivals were above all festivals of initiation, which brought into social intercourse the young people hitherto confined within their family hamlet: betrothals and marriages, which lessened the isolation of local groups, were concluded there for the benefit of the community and under its supervision. The bands that the tournaments opposed were made up of young people who were to be neither from the same village nor of the same sex..." (Op. cit., p. 11.)

Here again, Chinese philosophy explains the rise of "amorous desire," like the swelling of the waters and the renewal of nature, by the growth of the *yang* and *yin* principles. The Indo-European myth does not express as much, but it dimly implies a similar belief when it shows the same demon drunk with ambrosia and with love.

(b) Scenes of combat.

These rites are no less essential than the preceding ones. M. Granet mentions the *"principal contests"* — crossing the water and climbing the mountain, around which gathered other games — fishing, chases, gathering of herbs, battles with plants...

"One feels that in all these exercises there must have been a great spirit of emulation, and that the climbing, the chases, the gatherings were all occasions for struggles and contests; people exchanged invitations and challenges. Yet the joyful excitement of this gathered youth did not take place in disorder; these were not mere scuffles, nor were the challenges confused shouts: the movements and the voice followed the sound of the instruments; the drum was beaten, the clay tambourine resounded, and to the rhythm they gave, along the water's edge and on the slopes of the hills,

processional dances unfolded in song." (J. Granet, *Fêtes et Chansons*, p. 135.)

There were contests in the water, carried out in various ways — sometimes even in the form of boat races (Id., *Religion des Chinois*, p. 34).

Before such a spectacle, we can imagine what ambrosian rites of contests and combats may have given rise, in the corresponding cycle of legends, to the themes of the sea duel, of the challenge and quarrel at the gods' table, and finally of the struggle between gods and demons.

The verbal battle, the exchange of challenges that fills the *Lokasenna* or opens the Hesiodic episode of Prometheus, becomes clear when one recalls the "sung contests" of the ancient Chinese. In any case, there is here a shared feature of both Indo-European and Chinese rites, and we may say of the former what M. Granet says of the latter (*Fêtes*, p. 204):

"In our festivals, every ritual activity — whatever its material form — took the shape of a contest, and over everything they engaged in ceremonial struggles..."

⁂

Finally, just as the Chinese spring festival was a vegetation festival, so too the Festival of Ambrosia must have concerned the fertility of the fields and the growth of useful plants.

Thus we can explain the presence, in our legendary cycle, of two episodes — the expedition of the god disguised as a woman, and the expulsion and slaying of the thieving demon — which, in their very form and apart from any interpretation, correspond exactly to two common rites of vegetation festivals.

∗∗∗

It remains for us to understand how these various rites — of water, of communion, of sexuality, of combat, and so on — which we already find grouped together in non–Indo-European spring festivals, came to be interpreted among the Indo-Europeans in such a way as to form the legendary cycle of ambrosia.

In other words, we must try to understand how one of these rites — the communal feast — came to assume within the festival, within the ritual sequence, such an important place that all the other rites became merely its preparation or its continuation.

II. The Festival of Ambrosia and the Potlatch

We know the considerable importance that questions of food hold in the concerns of every primitive society. *Primum vivere* — first, to live. The very organisation of the clan reflects the upheavals and revolutions of food supply: successful hunting or fishing, the abundance of banquets offered by fortunate hunters or fishers to their clan, appear today as an essential factor in the individualisation of power.

Much more than a magician, the first chief was an able provider of nourishment (see, most recently, Davy, *Des Clans aux Empires*, Part I, ch. VI, "*Les Conditions de l'individualisation du pouvoir,*" pp. 106–132). What wonder, then, that mythology reproduces in its legends the same concerns, the same scenes?

"He who aspires to become chief," writes M. Davy (ibid., p. 124), *"must be for his clan a great provider of food. He must have, above all and always, the most fruitful fishing and hunting. Mythology (American) gives us the most significant indications on this point. We see, in fact, almost all the stories of heroes begin in the same way: the clan or the tribe finds itself in the utmost famine — destruction is certain — when one member of the group disappears and goes to be initiated by one of the numerous supernatural beings — spirits of the sea, of the canoe, or of the forest — into a fishing or hunting of extraordinary abundance. He then returns as saviour, bringing back not only the produce of this supernatural hunt or fishing to meet the first needs, but also secrets of hunting or fishing which will henceforth put the group beyond the reach of any famine. The collections of Boas and Hunt for the Kwakiutl, as well as those of the Tlingit or Haida, abound with such stories."*

This pattern of nourishing legends from North America illuminates the first part of the Indo-European cycle of ambrosia. In the latter, it is a specific drink to be prepared; in the former, it is simply a matter of fishing or hunting. But the drama is the same in both cases: threat of famine and death among the gods or among the members of the clan; the expedition of a heroic saviour to a marine figure, who eventually grants him the means to avert the famine; the triumphal return of the hero; the feast.

Among the Indo-Europeans, since the story concerns a drink to be brewed, the hero brings back from his expedition a vessel, the "Vessel of the Sea" — an original but recognisable adaptation of the tale of nourishing initiation.

The duel of transformations (the contest of metamorphoses) clearly reflects what is generally known about initiation rituals, in which the initiate confronts objects, forms, and beings of every kind, often shifting and unstable.

In this first section, then, the Indo-European cycle appears to derive from true "mysteries of ambrosia", or from ritual mysteries centred on a sacred drink meant to represent ambrosia — mysteries naturally involving an initiation, in the full social sense of the term.

※※※

Among the semi-civilised peoples of North America from whom M. Davy borrowed the pattern of the nourishing tale just described — that is, among the Kwakiutl, the Tlingit, and the Haida — these nourishing rites and collective feasts play an important, indeed a central role in social life. Retaining their indigenous name, sociologists have drawn from them an entire and highly interesting theory: the theory of the potlatch (see Davy, op. cit.; Mauss, *Anthropologie*, 1920, pp. 396–397).

According to these authors, the potlatch began as a special case within the system of total prestations that regulated relations within the tribe — that is, between its two phratries, the two halves of the tribe, each consisting of several clans, each forming a distinct moral personality, residing in different territories, and so forth. This system of total prestations governed the entire life of the two phratries:

A man of phratry A could only marry a woman of phratry B — therefore, each phratry had to supply the other with women. The same applied to all important circumstances of life.

"The potlatch," says M. Mauss (ibid.), *"is that institution, hitherto thought peculiar to the North-West of America, in which clans and phratries, set in rivalry, compete with one another in expenditure and even in the destruction of wealth, and which regulates the entire social, political, religious, aesthetic, and economic life of the Kwakiutl, Haida, Tlingit, etc. It forms part of the system which we have proposed to call the system of total prestations — a system normal in all clan-based societies. For exogamy is an exchange of all the women among clans united by kinship; rights, things, and religious rites, and indeed everything, are exchanged between the clans and among the generations of the various clans — as is evident, for example, among the Warramunga of Central Australia, where everything is done from actor phratry to spectator phratry."*

But the potlatch distinguishes itself by its ostentatious, usurious, and agonistic character — by the competitive nature of these exchanges, which take the form not merely of peaceful reciprocal contracts but of a real struggle, at times almost to the death, between the phratries.

The aim of the potlatch, at this stage of social life, is in fact for the phratry that offers it — under the obligation of future reciprocation — to affirm its power, its credit, until the other phratry, by an inverse potlatch, has regained the advantage. Hence the agonistic character noted by M. Mauss:

"The potlatch," writes M. Davy (op. cit., p. 107), *"transforms the primitive fundamental rites of obligatory prestations between phratries by introducing the principle of challenge, the logical outcome of rivalry, and employs them to produce inequality, rather than to maintain equilibrium. Beneath its concrete appearances, the potlatch is a festival given under obligation of return, constituting a religious ceremony in which both the living and the dead of the concerned clans commune and confront one another. This festival consists in a solemn distribution of food and gifts, which automatically renders the giver creditor of analogous future distributions, and confers upon him the right to appropriate a part of the names, emblems, and privileges of the rivals whom his lavish generosity has eclipsed and publicly placed in the impossibility of replying to his challenge."*

In this latter definition, M. Davy already indicates the natural and inevitable evolution that transformed the potlatch — almost everywhere it is observed — from a collective exchange of prestations between phratries into a distribution of food offered to the clans by a single individual.

M. Davy (op. cit., pp. 108 ff.) has shown how the potlatch thus became the principal mechanism for the individualisation of power in primitive societies.

And since it is well known that mythological evolution and

political evolution proceed hand in hand, this change in the meaning of nourishing rites, this individualisation of power to the benefit of one member of the clan, must be contemporaneous with the formation of true mythology — that is, a mythology containing a hierarchy of personal gods, built upon the ruins of totemic religion.

Thus, in the Kwakiutl, Haida, and other mythological tales mentioned earlier (the expedition of the nourishing hero, the feast, etc.), the distribution of food really establishes a new social order:

"The hero of the miraculous hunt or fishing that is to save the starving tribe," says M. Davy (op. cit., p. 124), *"on his return — endowed with the prestige of the initiate and the great provider of food — proceeds to make distributions of nourishment, during which the quality of the pieces distributed determines the social rank of each of those who take part in this hierarchical distribution."*

⁎⁎⁎

To what extent is it legitimate to generalise these observations made among the Indians of the North-West Coast of America? We shall leave that question to others.

But among the Indo-Europeans, the existence of similar "nourishing contests", and the social value of feasts offered by a successful hunter or a wealthy farmer, does not seem to us at all improbable.

To confine ourselves to Russia, a land whose conservative spirit can be observed even through its most violent revolutions, the *byliny* introduce us to an ancient hero, Volkh Vseslavievitch, whose great merit lies in feeding his entire *droujina* (band of companions) sumptuously and miraculously through hunting and fishing.

Another hero, the quintessential peasant, Mikula Selianinovitch, when asked his name, immediately recounts a scene of "individualised potlatch":

"I go to plough my rye, to stack the sheaves, to haul the bundles home; my wife will grind the grain, make groats, brew beer; and I shall offer it to the peasants, who will greet me then as Mikoulouchka Selianinovitch."

We shall therefore limit ourselves to noting how the Indo-European cycle of ambrosia is illuminated in the light of the barbarian potlatch. There, too, we find two phratries — two related but rival clans — who, in connection with a feast, first collaborate, then enter into conflict, so that the feast ultimately ensures for one of them victory and power over the other.

After this distribution of food, a new social order reigns in the supernatural world: inequality is established among the distributor, the beneficiaries, and the excluded. The Feast of the Grail, the Promethean feast of Mekone, and the *sóma* feast each establish among beings a social hierarchy analogous to that which the potlatch is specifically designed to define.

Furthermore, this spring festival, in which not only the divine and demonic clans quarrel over participation in the feast, but in which the demons also demand goddesses as brides from the gods, recalls precisely that system of total prestations of which, according to M. Mauss, the potlatch is only one special case.

In any case, we see no better way to explain the double character of the feast of ambrosia — both contractual and agonistic, as M. Mauss says.

Everything happens as though, in the spring festival where the Indo-European tribe gathered, the central rite consisted of an alimentary scene analogous first to the collective, then to the individualised potlatch. If, at some very ancient period, division into phratries existed in Indo-European society, we can easily imagine how an annual drama could have developed around the feast, grouping together all the springtime rites and forming the legendary cycle we now recognise.

Given that every collective potlatch is offered under obligation of return, one may readily suppose that, each year, the roles of gods and demons, of "victors" and "vanquished" in the potlatch, alternated between the phratries — otherwise, the ambrosia festival would have marked the permanent subjugation of one phratry by the other.

But these are hypotheses on which there is no need to dwell. What is clearer — and pertains to a less remote past — is the prominent role given throughout the cycle to a single god: the one who wins the Cauldron, who punishes the demon at the gods' table, who disguises himself as a woman to deceive another demon. He stands apart distinctly from the anonymous multitude of his brothers — indeed, he is the only one who does so.

It is not a question here of a tendency toward monotheism; it is simply the mythological expression of a major social fact: the individualisation of power, the appearance of a personal chief within the clan or the tribe — through the mechanism of the potlatch.

∗∗∗

Before attempting to identify the human ritual drink of which the Ambrosia in the legendary cycle must be the transposition, we must first show how this drink — whatever it may have been — came to be credited with the marvellous power of immortality. Here again, the beliefs of so-called "semi-civilised" peoples help us understand the Indo-European phenomenon:

"This conquest of food intended to supply the potlatch," explains M. Davy (*Des Clans aux Empires*, p. 125), *"does not correspond solely to an economic function, but equally to a magical activity... The food takes on a kind of mystical value at the same time that the one who has brought it back becomes surrounded with prestige. Food is life and strength; it is mana. He who gives food, or he who eats it, accumulates strength and produces life. And food itself, by an extension corresponding to primitive mystical thought, becomes one of the categories through which domination and possession are conceived: one eats one's dead enemy in order to assimilate his substance, his mana, as food. Polynesian mythology, for instance, tells of great battles between the sons of Heaven and Earth, in which one triumphs over all his brothers — except the one he has failed to*

transform into food."

This helps us understand the double meaning of ambrosia in the Indo-European legendary cycle: it is both the food of life par excellence, the food of endless life, and at the same time the great instrument of domination by which the gods assert their power over their rivals.

We understand, at the same time, a Chinese ritual that closely recalls the Roman peasants' prayers on the day of Anna Perenna: the ancient Chinese, gathered in spring for the ritual feast, passed around a great drinking horn, saying: *"Ten thousand years of life! A life without end!"*

This Chinese rite represents an intermediate stage in the evolution that, pushed to its limit among the Indo-Europeans, transformed a certain ritual beverage into the "drink of immortality."

It is this real ritual beverage that we must now attempt to determine.

III. Ambrosia and Beer

We no longer need to justify this final problem: everything that precedes necessarily implies a close connection between the communal feast and the legendary cycle, and consequently between the drink of the feast and that of the myth.

It is, moreover, a universal fact that every society, imagining the invisible world on the model of the visible, attributes to its gods its own passions, its own forms of activity, and — among other things — its culinary tastes.

The Mediterranean gods enjoy wine just as their worshippers do; and the "blessed bread" consecrated to the Lord varies in flavour from one province to another. Sometimes, by way of reaction, these foods and beverages once attributed to the gods take on a sacred character that excludes them from ordinary use: this is the case with the Indo-Iranian *sóma*.

More often, the drink of the gods simply acquires, on the human level, a special prestige: this was the case with beer among the Scandinavians (see Cahen, *La Libation*, p. 21).

What, then, could have been the drink used by the Indo-Europeans during their spring festival? One immediately thinks of the ancient fermented beverage, mead (hydromel, **medhu*), whose name has survived almost everywhere — either in its original sense or to designate the honey from which it was made.

That this **medhu* was regarded as a divine drink, a libation substance, is certain; there may even have existed a "Cycle of the Mead", narrating the making and adventures of this beverage. Certain Eddic episodes and some Hindu traditions suggest as much.

The Greeks, who used the word μέθυ (*méthy*) for any fermented drink, especially wine, knew that it was not to be offered in libation to infernal deities (Sophokles, *Oedipus at Kolonos*, v. 481); perhaps this is a verbal remnant of ancient prohibitions.

However, from what we have been able to reconstruct of the cycle of ambrosia, nothing in it recalls the properties or preparation of mead. If the Greeks early confused ἀμβροσία (*ambrosia*) and μέθυ, it is because both had lost their precise meanings. Similarly, if in the *Vedas*, *madhu* and *amṛta* sometimes overlap, it is due to the influence of soma; but later, in the *Amṛtamanthana* of the epics — where *amṛta* regains its independence — nothing recalls *madhu*.

We must therefore look elsewhere.

Above all, the presence in the Cycle of Ambrosia of themes covering ancient, evidently vegetative rites (the expulsion and killing of the demon, the god's disguise as a woman) proves that Ambrosia must originally have corresponded to a ritual drink of vegetal origin.

⁂

It may be observed that among the Indo-European peoples whose migrations carried them southward, the mythical name of Ambrosia was well preserved, but the drink designated by that name underwent one of three fates:

Either the divine drink was assimilated to a new human beverage, specific to the new homeland of these peoples (*sóma* among the Aryans, sometimes wine among the Greeks); or it became an imaginary drink with no earthly counterpart (the epic *amṛta*, the Greek ἀμβροσία); or it was personified, becoming a divine being (the Ameša Spənta Amərətāt, the Okeanid Ambrosia, or Anna Perenna).

Conversely, among the Indo-European peoples who remained in the North, the mythic name of ambrosia fell out of use, yet the divine drink itself was consistently identified with a human beverage — namely, beer: the beer of the Tuatha Dé Danann in Ireland, the beer of the Æsir in Scandinavia, and, similarly, the beer of Vladimir-the-Sun's feasts among the Russians.

It would be premature to draw a definite conclusion from this single phenomenon. However, it suggests the following three-part hypothesis:

1. In the period of common Indo-European life, the Indo-Europeans knew, alongside mead, a fermented drink made from cereals (probably barley), which they perhaps consumed only ceremonially, during the spring festival. Because of this solemn use, the drink acquired a religious character and a ritual name (**Nmrto-* or a similar term).

2. The Indo-Europeans who migrated southward, owing to various geographical circumstances — the encounter with the vine, the *sóma* plant, and others — abandoned the preparation of this cereal-based beverage, replacing it with drinks more common or easier to produce in their new climates, namely *sóma* and wine.

The legendary cycle of ambrosia adapted itself to this ritual transformation: the themes of *amṛta* were transferred to soma, and ambrosia was assimilated to various kinds of wine. Where this adaptation did not occur, the ambrosia ceased to correspond to any human reality and became a mythical essence, a fanciful liqueur, a proper name ready to be personified.

3. Conversely, the Indo-European peoples who remained in the North generalised and, to a certain extent, secularised the use of the cereal-based beverage. Neither wine nor *sóma* existed there to compete with it, and barley cultivation flourished in those climates. They therefore made this drink their preferred beverage, often replacing the older mead.

But at the same time, the ritual and religious name — the "liquor of immortality" — was too solemn to suit everyday use, and thus gave way to simpler designations ("barley drink," for instance, or other names).

Moreover, this popularisation of the former drink of immortality, along with the disappearance of its sacred name, must have encouraged — among the Germanic peoples — the very evolution we noted earlier: from the beer of the Æsir as a divine beverage to an ordinary drink of the gods, stripped of any properly immortalising power.

Here, then, is the hypothesis suggested to us by a very general phenomenon — the distribution throughout the Indo-European world of beer on the one hand, and of the mythic name "ambrosia" on the other. A few observations will serve to support this hypothesis:

1. To begin with, one objection dismisses itself: it is almost universally accepted that the Indo-Europeans did not know beer, precisely because they have left no common inherited word for it in their descendant languages — unlike mead (*medhu*). However, if our hypothesis is correct, in the Indo-European period the only name for beer — or for the earlier cereal-based fermented drink that preceded it — was the sacred, ritual name "ambrosia."

The peoples who remained in climates favourable to the preservation of beer and secularised its use later chose new names independently. Those who, like the Greeks, rediscovered beer at a later period likewise invented new terms for it.

Schrader, in his *Reallexikon* (entry "Bier"), nevertheless recalls that certain technical terms are common to two or more Indo-European peoples:

1. Old High German *briuwan* "to brew"; Thracian-Phrygian βρῦτον, βροῦτος ἐκ κριθῶν πόμα — "a drink made from barley" (Hesykhios); Latin *defrutum*. 2. Old High German *trestir* "yeast"; Latin *fraces*. 3. Old English *ealu*, Old Norse *öl* "beer"; Lithuanian *alus* (whence Finnish *olut*); Old Slavic *olu* "beer"; cf. Old Prussian *alu* "mead."

But what would indeed be astonishing — what is impossible, in fact — is the unanimous agreement among these terms, which are all of relatively recent formation.

2. Setting aside the question of names, it is by no means improbable that the Indo-Europeans knew a beverage made from

barley. The use of unhopped beer is attested in northern Europe long before the Christian era.

Barley was certainly known to the Indo-Europeans, since the same root appears in Greek κρῖ, κριθή, Latin *hordeum*, Old High German *gersta*, Armenian *gari*, and in the Celtic names for beer (*koúrmi*, *kórma* according to the ancients; Gaulish *cervesia*, Old Irish *cuirm*, Welsh *cwref*, etc.).

There is therefore no material impossibility in supposing that they may have once a year, at the spring festival, prepared a fermented beverage based on barley.

3. Among the Greeks there are traces of this ancient sacred drink. Without returning to the relationship already noted (above, p. 262) — according to Athenaeus — between the *pankarpia*, the cereal-based *thargelos*, and the ambrosia, we may simply recall the well-known passage from Miss Harrison's *Prolegomena* (p. 414 ff.). There, in studying the epithets of Dionysos, she shows that the adjectives Βρόμιος (*Brómios*), Βραιτής (*Braitês*), and Σαβάζιος (*Sabázios*) testify to an earlier stage in which Dionysos was not yet the god of wine, but rather the god of a fermented cereal drink (βρόμος = "oats"; Βραιτής cf. Late Latin *braesum* = "malt"; Σαβάζιος cf. Illyrian *sabaia, sabaium* = "a kind of beer").

Is it then mere coincidence that, in Hyginus (fab. 182), where Ambrosia is named among the Oceanids who nursed Zeus or Dionysus, we also find, immediately beside Ambrosia as her counterpart, a Bromia (cf. Servius *on Ecl.* VI 15: *Brome*)?

This same, unfortunately fragmentary, text also tells of a scene of gender transformation involving Ambrosia, Bromia, and their sisters — a scene which, though it does not precisely reproduce the ambrosian episode of the god disguised as a goddess, is nevertheless intriguing in this context: as Ambrosia, Bromia, and their sisters begin to age, the god they have nurtured has them changed by Medeia into young men.

Perhaps, as we have suggested, this reflects a special Dionysian form of the Indo-European ambrosia cycle and festival. But for our present purpose we need only retain the pair Ambrosiē–Bromiē, that is, without capitalisation, "drink of immortality – drink of barley."

This pairing confirms both Miss Harrison's hypothesis and our own. Finally, Miss Harrison also wondered whether the Homeric epithet of the Earth, ζείδωρος ("giver of spelt"), so remarkable in its precision, might not itself derive from the ritual use of that particular grain.

4. Even Vedic India, where the *sóma* plant and the drink extracted from it had — according to our hypothesis — replaced barley and the barley-based beverage, seems to have preserved the memory of the earlier state of things.

It is well known how countless variants the *Brāhmaṇas* give of the *sóma* battle between the Deva and the Asura: sometimes the moon, sometimes the *udumbara* tree, sometimes the sacred meter *gāyatrī*, sometimes the sun, sometimes the seasons, and so forth, become the stakes and the instruments of victory in the conflict.

Now, among these accounts there is one in which barley is exalted above all other plants and plays in the struggle precisely the role of the *amṛta*:

"When the Deva and the Asura were in rivalry, all the plants deserted the gods; only the barley remained faithful. The gods triumphed, and with the barley they won back from their rivals the other plants." (*Śatapatha Brāhmaṇa* III, 6, 1, 8–9)

5. Beer, by natural fitness, was the designated drink for spring festivals. The best beer is brewed in March, for it is then that the germination of barley and the accompanying chemical transformations occur under the most favourable conditions. The expression "March beer" is still in common use today to designate the finest brew.

Moreover, M. Cahen (*La Libation...*, p. 107) has already emphasised — though presenting it as a Germanic innovation — the profound difference between **medhu-* and beer: beer is a beverage generally brewed by women, using grain likely cultivated by women themselves.

Now, the spring festivals, including that of the Ambrosia, were mixed celebrations, and women often played an essential part in them. Thus, as a March beverage, and as a drink prepared by women, beer naturally finds its place within the cycle of the Ambrosia.

6. Finally, if we are right, there ought to be found, within the

cycle of the ambrosia, among the themes of "fabrication," certain details that can be explained only in reference to beer.

We will not take into account here the Scandinavian account, where the drink is quite explicitly presented as beer; we shall consider only the fantastic description left by the epic poets of India of the churning of the *amṛta*.

For them, this operation has no real equivalent in human practice; they seem indeed to be thinking of the churning (*manthana*) of milk in a jar, yet their description quickly outgrows those narrow bounds, and one would be hard pressed to recognise, in the verses of the *Mahābhārata*, the humble domestic labour of making butter.

Now, there exists a Finnish poem — the twentieth rune of the Kalevala — which, likewise expanding it to fantastic proportions, describes the brewing of beer. When one compares it to the Indian account, one cannot fail to recognise the analogy between the two scenes, though they belong to entirely different cycles.

The house-mistress of Pohjola, preparing the wedding feast for her daughter, "*brews the mighty drink in the new vessel, in the birchwood vat.*" (trans. Léo Leouzon Le Duc)

"*For a month the stones of the hearth glowed red beneath the fire; the water boiled through several summers; the great forests were laid waste to feed the flame, the springs were exhausted to supply the water...*

"*The smoke rose above the island, the flame shone from the top of the* headland; the smoke whirled, a thick cloud in the sky, from the heart of the powerful hearth, from the immense fire; it filled half the land of Pohja, it darkened all the region of Karelia.

"The people looked upon this sight, they looked and were seized with wonder: 'What is this smoke that rises? What is this mist that whirls in the air?...'"

Even better, the Finnish account may perhaps explain the strange Indian detail of the poison — the one born from excessive fermentation, threatening to bring death to the worlds — a detail that, from certain traces in Avestan literature, can be traced back to the Indo-Iranian period.

Once the brewing was complete, the beer was put into a barrel. But the beer began to stir:

"If only someone would come now to drink me, to exhaust me; if someone would come to sing my praises, to celebrate me gloriously!"

In vain they searched for the desired singer... Then,

"The red beer cried out threats, the fresh drink swelled violently in the oak barrel, beneath its copper hoops: 'If no singer is brought to me — a good singer, one able to sing skilfully, to raise a solemn song — I shall break all my bonds; I shall swell so greatly that the barrel will fly into splinters!'"

At once, the mistress of Pohjola sends her maidservant to carry invitations to everyone — the crippled, the wretched, the blind —

but especially to Väinämöinen, "*so that he may let his fair songs be heard.*" And thus, the peril is averted.

It is in exactly the same manner that, at the end of the preparation of the *amṛta*, the ocean, continuing to ferment, produces a poison that threatens to overflow the worlds, and Viṣṇu, overseeing the operation, implores Śiva to absorb the poison.

In both cases, the ritual memory — or rather, the everyday sight of what occurs during the brewing of beer — seems to have suggested to the poets the features of their fantastic descriptions, and in particular this detail of the excessive fermentation that must be stopped.

*
* *

The hypothesis is certainly not proven by this collection of mere presumptions. In any case, we see no better way to establish the necessary correspondence between the legendary cycle and the spring festival of Ambrosia. Here is how the solution we propose may be summarised:

Everything happens as if the cycle of Ambrosia translated into legendary form a spring festival whose central episode was a kind of beer potlatch — or, more generally, a ritual feast involving a fermented drink made from cereals.

General Conclusions

At the end of this study, it is important to draw some general conclusions — and, above all, to formulate certain methodological rules that may have broader applications.

1. The first is not new, but it finds here a strong confirmation: it is by starting from the rites that one must seek the explanation of the legends.

As long as we merely identified and catalogued the ambrosial legends among the various peoples of the Indo-European family, we were not yet in a position to interpret them. But once they were considered as original translations of springtime and communal rites, all their strangeness vanished, and their profound unity became apparent.

The reverse operation — an attempt to explain the rites by means of the legends — would have produced no result.

2. Comparative mythology (in the narrow sense of the term, i.e., within linguistic or cultural families) holds a necessary place in the science of religions.

If, for example, one were to take the myth of Pandora and

attempt to interpret it directly in light of Australian or African ethnographic data — that is, by immediately applying the ethnographic method — one would arrive at an entirely artificial explanation. On the other hand, if one limited oneself to studying it purely historically, one would clarify neither its formation nor its constituent elements.

The comparative method (in the strict sense) has allowed us to avoid both pitfalls: it has shown us that the story of Pandora and the *píthos* is an adaptation of the Indo-European story of the False Bride and the Vessel of Immortality.

This approach first made it possible to extend the historical study of the myth back into prehistory; then, having thus established the Indo-European foundation, we could apply the ethnographic method — that is, we could relate it to universally attested religious phenomena (such as sexual rites, spring processions of effigies or men disguised as women, and the various games and contests associated with ceremonies of exchange and prestation).

This comparative method must, of course, be applied with caution: there are countless Greek and Latin legends that have nothing Indo-European about them and therefore fall outside its scope.

Yet up to now, in reaction against Max Müller or Regnault, scholars have perhaps gone too far in the opposite direction.

The example of Ambrosia serves as a timely reminder that it is indeed possible to reconstruct, if not a full Indo-European mythology, then at least certain well-defined groups of Indo-European legends, connected with parallel groups of rites. One has only to look for them.

3. It would be easy, by classifying all the forms and accidents of evolution of the legends — as we have recorded and explained them throughout the second part — to derive several general "laws" of this evolution.

One could thus study: *Mechanical* accidents and their consequences (the loss or atrophy of an essential detail; the splitting of themes; confusions, substitutions, contaminations, etc.); *Psychological* accidents (the personification of an object; changes in the moral quality of characters — for instance, a sympathetic figure taking the place of an originally hostile one, or a single character substituting for two originally distinct figures); *Sociological* accidents (the introduction of philosophical or social ideas; the "national stamp" impressed on the legends — such as a taste for the colossal, a satirical spirit, or mysticism); *Geographical* accidents (the fusion or merging of local variants, and so forth).

However, after the analysis of a single cycle, it would be premature to pursue this theoretical study in detail. It is highly probable that we have not yet encountered all the possible modes of transformation of legends.

4. The Indo-European mythology we have glimpsed has nothing primitive about it. We have said that the legends of Ambrosia are an original, poetic interpretation of pre-existing rites.

How did this interpretation arise? It is deliberately that we have spoken of poetry.

We have proof that — from India to Rome, from Greece to Armenia — songs and recitations accompanied the mimed episodes of the cycle: the expedition of Anna disguised among Mars's followers, the procession of the Εἰρεσιώνη, the sending of Vāc to the demon Viçoávasu, the making of the effigy *Vicak*, not to mention the adventure of Thor disguised before Thrym — all of these gave rise to ritual tales or songs, of which we sometimes retain curious fragments.

It must have been the same among the Indo-Europeans; the imagination of individuals, of poets, must already at that time have been an important factor in the evolution of the legends. As in the case of the magico-religious dramas of the Australians, where *"the scenarios are invented by individuals we know"* (A. van Gennep, *Formation des Légendes*, p. 116, citing *Mythes et Légendes d'Australie*), so too among the Indo-Europeans the shaping of legend was a creative process.

In any case, we are dealing with peoples who believed in multiple, well-individualised gods, beings related to but distinct from the forces of nature. These semi-civilised peoples, at least in their spring festival, show us only survivals of totemism; at most, the episode of the False Bride may suggest an ancient exogamic law, and the ambrosial potlatch, an old organisation into clans and phratries.

Finally, if the episode of the punished demon seems indeed a new interpretation of an ancient rite of vegetal or human sacrifice, that rite, even before the dislocation of the Indo-European community, had already been reduced to a joyful simulacrum. We must therefore abandon the notion that Indo-European mythology, like the Indo-European language, is in any sense primitive.

5. All the more reason, then, must we abandon this illusion when it comes to the Vedic, Greek, and other derived mythologies. We have seen, for example, that the legend of the fatal fiancée in India, by the end of the Vedic period (the legend of Vâc), was already as developed, almost as humanised, as it would be in Rome around the beginning of the Christian era (the legend of Anna).

Likewise, the naturalistic effusions of the *RgVeda* are nothing more than the deliberate, systematic elaboration of a tendency already perceptible — but still secondary — in the Indo-European myths.

6. Finally, we cannot conclude this study without emphasising the exceptional human value of Greek mythology. In exploring its obscure foundations too long, one risks forgetting how high it rose — both poetically and philosophically.

Nowhere — not even in India, not even among the Celts — could one find a creator who, like Aiskhylos, was able to raise from merely two or three episodes of the ancient cycle a Promethean drama. We have heard the mocking laughter of the excommunicated Loki, the incantations of the defeated Ahriman. Undoubtedly, the wrath of Prometheus Bound stems from the same origins. But when that has been said, everything has not been said.

The danger of studies like ours lies in blurring the sense of values, in establishing a dull equality among all the fantasies born of all human minds. Since it is Greece that is in question, such levelling would be sacrilege; far from serving the progress of understanding, it would mark a regression.

When Racine or Goethe, reading Sophokles or Aiskhylos, entered into communion with the Greek myths — without knowing or seeking their humble beginnings — they made better use of our human treasure than we would if, satisfied with recognising in Pandora the springtime effigy, or in Prometheus the common Indo-European punished demon, we forgot all that had later been gathered and crystallised upon them: thought, aspiration, wisdom, and beauty.

We must therefore not misunderstand the scope of the work we have just accomplished: the subterranean foundations of the temple have been cleared, but its columns and their harmony, its friezes, its altars, and its gods belong to others — the humanists, who have chosen the better part.

Tables of Correspondence

To facilitate a general and rapid examination of the Indo-European Cycle of Ambrosia, we bring together, in these final pages, the most characteristic testimonies drawn from the various Indo-European mythologies.

Since these testimonies have been examined in detail in their respective places throughout the book, their juxtaposition here requires no further commentary.

1. The Hindu Cycle (Amṛta)

I. — The Deva, fearing death, deliberate on the means of preparing the food of immortality, the *amṛta*. Advised by Viṣṇu, they decide to churn the ocean within its "vessel." For this task, they reach an agreement with the Asura.

Conquest of the instruments: The Deva, among other things, ask the Lord of the Waters to lend them the ocean for the operation.

They churn the ocean. From this churning emerge the *amṛta* itself and various divine beings (such as Lakṣmī). A poison, born from the excessive agitation, threatens the world; it is absorbed by Śiva.

III. — The Asura have stolen the *amṛta*, and in addition, they demand possession of the goddess Lakṣmī.

Viṣṇu-Nārāyaṇa, taking on the appearance of Lakṣmī and followed by Nara, also disguised as a woman, goes to the Asura. Mad with desire, they give the *amṛta* to the false goddess, who carries it back to the Deva.

II. — The Deva, assembled together, drink the *amṛta*. The Asura Rahu joins them surreptitiously. Exposed, he is beheaded by Viṣṇu; his body, as it falls, defiles the earth.

IV. — A general battle ensues. The Asura, vanquished especially by Viṣṇu, are hurled into the waters and beneath the earth. The Deva retain permanent possession of the *amṛta*.

2. The Iranian Cycle (Amərətāt and Creation)

I. — Ahura Mazdā seeks to free his creation from death, hunger, and thirst. He offers an alliance to Angra Mainyu, who refuses. (In another version: it is a question of preparing a common feast — Eznik.)

The god Tištrya goes forth to conquer the Sea from the demon Apaoša, in a duel of transformations.

Ahura Mazdā then creates, from the Good Light (perhaps dwelling within this sea), the Ameša Spənta, the holy immortals — among them Amərətāt, the genius of immortality. (Compare

Gaokerena, the plant of immortality, which also grows in this sea.) A poison, born of this sea and threatening to destroy creation, is neutralised by Tištrya.

III. — Angra Mainyu seeks to take from Ahura Mazdā's creation its health, life, and all that sustains it (cf. Amərətāt).

His daughter, Daēva Jahī, goes forth on an expedition against humankind and against creation itself, stripping them of these gifts.

II–IV. — Angra Mainyu then invades Heaven, but Ahura Mazda casts him down. A battle ensues between the Daēva and the Yazata; the Daēva are crushed, and Angra Mainyu is bound to Mount Arezura.

3. The Scandinavian Cycle (The Æsir's Ale)

I. — The Æsir have nothing to eat. They deliberate. On Thor's advice, they decide that Ægir, the god of the sea, shall brew beer for them. Ægir, however, asks that they first procure a great vessel.

The conquest of the vessel: Thor and Týr go to the giant Hymir (the genius of the wintry sea) and, after a series of trials, bring back the immense Cauldron of the Sea. (Thor kills the black bull, fishes up the serpent, etc.)

In this cauldron, Ægir brews the beer of the Æsir.

II. — The Æsir, assembled, drink the beer. Loki, the outcast, joins them and demands to drink. After a scene of insults and quarrels, the Æsir expel Loki and bind him to a rock. Through his convulsions, Loki causes earthquakes.

III. — The giant Thrym has stolen the object that alone ensures the Æsir's power and endurance: Thor's hammer. Thrym declares that he will return it only if they give him the goddess Freyja as his bride.

Thor, disguised as Freyja and accompanied by Loki, goes to Thrym's dwelling. Mad with desire, Thrym gives the object of permanence to the false bride.

IV. — Thor then slaughters Thrym and the Giants.

4. The Greek Cycles (ambrosia and Ambrosia)

I. — The gods are in need of nourishment — or, in certain versions, Zeus or Dionysus requires a nurse.

This nourishment is the ambrosia produced by the Ocean, or else this nurse is the Oceanid Ambrosia herself.

II. — A mortal (such as Tantalus) sits at the table of the gods. He steals the ambrosia. For his sacrilege, the gods crush him under a mountain (Mount Sipylus), or condemn him to the torment of a rock suspended above him.

III. — Ambrosia, the nurse of Dionysus, grows old. Then Dionysus restores her youth by transforming her into a man.

IV. — In the war of the Gods and the Titans, the ambrosia ensures the victory of the gods, through the alliance of the Hecatonkheires (compare the *phármakon* of immortality used in the war of the Gods and the Giants).

4 *bis*. A Greek Cycle, Probably Boiotian (Prometheus and the Jar of Immortality)

I. — The gods (gathered around Zeus) and the men (gathered around Prometheus) come together for a solemn feast.

Prometheus prepares the food. (According to Aiskhylos, there is an unspecified collaboration between Prometheus and Okeanos.)

II. — Prometheus, by trickery, gives to men the portion of food that rightfully belongs to the gods. In revenge, Zeus hides the grain, and also the fire necessary to cook this food; Prometheus steals the fire. The gods seize Prometheus and bind him to a mountain.

III. — Prometheus and Epimetheus have stolen from Zeus the jar (*píthos*) that contains "the absence of death" (or, in another version, "the mortal diseases"). The gods then fashion a mysterious feminine being, Pandora, and send her, escorted by Hermes, as a bride to Epimetheus. Pandora, driven by love, opens the jar, from which "the absence of death" (or "the mortal diseases") escapes.

IV. — The gods punish the brothers of Prometheus and Epimetheus: Menoitios and Atlas.

5. The Latin Cycle (Anna Perenna)

I. — The Plebeians, besieged on the Sacred Mount, are threatened with starvation. Anna Perenna, the "nurse of permanence", prepares and brings them food.

(The Latinian cycle has preserved here the trace of a maritime duel: Battus, king of the island of Melite, is summoned to surrender Anna Perenna.)

Anna Perenna is elevated to divine status.

III. — Mars demands Minerva as his wife. Anna Perenna, disguised as Minerva, and accompanied by the usual bridal procession, goes to Mars's dwelling. Mars is deceived — and a great burst of laughter ensues. (On the *cista* of Praeneste, Minerva is shown going to Mars to recover, through a "love duel," a *dolium* containing a liquid substance.)

II. — (The episode of Mamurius — i.e. Mars — being expelled and scourged belongs to another cycle.)

5 *bis*. The Latin Christian Cycle (Anna Petronilla)

I. — The Christians, gathered at the house of Saint Peter, are in need of food. Anna Petronilla prepares and serves them the meal.

III. — The pagan Flaccus demands Petronilla as his wife. Rather than yield, Petronilla lets herself die of hunger. When the bridal procession comes to fetch her, they find her dead — Flaccus is deceived and confounded.

II. — The pagan Flaccus, having caused the massacre of one of Petronilla's companions, Nicodemus secretly gathers the remains of the martyred woman. Flaccus has Nicodemus arrested and scourged, and finally thrown into the Tiber.

6. The Welsh Christian Cycle (Grail)

I. – The Christians (Fishermen and Saints) are threatened by famine. Joseph consults the Spirit, who orders him to prepare a mystical feast around the Grail, and to send a Saint on a fishing expedition.

A Saint, "the Rich Fisherman," brings back from a pond a fish which is not eaten, but which is placed near the Grail (formerly, the Grail itself?).

II. – The Saints assembled are filled by the mystical feast. A Fisherman, Moses, joins them. Hardly has he sat down when he is swallowed up and buried under a burning rock.

IV. – The Fishermen Simeon and Canaan try to massacre all the Saints. They are seized and put to torture.

III. – Mordrain is on an island, possessor of the "Grace" that baptism has just conferred upon him. The Devil, disguised as a woman, comes to steal it from him (but Christ intervenes).

&. The Russian Cycle (Maria-White Swan)

I. – The Paladins of Kiev, gathered for a feast, are in need of food. Vladimir-the-Sun sends Mikhailo Potyk to the Sea to fetch the finest food of Russian tables, the White Swan.

Mikhailo Potyk captures upon the sea the Swan-Woman, Maria. [Variant: he wins this "princess" in a game of chess played with a king from beyond the sea.] He brings back to Kiev and marries Maria–White Swan, who (after an adventure in which life-giving water intervenes) passes for immortal. Feast at Vladimir's; naturally they eat something other than the personified White Swan, Maria.

III.–IV. – One hundred and sixty foreign princes march upon Kiev and demand that Maria–White Swan be handed over to them. Mikhailo Potyk disguises himself as a woman and goes to the suitors, who, blinded by love and without suspicion, let themselves be massacred one by one.

II. – A foreign prince has carried off Maria (this time with her consent). Mikhailo Potyk arrives at their camp. The cunning Maria welcomes him kindly, gives him a cup of "green wine" that puts him to sleep. Immediately Maria turns him to stone, and the stone sinks beneath the earth.

The Feast of Immortality

A Study in Comparative Indo-European Mythology

Was written by Georges Dumézil
and translated into English by Tom Billinge.

Learn more about Tom at **TomBillinge.com**.

If you enjoyed this book, consider reading *WarYoga: Palaístra*
and the *Heroes of Greek Myth* series by Tom Billinge.

Watch for future translations by Tom from
Sanctus Arya Press.

EX UMBRA IN SOLEM

From the translator of this book...

HEROES OF GREEK MYTH

Written by Tom Billinge

The *Heroes of Greek Myth* series explores the heroic archetypes and metaphysical lessons taught in the mythology of Ancient Greece. Spanning several generations of heroes, Tom Billinge examines the timeless truths handed down to us through the millennia.

Undying Glory: The Solar Path of Greek Heroes is the first of Billinge's books. More than just a recounting of the tales of Greek heroes, it is a blueprint for modern to men to follow. The work focuses on six heroes in particular as they traverse the Solar Path, each aiming to become Solar Man — a state above the gods.

Age of Heroes: Beyond the Solar Path lays out a framework of the Ancient Greek Heroic Age as a model for a return to the values of that time. It analyzes concepts that can be gleaned from the Iliad and Odyssey, placing them in their original context within the complete Epic Cycle. With esoteric lessons drawn out from the Homeric material, this is a manual for the modern-day heroic aspirant looking to reach greatness.

Return to Hyperborea: The Heroic Initiate culminates the trilogy, postulating the hero Orpheus as transmitter of ancient Hyperborean mysteries to the Hellenic people. Looking at the Indo-European Wolf Cult in the context of Ancient Greece, this final installment in the series delves into the mystery traditions of both Samothaki and Eleusis before piecing together a Hyperborean initiatic lineage handed down through Orphic mystery rites and theogonic material.

The highly acclaimed ***Heroes of Greek Myth*** series is a triumphant call for a resurgence of true heroism in a time that so critically needs it.

Pickup your copies now at major booksellers.

Tom at the Sanctuary of the Great Gods in Samothrace, Greece

About the Translator

Tom Billinge is originally from England and lives in the USA. He grew up surrounded by Ancient Greek mythology, culture, archaeology and history, as his father was a historical geographer and his mother was Greek. After graduating with a degree in archaeology, Tom moved to Asia, where he explored temples and immersed himself in the martial and spiritual traditions of the East.

Following several years travelling the world and writing for a living, Tom returned to the West and to his roots. This led to his first book, *Undying Glory: The Solar Path of Greek Heroes* that examines the first heroes of Greek mythology. Tom then continued the series with an exploration of the Homeric material in *Age of Heroes: Beyond the Solar Path*. The final book of the trilogy, *Return to Hyperborea: The Heroic Initiate*, examines the Orphic tradition.

With a particular interest in Indo-European matters, Tom spends much of his time making connections between the spiritual and martial impulses of the various Indo-European cultures. His book *WarYoga* explores the Indic branch of the Indo-European physical alchemical practice, while the sequel, *WarYoga: Zurxāne* deals with the Iranian tradition. The third part, *WarYoga: Palaistra*, was released in 2025. These works are the culmination of years of academic, spiritual, and physical research.

Tom has also translated several works including the Iranian epic *Garšaspname*, *The Aryan Männerbund* by Stig Wikander, and *The Feast of Immortality* by Georges Dumezil. *Varuna-Ouranos* by Georges Dumezil, *Pythagoras and Orpheus* by Karl Kerenyi, and *Theophania* by Walter Otto are slated for future release by Sanctus Arya Press.

In addition to authoring books, articles, and essays, he teaches Muay Thai, Jiu Jitsu, Old English bareknuckle, Ancient Greek Pankrátion, and works as an editor in combat sports media. Tom is a Fellow of the Royal Asiatic Society.

For more information about Tom Billinge and his work, visit his website at **TomBillinge.com**.

www.ingramcontent.com/pod-product-compliance
Lightning Source LLC
Chambersburg PA
CBHW071732150426
43191CB00010B/1547